I0037573

'Sets the stage for practicality in the most stimulating way. Beginning with a well-researched "state of the industry" to ground us in the challenges and obstacles we all face regularly, Joanna Parsons then provides tangible, clear examples and actual, functional solutions to break down barriers and make room for innovation, no matter the circumstances. I have pages and pages of notes and my mind is still buzzing with all the possibilities of applying these learnings in my work, both in the short and long term. A must-read for any internal communicator.'
Laura Kennedy, Director, Team Member Communications, Life Time

'Internal communications has been a misunderstood and ill-defined profession since the beginning. Even those of us who do it for a living had a hard time explaining what we do, much less defining the business value of it – until now. Joanna Parsons is a wonderfully talented voice in our profession, with the uncanny ability to cut right to chase and with the audacity to believe that internal communications can actually be innovative. This work is refreshing, provocative, honest and from the heart.'
Jason Anthoine, Managing Founder, Audacity

'Serves as a rallying cry to be bold, confident and execute for your organization. Joanna Parsons' book builds the case for empowered internal communicators through peer insights, expert opinions and academic perspectives, alongside the business rationale for leading with innovation. This book not only leaves the reader with proven insights on leading internal communication practices, but also serves

as a guidebook as to how to position internal communications as a key strategic partner within the business.'
Laura Edgerton, Head of Internal Communications and Employer Branding, Goodbody

'Joanna Parsons is not only an expert in the area of internal communications but a thought-leader. This book is crammed with practical advice for internal comms professionals whether they are a novice or a veteran.'
Eoghan Tomás McDermott, Managing Director, The Communications Clinic

'A must-have book for any internal communications professional – the ultimate guide to transforming internal comms practice! It is a truly refreshing and easy read, and once I started I couldn't put it down. I felt so invigorated afterwards – it gave me so many bitesize tips on ways I can start innovating today and improving my internal comms practice. Thanks so much, Joanna, for writing this brilliant book, I will be keeping this handy friend close by to refer back to!'
Gemma Pike, Internal Communications Manager, Amnesty International

'Joanna Parsons challenges internal communicators to move beyond restrictive models of best practice, step out of their comfort zones and use innovation to deliver great outcomes, rather than tactical outputs. She does so with her signature warmth, humour, empathy and wit – you know she gets it and she's on your side!'
Liz Davies, Global People Communications, Unilever

'Having overseen internal communications in three big organizations I thought I knew most things about the profession. But with the turn of every page I learned something new. Beautifully written and insightful, I recommend Joanna Parsons' book to anyone in communications, regardless of their level of experience, ability or seniority.'
Alastair Campbell, Communications Director, Local Government

'In her thoroughly researched book Joanna Parsons challenges the norms of internal communications, inviting you to dismantle "best

practices" to chart a path for genuine innovation. She dares you to cast aside convention, rethink everything you know about your role, and embrace curiosity to engage your work on a deeper level. *Innovative Internal Communication* is a must-read for rookies and veterans alike.'
Shaun Randol, Founder, Mister Editorial

'This book stands as your ultimate guide, whether you're starting out in your career journey, are a seasoned professional, or simply curious about the world of internal communication. It seamlessly blends thought-provoking insights with relatable anecdotes, offering practical advice that is enriched by data and research. This is a book you'll revisit for timeless wisdom and guidance!'
Faye Banks, Internal Communications Manager, Card Factory

'Full of practical, easy-to-understand advice for communicators who want to demonstrate impact in their work. If you're an internal communication professional who wants to progress in your career and lead with a curious mindset, this book is for you!'
Advita Patel, Founder, CommsRebel

'Provides a compelling call to action to lead with curiosity so we can bring competitive advantage not just to ourselves but to the organizations we serve as well. Let's throw out best practice and innovate!'
Jon Bates, Employee Communications Lead, Microsoft

'Don't let the title of this book fool you. It's not about how to be more innovative in your internal communication in terms of your channels and technology. It's much more about how you can be more curious as an internal communicator. Joanna Parsons discusses what innovation really is and how curiosity and measurement go hand in hand. The book is a great read for anyone getting started in internal communication, looking to understand the importance of asking the right questions and having the right mindset to lead internal communication in the future.'
Jenni Field, CEO and Founder, Redefining Communications

Innovative Internal Communication

How creativity, curiosity and technology can create lasting impact

Joanna Parsons

KoganPage

First published in Great Britain and the United States in 2024 by Kogan Page Limited

2nd Floor, 45 Gee Street
London
EC1V 3RS
United Kingdom
www.koganpage.com

8 W 38th Street, Suite 902
New York, NY 10018
USA

Kogan Page books are printed on paper from sustainable forests.

© Joanna Parsons, 2024

The right of Joanna Parsons to be identified as the author of this work has been asserted by her in accordance with the Copyright, Designs and Patents Act 1988.

ISBNs
Hardback   978 1 3986 1646 2
Paperback   978 1 3986 1644 8
Ebook   978 1 3986 1645 5

British Library Cataloguing-in-Publication Data
A CIP record for this book is available from the British Library.

Library of Congress Cataloging-in-Publication Data
Names: Parsons, Joanna, author.
Title: Innovative internal communication : how creativity, curiosity and
   technology can create lasting impact / Joanna Parsons.
Description: London ; New York, NY : Kogan Page, 2024. | Includes
   bibliographical references and index.
Identifiers: LCCN 2024020129 (print) | LCCN 2024020130 (ebook) | ISBN
   9781398616448 (paperback) | ISBN 9781398616462 (hardback) | ISBN
   9781398616455 (ebook)
Subjects: LCSH: Communication in management. | Creative ability in
   business. | Diffusion of innovations–Managment.
Classification: LCC HD30.3 .P386 2024 (print) | LCC HD30.3 (ebook) | DDC
   658.4/5–dc23/eng/20240503
LC record available at https://lccn.loc.gov/2024020129
LC ebook record available at https://lccn.loc.gov/2024020130

Typeset by Hong Kong FIVE Workshop, Hong Kong
Print production managed by Jellyfish
Printed and bound by CPI Group (UK) Ltd, Croydon CR0 4YY

CONTENTS

Introduction

When I was 7 or 8 years old, I asked my mother a question that probably shaped the course of my whole life.

'Do I *have to* go to church with you?'

Let's back up and I'll explain everything.

I was born in Ireland in the early 1980s to parents of different religions – my mother was a Catholic and my father a Protestant. That doesn't seem like a big deal now, but when they married in 1969 that was quite the scandal in Catholic Ireland. Their marriage in a Catholic church was only permitted on the condition that any children borne of the marriage would be raised as Catholic.

The religious diversity in our home sparked my curiosity, even as a young child. I remember Christmas morning when I was a small child, when my mother was getting us ready to go to Catholic mass after breakfast. It was freezing cold, I was in a stiff new dress and hard, shiny shoes and it was raining outside. Needless to say, I wasn't best pleased to be going to a cold church in the rain when I had new toys at home to play with and tons of chocolate to eat.

My Dad, being a non-practising Protestant, wasn't going anywhere. I can picture him in that moment perfectly to this day: sitting by the roaring fire, new slippers on his feet, book in hand. The image of contentment.

And at that moment as a young child I got deeply curious: was going to church optional? Did I *have to* go? How much choice did I have in this situation?

I had already been raising fairly significant questions about the existence of God and about the religious stories we were fed in school, and my parents tirelessly indulged my curiosity, answering my questions as best they could and encouraging me to come up with answers for myself.

So that cold, wet Christmas morning I asked my mother that fateful question. 'Do I *have to* go to church with you?' She hesitated, thought for a moment, and gave the answer that cemented my curiosity-fuelled approach for the rest of my life: 'I think you're old enough to decide for yourself.'

I had *agency*. I didn't have to do what the others were doing. I could think and decide for myself – and I could decide my own fate by asking good questions. What an absolute light bulb moment.

As a result of that moment of curiosity, that was the last time I ever went to mass.

The point here is nothing to do with religion or belief. The point is that I was always curious and I was always encouraged to ask questions and think for myself. It was okay in my household to ask difficult questions or to challenge accepted ideas or norms. It was more than okay – it was encouraged, recognized and rewarded. (Yes, my parents were incredibly patient.) This space to be curious gave me an innovator's mindset from an early age. I valued learning and understanding problems and generating new ideas and I was rewarded for it.

As I reflect now as an adult, I recognize that curiosity has been an enduring theme of my life and has significantly shaped my career. Asking questions, listening intently, being curious… these are the foundations upon which my success has been built. I even named my business 'The Curious Route'. I firmly believe curiosity is the fuel that propels us towards new ideas and a greater understanding of the world. It is what sparks ideas for innovative solutions to the world's problems.

Writing this book has been a deeply enjoyable indulgence of my curiosity with the internal communication profession. I was struck by our profession's deep love affair with 'best practice', a complex relationship that had us all peering over our shoulders to assess what others were doing so we could mimic them. This seemed like the antithesis of curiosity and innovation in what is an innately creative profession.

I couldn't stop rolling the concept of 'best practice' around in my head: How can we be innovative whilst also accepting that there were 'best' ways to do things?

I began to see an inherent paradox emerge. Internal communicators are creative professionals. They are writers, creators, designers, strategists and leaders who are capable of creative thinking and thoughtful problem-solving. And yet here we are, an industry of creative thinkers, mired in a sea of 'best practice' and a frenzy of imitation. Perhaps internal communication professionals are using 'best practice' as a security blanket, finding safety in its norms.

As I got increasingly curious and conducted more research, it became clear that this is not an individual problem. This is a structural problem. Communicators told me, again and again, that it's not a lack of desire that's stopping them from experimenting or innovating. It's a structural system of obstacles and blockages that prevents it from taking place. I followed this thread down a rabbit hole and documented 10 clear obstacles to innovation in internal communication.

I spoke to professional communicators all over the world and heard their dismay and disillusionment. Time and time again, I heard of the frustration with how internal communicators seem to have accepted their position as order-takers and output-producers, rather than as creative problem solvers, business advisors or innovative strategists.

The desire to innovate is there. The time to change is now. Innovation is not a special reserve of the elite. Anyone can innovate. We must first start with our mindset and give ourselves the space, permission and confidence to ask questions and get curious.

This book will help you get started. This is a practical book, but it is not a prescriptive 'how-to' book. It will intentionally avoid creating a set of 'best practices' for you to follow, but rather will give you some starting points to find your own path to 'how'. This book is intentionally light on case studies, to encourage you to forge your own path, but is deliberately heavy on quotes and thoughts from a variety of professionals, both from within our own profession and from outside it.

The book is a rousing call to arms, a manifesto for revolutionizing the internal communication profession through embracing the innovator's mindset. This book will help you to understand why innovation is so crucial and will encourage you to embrace curiosity to begin the revolution in your own organization. I will encourage you to adopt the innovator's mindset, equip you with the confidence to challenge best practices and help you to fall in love with curiosity as a communicator's superpower.

If you are an internal communicator who finds comfort in best practice, this book is a step outside your comfort zone and an opportunity to think about things differently. It will help you throw off the shackles of best practice and take baby steps into the world of the unknown. At the end of this book, you will feel well positioned to be more curious, open-minded and willing to explore new territories. I'll show you how to conduct measurable experiments, how to learn from failure and how to drive innovation in your work.

By embracing innovation in this way, you'll not only find your work more rewarding, but you'll also drive organizational success through your work. Innovating in internal communication can enhance the employee experience and ultimately contribute to the delivery of organizational strategic goals.

By the end of this book you will:

Know: You'll know the power of innovation and how to cultivate an innovator's mindset.

Feel: You'll feel less intimidated by the idea of innovation and more emboldened to try new things.

Do: You'll embrace your curiosity and look at your work with a new lens, asking questions and experimenting with new ideas.

01

What on earth is internal communication?

It seems remiss to write a book on internal communication without stating clearly what internal communication *is*. I see so many different definitions of internal communication, some that directly contradict each other, that it's worth taking the time to unpack key concepts before diving headlong into a discussion of innovation.

When I teach students about internal communication, I always take the time to ask them for their understanding of key terms. I get them to work in small groups and come up with answers for three seemingly simple questions:

1 What is internal communication?

2 What is employee engagement?

3 Are they the same or different – and how?

These questions seem easy at first glance, but the conversations always prove more difficult than expected. Students struggle to agree on a clear definition for internal communication. Some focus on internal communication *activity*, others lean into the *purpose* of internal communication, some go with a mixture of both. Before we go further, I suggest you pause here and write down your own definition of internal communication. What does it mean for you? Do the same for employee engagement. Then come back and read on.

If you did that exercise, well done. That's your first indulgence of curiosity – getting curious about the scope and purpose of our work and attempting to put some clarity on it. I often say that clarity is kindness, because being clear on what we're talking about gets everyone on the same page and reduces friction caused by confusion.

I'm always so fascinated by this exercise of defining key terms. Students may struggle to answer these questions and they often have challenging group conversations when attempting to create an agreed-upon definition of internal communication or employee engagement. It's intriguing to listen to professional communicators argue about what their own profession is and what it's for. Here are some of the answers I hear when I ask communicators to define internal communication:

> 'Internal communication is about sharing information with employees.'
>
> 'Internal communication is about building a great culture.'
>
> 'Internal communication is about motivating employees to do great work.'
>
> 'Internal communication exists to bridge the gap between employees and leaders.'
>
> 'Internal communication is about communicating the bigger picture.'

The Gallagher (2023) *State of the Sector* report surveyed thousands of internal communication professionals and asked them: What is the purpose of internal communication in your organization? The top three answers were:

- 74% said the purpose is culture and belonging: creating an inclusive workplace where employees feel valued and energized.
- 67% said it's about strategic alignment: creating clarity around your strategy and a sense of ownership.
- 47% said it's organizational agility: supporting the adoption of new behaviours, systems and processes.

This gives us a flavour not just of how academics understand internal communication, but how in-house practitioners are actively experiencing it.

The results from my curious questioning with my students as well as the findings from the Gallagher report indicate that internal communicators don't necessarily agree on what internal communication is all about. There's rarely consensus in an exercise like this, even amongst experienced internal communication practitioners, academics and professionals. Bates and Patel (2023) conclude the same in their book, *Building a Culture of Inclusivity*, stating, 'each professional body, theorist, academic and influencer had their own take on the [internal communication] profession'.

I see even more variation in the answers when it comes to explaining employee engagement. This is often where the group conversations between students become even more challenging, as communicators struggle to unpack the two concepts, define them and interrogate the overlaps and boundaries between them.

Here's a sample of what internal communicators tell me their definition of 'employee engagement' is:

'Employee engagement is about keeping employees happy and satisfied at work.'

'Employee engagement is about how much effort people bring to their role.'

'Employee engagement is about getting everyone on the same page.'

'Employee engagement is about reducing employee turnover.'

'Employee engagement makes an impact on profits and the bottom line.'

Again, totally fascinating. There is a lot of disagreement about what this concept means. For some people employee engagement is about happiness. For others it's about effort and productivity. And for others it's about employee retention and profit.

Because I am simply tortuous as a lecturer, I then get my students to go one step further: What's the difference between internal communication and employee engagement? Are they the same? And if not – what's the difference? This is usually where the arguments start and things get more heated. (That's usually a sign you've asked a really good question, by the way.)

There is rarely agreement on the difference between internal communication and employee engagement. Students can find it excruciatingly difficult to identify a hard line that makes the boundary between them clear. Some students tell me that internal communication and employee engagement are the same thing dressed up in a different language. Others feel that internal communication and employee engagement are different but can't quite articulate how or why. Some indicate that the two concepts are interlinked but not the same. Five points for effort to the communicator who once sent me a hand-drawn Venn diagram which attempted to show the overlap between the concepts. I've seen others attempt to draw the ideas in a hierarchy to show how internal communication has a tiered relationship with employee engagement.

Why not give this a go yourself before reading further – do you think they're the same or different, and why? Do you find the question easy or difficult? Can you draw an illustration of the relationship between internal communication and employee engagement?

There's little agreement on the answer, in my experience, and this is a problem. We are clearly not all on the same page about the fundamentals of our profession and why we are here doing this job. Let's fix that now by creating a common understanding of what internal communication is, what employee engagement is, and how they intersect. This will get us aligned on the key concepts we need to explore innovation in internal communication.

Understanding internal communication

I liken internal communication to the oil in an engine: it reduces friction, makes everything run faster and keeps things running smoothly. This is what effective internal communication will do for an organization. Sure, you can run an organization without it – but would you really want to? A car engine can run without oil for a time, but the effects are so damaging that it will quickly start to break and fail. Your organization is no different.

Bates and Patel (2023) argue that 'internal communication is the backbone in any organization, large or small'. Increasingly, organizations are realizing that internal communication is not a support function that can produce pretty outputs, such as PowerPoint decks or digital posters, but that it is a critical driver of strategic business outcomes. Effective internal communication can result in greater alignment and adaptability, and improved organizational performance and employee retention.

Communication can align employees around a common purpose – the vision, mission, values and strategic goals of an organization. These should act as the North Star for all employees, guiding their actions and helping them make decisions. Internal communication helps employees understand and commit to this shared vision, clearly explaining the 'why' behind what the organization does. When employees are on the same page about the organization's overall purpose, they're more likely to align their efforts and work collaboratively across teams and departments to achieve common goals. Getting all employees on the same page, aligned to the strategy and rowing in the same direction makes organizations work more effectively and produce better results. But there's a gap to be filled here, as the Institute of Internal Communication's Index Report (2023) found that one in four UK workers neither understand nor believe in their employer's strategy.

Communication can also help organizations to adapt and change. If Covid-19 did nothing else, it proved the importance of organizations being adaptable and agile when faced with a crisis. Internal communication became a hot ticket during the pandemic due to the urgent need to effectively communicate changes, updates, safety protocols, working arrangements and new processes to employees so they could adapt quickly to the new normal. As the pandemic raged on, effective communication facilitated employee behaviour changes which in turn enabled many organizations to pull through the crisis successfully.

This is not just contained to crisis situations. The business world is changing constantly and organizations are undergoing digital transformations and change programmes to stay relevant and competitive with increasing frequency. Internal communication can ensure that employees understand what is happening, what it means for them and what behaviour is expected of them as a result.

Communication is good for organizational performance and the bottom line, too. According to recent research, ineffective communication costs organizations $2 trillion every year – and that's just in the United States (Axios HQ, 2023). That's an average of $15,000 per employee per year. A report from Steven G Rogelberg (2022), a professor at the University of North Carolina, found that ineffective communication through too many unnecessary meetings is costing large businesses up to $100 million a year. A well-designed, intentional system of internal communication would provide more effective, efficient methods of communicating which would save significant amounts of money for organizations.

Yates (2006) found convincing evidence that organizations with good systems of internal communication produce superior financial results. For example, companies with effective internal communication produced a 57 per cent higher total return to shareholders over a five-year period than companies without. This study found that effective communication is a leading indicator of financial performance. Watson Wyatt (2004) found that companies with effective communication have a 29.5 per cent increase in market value.

There's more money to be saved through communication when you consider its effect on employee retention. It's never been harder to retain employees. In 2022, nearly 51 million people voluntarily quit their jobs – a huge increase from the previous year's recording-breaking figure of 47 million people (Work Institute, 2023). In their report, Work Institute found that organizational culture and communication come up again and again as reason for resignation. Management communication is a particular driver of resignations and has been continuously on an upward trend in the Work Institute report since 2020. The Institute of Internal Communication Index (2023) found that employees' intent to leave within the next two years is 13 points lower among those who work for an organization with an internal communication team in place.

Replacing people who quit their job is expensive. It costs approximately 33 per cent of an employee's annual salary to replace them successfully (Work Institute, 2023). In companies with effective communication, employee turnover is up to 20 per cent lower than that of their competitors (Yates, 2006). Conner (2018) argues that strong communication inside a business helps to avoid preventable turnover.

Definitions of internal communication

Now that we know that internal communication is important, let's create clarity on what it is and look at how it's different to employee engagement.

There are so many different definitions of internal communication across various literature. I've pored through lots of them to save you the trouble. Let's unpack some of the themes that emerge from the literature.

Is internal communication just an internal postal service?

In a word… no.

If someone offers you an internal communications job and they tell you the crux of the role is distributing information around the company, then you should see this as a massive red flag waving. Yes, our job does involve running communication channels and distributing content within them – but we are not simply an internal postal service. Distributing information is a task, an activity. It is not an outcome or a result. In theory anyone could distribute information or perhaps it could even be automated. Why would you need to hire an internal communications team just for that?

Internal communication isn't just about information sharing. We are not the organizational postal service, delivering messages from one department to another (at least we ought not to be). Simply sharing information suggests one-way, broadcast communication in which information is pushed blindly at employees. In this scenario, employees are passive recipients of information. Thinking of internal communication simply as information sharing reduces it to a simplistic, top-down broadcast or postal system in which we complete tasks but don't deliver business outcomes.

As FitzPatrick and Dewhurst (2022) note, 'Great communication is about more than an efficient distribution system'. Communication is about *more* than channels or tactics or messages. The role of internal communication, according to Quirke (2016), is 'to provide employees with the information they need to do their job, and to paint the bigger picture and tell the fuller story that puts that information into context'.

Reducing internal communication to information sharing fails to capture the emotional and motivational aspects of communication. Effective internal communication not only keeps employees informed, but can also inspire and motivate them, instilling a sense of purpose and commitment to the organization. This can be particularly important during times of transformation or change when employees require more than just the sharing of information. They need reassurance, comfort, context and a sense of direction. They need to feel valued.

We are highly influential in our organizations

How do you feel about the word 'influencer'? Because if you're working in internal communication, then you probably are one – whether you realize it or not. Internal communication is about influencing employee behaviours. This is where we really add value and earn our salaries. This is where we deliver value for the business, no matter what kind of organization or industry you work in.

Think of internal communication as a force of influence inside organizations. Effective internal communication can significantly influence the knowledge, attitudes and behaviours of employees (FitzPatrick and Dewhurst, 2022). Here we move beyond activities and channels and distribution of information into something deeper; influencing what employees know, what they do and how they feel.

Arguably the most powerful aspect of effective internal communication is its capacity to influence what employees *do*. It can significantly impact employee behaviours and decisions. Effective communication can systematically drive desired specific behaviours, for example adherence to safety measures, ways of collaborating together or approaches to interacting with customers. Communication can be used to embed new behaviours into an organization, for example a traditional, conservative organization could harness internal communication to drive a culture of innovation by encouraging employees to share their ideas, communicating failures openly or encouraging people to run measurable experiments and post their results in an internal channel. The ability to influence employee behaviour is incredibly important and is key to what our profession does.

I saw this myself first-hand when I worked as Head of Internal Communications in the Irish national police service during the Covid-19 pandemic. The fast-spreading virus had the potential to significantly disrupt the police service through decreased number of police officers available for duty through illness or self-isolation after close contact with a Covid case. Police behaviours needed to change in a range of areas and they needed to change fast, in order to keep the police service running and to be able to deliver on the organizational mission of Keeping People Safe. And key to driving these behaviour changes was internal communication. Clear, direct and easy-to-understand communication drove significant behaviour change in police officers, for example wearing face masks, social distancing or wearing specific items of protective equipment at crime scenes. These behaviours were vital to protect police officers from the virus and in turn to keep the entire operation functioning – communication was key to keep the police service operating effectively throughout the crisis. So you can see that internal communication is more than just sharing information. It's about influencing what employees *do* and how this has a direct impact on the performance of an organization.

Communication can also play a critical role in shaping how employees *feel* about their workplace, their colleagues and the leadership team. Communication can inspire and motivate employees and in this way can contribute to a positive organizational culture in which employees feel a greater commitment to achieving organizations goals. It can go the other direction too – poor communication can cause employees to feel undervalued and mistreated. Think of the example of the internal communication from Internet Brands, the parent company of WebMD, that went viral in January 2024. This was an internal video in which the CEO and other senior leaders communicated to their workforce that they had to come back to the office. Their intent appears to be influencing employee behaviour (come back to the office) but their threatening tone and lack of empathy for employees most likely had a brutal impact on how their employees feel. In the video, the CEO says 'We aren't asking or negotiating at this point. We're informing' (Kelly, 2024). Ouch. I would have loved to be a fly on the wall when they were developing the idea for this video. It seems like someone did ask 'What do you want people to *do* as a result of this communication?' (come back to the office) but they neglected to interrogate 'What do you want people to *feel* as a result of this communication?' If I was one of their employees I would probably have felt threatened, undervalued and downright annoyed. But who knows... maybe that's what they were going for?

Don't underestimate the impact and influence you can have in your organization as an internal communicator. Your actions and work can make a huge difference to how people feel about working in the organization and what they do during the course of their day.

The communicator as a curator

An interesting take on our role is that we act as a curator. Field (2021) states, 'Internal communication includes everything that gets said and shared inside an organization. As a function its role is to curate, enable and advise on best practice for organizations to communicate effectively, efficiently and in an engaging way.'

Field's definition introduces the concept of *curation*. Curation suggests the presenting or organizing of something. This makes sense, given that we live in a digital age with vast quantities of information available to us, but not all information is relevant to or of interest to all employees. An internal communicator, as a curator, can sift through the expanse of organizational information, selecting and presenting the most relevant and valuable information for different internal audiences. This targeted, tailored approach to communication can meet the needs and interests of different employee groups.

For example, if an organization introduces a new marketing strategy, the internal communicator doesn't simply distribute the marketing strategy document. Instead, they could curate it. They may extract key takeaways, distil complex concepts into digestible nuggets, translate ideas into language that their audience will understand and present the information in a way that will resonate with different internal audiences based on what they need to know and their ability to understand different levels of complexity.

It's not a million miles away from what Quirke (2016) says when he claims that internal communication is a process of conversion. He states, 'Just as an assembly line worker converts, or adds value to, a component he receives from up the line, so we have to convert information we receive into meaning in order to help employees make the right decisions'.

Field (2021) also talks about the concept of *advising* in her definition of internal communication. In our role we also act as advisors and internal consultants. This again helps us to understand that internal communication is more than simply sharing information; it's also about giving guidance and counsel, and acting as a strategic advisor to managers and leaders. We advise leadership on communication techniques, approaches and strategies to help them communicate effectively with employees. We also advise on behalf of employees – we are often the people inside an organization with the deepest, richest and most insightful understanding of the employees. We are the bridge between employees and senior leaders, and can help to advise leaders on decisions and communications that will align employees, reduce frustrations and optimize how the business runs. Our insights into the perceptions and sentiments of employees can be immensely valuable to leaders, and often we are the only one in the entire organization with such a rich knowledge of various employee groups. We cut across all departments and silos in the business and have a view of all employees, not just our own team.

Internal communication creates alignment

At the heart of it, internal communication is fundamentally about creating alignment in organizations. I'm sure you've all probably experienced working in an organization that did not have alignment. It usually manifests as things like:

- Teams won't collaborate with each other.
- Departments are competing for internal resources.
- The leadership team communicate mixed messages.
- Work is being duplicated in different parts of the business.
- The day-to-day work of teams has no relevance to the overall goals of the business.

This is often symptomatic of a lack of alignment, a lack of what Quirke (2016) calls 'a shared understanding' of the big picture. Employees in organizations like this often don't understand the broader context of the organization or what they're actually there to achieve. For example, they don't have a clear understanding of why the organization exists (the vision) or what the organization is trying to do (the mission) or how employees are expected to behave to deliver on that mission (the values) or what the big important priorities are for the next few years (the strategy).

Helping employees to develop a common understanding of these elements can enable them to see how they fit into the bigger picture and how their own daily work is helping to contribute to the achievement of much bigger goals. It creates purpose and meaning. It can help employees at all levels feel part of something bigger than themselves, and can help them to align their work with the overall goals of the business. Without this common understanding, each team or department will simply do their own thing and may work at cross-purposes, to the detriment of the business. Internal communication plays a vital role in deterring that and creating this essential sense of alignment in the company.

This theme of alignment can be seen in Allman's (2021) book, *Better Internal Communication*. Allman (2021) states, 'Internal communication is about ensuring that employees know what they need to do to deliver the company strategy.'

This definition from Allman is short, it's direct, it encapsulates nicely this idea that internal communication drives organizational alignment. Creating a common understanding amongst employees involves bridging the gap between the vision of the leadership team and the perception of employees. It involves translating abstract concepts, complex topics and technical details into relatable and actionable ideas.

Think about company core values, for example. You want employees to have the same understanding of what they mean and what the company expects from employee behaviour as a result.

According to Quirke (2016), internal communication should help to translate the organizational strategy into the day-to-day actions of employees. This, he argues, is where internal communication can deliver the most value. Think about the example of internal communication in a police service again. The internal communicator's role isn't just to churn out endless updates and newsletters and blog posts. Their role is to help employees understand what matters most to the organization and what their role is in delivering it. In the case of the Irish police service, where the organizational mission is Keeping People Safe, internal communication can help create a common understanding of what that mission means, why it matters and how every employee can contribute towards it in the course of their work. In Quirke's (2016) words, 'The real value of internal communication is to deliver business ends by enabling employees to turn strategy into action'.

So remember, internal communication is not just a broadcast system or a postal service. It's not a nice-to-have or an optional bolt-on when there's extra cash lying about. Internal communication is a critical business function that enables organizations to deliver on their strategies. As internal communication professionals, we have the power to deliver enormous value for our leaders, our employees and the organization's bottom line.

What about employee engagement?

Let's also define employee engagement. Is it the same as internal communication, as some of my students suggested? Are there overlapping areas between the two concepts, like the centre of a Venn diagram? Are there clear boundaries we can draw between them or could we position them in a hierarchical relationship?

As with internal communication, defining employee engagement isn't straightforward. There are multiple definitions of the term, which would explain why so many people seem to be confused about what it is and whether it's the same as internal communication.

One of the earliest definitions is Kahn's in an article published in *The Academy of Management Journal* in 1990. His research set out to explore the idea that people invest different levels of their physical, cognitive and emotional selves in their work, which impacts their experience of work and their work itself. He concludes that there are 'three psychological conditions – meaningfulness, safety and availability' which are at the heart of employee engagement (Kahn, 1990). The idea of psychological conditions is a common theme across employee engagement literature. A study of employee engagement in the NHS, for example, outlined that engagement is a psychological state experienced by employees (Bailey et al, 2015).

In 2009, the *Engaging for Success* report was published by MacLeod and Clarke which sparked widespread interest in the concept. Their definition of employee engagement is still widely cited today:

> 'Employee engagement is a workplace approach designed to ensure that employees are committed to their organization's goals and values, motivated to contribute to organizational success and are able at the same time to enhance their own sense of well-being.'

This definition includes the idea that engagement is fundamentally about a deep commitment to the organization's goals and values. It suggests that engaged employees do not just complete tasks in a transactional exchange of labour for money; they are emotionally invested in the success of the organization – an echo of earlier ideas that engagement is a psychological state. This commitment is manifested in displays of loyalty, dedication and discretionary effort. Employees may willingly go the extra mile because they believe in the vision and mission of the organization. The behaviours you might see in an engaged, motivated employee include employees speaking positively about the organization to people outside of work, seeking opportunities to contribute to organizational success even when the work falls outside of their job scope, or taking the time to find creative solutions to challenges.

McLeod and Clarke's definition also includes *motivation* – the idea that engaged employees are motivated to contribute to organizational success. This implies intrinsic motivation – not being driven by bonuses or external rewards, but the idea that engaged individuals are driven by an internal desire to contribute positively to the organization. They find meaning and purpose in their work, which fuels their enthusiasm and involvement. Motivated employees may be more productive, more innovative and more likely to take calculated risks. Engaged, motivated employees also have a thirst for continuous learning and self-improvement, which benefits both the individual and the organization.

The third concept in McLeod and Clarke's definition is well-being; they claim that engaged employees can enhance their own sense of well-being. This broadens out the scope of the concept, adding a sense of fulfilment and satisfaction at work which contributes to the overall psychological and emotional well-being of employees. Engaged employees feel supported and looked after, and in this way their work enhances their sense of well-being.

MacLeod and Clarke say that employee engagement is ultimately about 'how we create the conditions in which employees offer more of their capability and potential'. This understanding of employee engagement paints a multi-faceted picture of commitment, motivation and well-being.

Gallup (2023) states that employee engagement is 'the involvement and enthusiasm of employees in their work and workplace'. And Kruse (2012) states that employee engagement is 'the emotional commitment the employee has to the organization and its goals'. Kruse is at pains to outline that employee engagement does not mean employee happiness, but rather it's about employees caring about their work and feeling invested in the company. He argues that there's an emotional aspect to their employment which is visible through their displays of discretionary effort at work.

If we understand that internal communication is 'about ensuring that employees know what they need to do to deliver the company strategy' (Allman, 2021) and we use McLeod and Clarke's definition of employee engagement, which is 'Employee engagement is a workplace approach designed to ensure that employees are committed to their organization's goals and values, motivated to contribute to organizational success and are able at the same time to enhance their own sense of well-being', then it becomes clear that internal communication and employee engagement are not one and the same.

Employee engagement is more than internal communication. It's bigger. Let's have a look at how the concepts intersect.

The relationship between internal communication and employee engagement

Internal communication plays a key role in employee engagement. McLeod and Clarke put forward four key drivers of employee engagement, some of which are heavily influenced by communication (for example, employee voice and strategic narrative). So it's reasonable to deduce that internal communication may influence the engagement level of an employee.

Field (2021) suggests that 'employee engagement is an outcome of good internal communication'. This views employee engagement as an *outcome*. This is a useful way to position the terms in a hierarchy: employee engagement at the top and communication underneath, serving as a driver. This definition reinforces the relationship between communication and engagement, whilst also very strongly differentiating between them. But communication alone is not enough to drive engagement.

Nicholas Wardle and Mike Sharples, authors of *Monetising the Employee Experience* (2021), echo the idea that employee engagement is an outcome, stating that 'employee engagement, morale and productivity are all outcomes of a good employee experience'. In this definition, employee engagement is the outcome of a range of employee experiences. The employee experience may be comprised of many things: development opportunities, compensation, benefits, promotions, flexibility, effective management, levels of autonomy, recognition, inspiring leadership, decent IT equipment... the list goes on. Internal communication, while critical, is not the sole driver of engagement.

For example, you might have an organization with a clear set of core values. They're well communicated, outlined in clear behaviours that are expected of all employees, and serve as the basis for the employee recognition scheme. Employees understand them and know what is expected of them at work. The communication of the values is effective. But what happens if the leadership team do not role model the values? What if leaders display contrary values through their actions and behaviours? We know that leaders play a key role in creating and maintaining culture (Trice and Beyer, 1991) and that leadership behaviours are scrutinized closely by lower-ranking employees, who in turn will mirror those behaviours (Amabile and Kramer, 2012). Leadership is one of the most important predictors of how well organizations function (Pearson-Goff and Herrington, 2013) and arguably is essential for employee engagement. So even if the internal communication of the core values is effective, the leadership behaviours may undermine that communication. Thus, internal communication is only one piece of the puzzle. Leadership behaviour will also have a significant impact on employee engagement.

Let's look at another example. Perhaps there's an organization with a brilliant internal communications team. They work hard to communicate the organizational strategy in a way that is accessible and interesting in order to align employees around shared goals. They have a range of two-way channels, they use a variety of visual and written tactics and they regularly listen to employees. This all sounds great, right? But what if that same organization has terrible, outdated hardware and software for employees that causes enormous frustration and complaints on a daily basis? Perhaps it takes 10 minutes for your computer to load up in the morning and the most-used software crashes every hour. All the communication in the world isn't going to make those employees feel engaged. Internal communication can certainly help to improve the employee experience, but it's not a silver bullet and can't make up for shortfalls in key areas such as malfunctioning technology or poor leadership behaviours.

Internal communication is one of many ingredients needed for employee engagement

Let's agree, then, to position internal communication as an essential *ingredient* of employee engagement. Employee engagement is an outcome of effective internal communication, but communication alone is not sufficient to drive engagement. Engagement is influenced by a variety of factors, including leadership, workplace culture, autonomy and management competence.

KEY TAKEAWAYS

- Definitions of internal communication vary, even amongst experienced practitioners and academics. This diversity highlights the complexity of our field.

- Internal communication is about more than just sending out information. It's about creating alignment and a common understanding amongst employees so they know how they play a role in delivering the company strategy.

- Employee engagement differs from internal communication. Employee engagement goes beyond communication and includes motivation, well-being, commitment and emotional attachment.

- There's a clear hierarchical relationship between internal communication and employee engagement: internal communication is an essential component of engagement but is one of many factors contributing to it.

- Internal communication plays a critical role in organizational success. It aligns employees with the company's purpose, creates clarity, reduces confusion, can help make organizations more adaptable, can improve financial performance and can reduce employee attrition.

REFLECTIVE QUESTIONS

1 What is your own understanding of internal communication, and how does it align with the various definitions discussed in this chapter?

2 How would you describe the purpose of internal communication in your organization?

3 Is there a common understanding in your organization of what internal communication is and the purpose of the function?

4 Consider the hierarchy outlined here, with employee engagement at the top and internal communication as a driver underneath. How does this perspective change your approach to internal communication?

5 How would you demonstrate the impact of effective internal communication to your organization's leaders? Can you link it to business objectives or overall business goals?

References

Allman, L (2021) *Better Internal Communication: How to add value, be more strategic and fast-track your career*, Rethink Press, Great Yarmouth

Amabile, T and Kramer, S (2012) How leaders kill meaning at work, *McKinsey Quarterly*, 1, 124–31

Axios HQ (2023) The 2023 state of essential workplace communications, Axios HQ, www.axioshq.com/research/2023-state-of-workplace-communications (archived at https://perma.cc/8G3W-Z2BY)

Bailey, C, Madden, A, Alfes, K, Fletcher, L, Robinson, D, Holmes, J, et al (2015) Evaluating the evidence on employee engagement and its potential benefits to NHS staff: A narrative synthesis of the literature, *Health Services and Delivery Research*, 3 (26)

Bates, P and Patel, A (2023) *Building a Culture of Inclusivity: Effective Internal communication for diversity, equity and inclusion*, Kogan Page, London

Conner, C (2018) How better communication prevents painful turnover, Forbes, 24 June

Field, J (2021) *Influential Internal Communication: Streamline your corporate communications to drive efficiency and engagement*, Kogan Page, London

FitzPatrick, L and Dewhurst, S (2022) *Successful Employee Communications: A practitioner's guide to tools, models and best practice for internal communication*, Kogan Page, London

Gallagher (2023) *State of the Sector 2022/23*, Gallagher Communication Limited

Gallup (2023) What is employee engagement and how do you improve it? Gallup, www.gallup.com/workplace/285674/improve-employee-engagement-workplace. aspx (archived at https://perma.cc/VBG9-RNXX)

Institute of Internal Communication (2023) *IC Index 2023 Report*, IIC, Ipsos Karian and Box

Kahn, W A (1990) Psychological conditions of personal engagement and disengagement at work, *The Academy of Management Journal*, 33 (4)

Kelly, J (2024) WebMD parent company's cringe video is a masterclass in how not to call workers back to the office, Forbes, 16 January

Kruse, K (2012) What is employee engagement? Forbes, 22 June

MacLeod, D and Clarke, N (2009) *Engaging for Success: Enhancing performance through employee engagement. A report to Government*, Department for Business, Innovation and Skills, dera.ioe.ac.uk/id/eprint/1810/1/file52215.pdf (archived at https://perma.cc/UFV3-GT93)

Pearson-Goff, M and Herrington, V (2013) Police leadership: A systematic review of the literature, *Policing*, 8 (1), 14–26

Quirke, B (2016) *Making the Connections: Using internal communication to turn strategy into action*, 2nd edn, Routledge, London

Rogelberg, S G (2022) *The Cost of Unnecessary Meeting Attendance*, Otter.ai.

Trice, H M and Beyer, J M (1991) Cultural leadership in organizations, *Organizational Science*, 2 (2), 149–69

Wardle, N and Sharples, M (2021) *Monetising the Employee Experience: How to prove the ROI for investing in your people and unlock lost productivity*, Brand Experiences

Watson Wyatt (2004) *Connecting Organizational Communication to Financial Performance: 2003/2004 communication ROI study*, Worldwide Research Report, Watson Wyatt, Arlington

Work Institute (2023) 2023 retention report: The complexities of employee retention, Work Institute, info.workinstitute.com/2023-retention-report (archived at https://perma.cc/ZR25-LRYG)

Yates, K (2006) Internal communication effectiveness enhances bottom-line results, *Journal of Organizational Excellence*, Summer

02

Innovation matters

When I started researching this book, I asked people what they thought about innovation. I was surprised at how divisive the word is. It lights up the faces of some, it causes severe eye-rolling in others. It seems that the word 'innovation' is a bit like reality TV: you either love it or you hate it, you either tune in or you switch off. Someone even suggested that putting the word 'innovative' in the title of my book would dissuade people from buying it!

(I kept it in – let's see how that goes.)

People seem *weary* of innovation. I spoke to people who work in conservative, bureaucratic organizations where it's impossible to try anything new without getting it approved by several layers of senior management – and yet those same organizations are proudly flaunting 'We are innovative' in their core values and in their employer brand. It appears meaningless.

People also seem *confused* about what innovation actually means. It's a bit of a buzzword, isn't it? Innovation seems to suffer the same challenge as internal communication: no one can quite agree on what it really means.

So let's start there. What's innovation and why should we care?

The challenge of defining innovation

In the previous chapter, we uncovered the plethora of wide-ranging definitions that exist for internal communication. Similarly, defining the term 'innovation' presents a challenge.

Ask a hundred people what innovation means and you're likely to get a hundred different answers, each focusing on a different aspect. This diversity reflects the broad scope of innovation, ranging from groundbreaking inventions to small yet meaningful improvements. Innovation can be big leaps by a visionary like Steve Jobs or small steps forward by anyone at all.

When I asked internal communication professionals for their understanding of innovation, many appeared frustrated with the concept. They felt it is just a fancy word for 'new stuff'. Many felt it is synonymous with technology – that innovation refers to a new app or a new digital platform. When I asked non-communication professionals in my network, I got much broader answers about what innovation is. People talked about improvements, changes, new products, new approaches to existing products, modern services... the list went on.

What I found so fascinating is that people were easily able to tell me about the *outputs* of innovation but struggled with a *definition* of innovation. (Sounds familiar, right?)

Definitions of innovation

Asking Google for a definition of innovation is either hilarious or maddening, depending on your point of view and how much coffee you've had. You'll get more than 1.9 billion search results containing conflicting and competing definitions of what innovation is. Google's built-in dictionary isn't much help either, offering up this definition: 'the action or process of innovating'. Hmm, thanks Google. The *Oxford Dictionary* is a bit more useful, stating that innovation is 'the introduction of novelties; the alteration of what is established by the introduction of new elements or forms'.

Definitions of innovation change depending on the industry of the definer. McKinsey (2022) take an unsurprisingly commercial view of innovation, stating that 'innovation is the systematic practice of developing and marketing breakthrough products and services for adoption by customers'. This definition focuses on creating something new that customers want and reflects a business-driven, economy-focused approach.

Groups that are not business consulting firms offer simpler and broader definitions of innovation. Eurostat (2023) state that 'innovation is the use of new ideas, products or methods where they have not been used before'. Lee and Trimi (2018) argue that innovation is about more than creating value for individuals or organizations, stating 'The ultimate purpose of innovation should be much more far reaching, helping create a smart future where people can enjoy the best quality of life possible.'

These definitions broaden out the scope of innovation beyond the creation of products or services for the market. They talk about the use of new ideas or methods, and about the purpose of innovation as bigger than the economy and transformational for society as a whole.

Matt Ridley (2020) says that innovation is a process of discovering different ways of arranging the world into forms that are unlikely to arise by chance. He argues that this must result in something *useful* to be considered innovation. The process of innovation should result in products, services, business models, strategies, processes that are both useful and valuable.

It's time to consult with some experts

I found so many different approaches to understanding innovation that I knew I needed to speak with some experts. I was lucky to meet with Dr Lollie Mancey, the Programme Director in the Innovation Academy in University College Dublin and an all-around fascinating and incredibly clever human being. She is at pains to tell me that she doesn't teach innovation; she *cultivates* it. She facilitates it.

Described on the Innovation Academy website as an 'educational provocateur with a wealth of entrepreneurial experience', I felt that Lollie must surely have the answers I was searching for. Could she help me make sense of this complex concept in a simple sentence?

I ask Lollie if she has a definition of innovation she uses for her students. You know what she tells me? She tells me *no*.

Oh.

'No, and I do that on purpose,' she says. 'You're better off to start with what innovation isn't. Innovation isn't doing the same thing that everyone else does and expecting success. It's not that I can't define it, I just don't want to.'

Lollie did tell me that innovation is about 'matching two things that shouldn't go together but suddenly do', which echoes Matt Ridley's idea of rearranging things that previously didn't go together, to put them together. She tells me that innovation is about creativity and curiosity and play, and ultimately about connecting two dots that were previously unconnected.

I pondered this and found myself agreeing with her, and I experienced an example of this the day after our interview. I was out for a walk with a Spotify playlist on, and it was randomly shuffling through rock music from the 1990s (don't judge – I'm old). The sound of 'Enter Sandman' by Metallica came into my ears, but with a twist… there was also a classical orchestra playing with them. In 1999, Metallica recorded a live album with a symphony orchestra, an absolutely perfect example of connecting two previously unconnected dots: heavy metal music and classical music. The album got very mixed reviews. One of the Google reviews I read opened with 'Why do I hate this album so much?' and a review on a website called Dead End Follies blusters 'This is not a successful album by any means'. I remember my own friends complaining about it when it was released, whilst I secretly loved it (and still do). The album is a masterclass of innovation; a dramatic clash of musical culture and styles. I'd never heard anything like it before. This is surely what Lollie was talking about when she told me that innovation is about giving yourself 'permission to see things upside down, to put crazy things together'.

I also interviewed Laurence Knell, Director of Strategic Innovation Partners and host of the popular podcast Brain for Business, Brain for Life. Laurence has 20+ years' experience working across a huge range of industries delivering innovation and change. He's an Associate Lecturer in the Open University Business School's Master of Business Administration (MBA) programme where he teaches in the areas of creativity and innovation.

I ask Laurence what innovation is. 'Definitions tend to focus on products or marketing', he tells me. 'But it's broader than that. Innovation is a process of continual improvement'. He likes the definition from the Massachusetts Institute of Technology (MIT) Office of Innovation: innovation is 'the process of taking an idea from inception to impact', because innovation is more than having a good idea. It's about making that idea into something useful that has an impact.

Laurence tells me that innovation is often viewed as something really big or groundbreaking, but a lot of the time it's not. It's often lots of small changes over time that build on each other.

He gives me the example of the Boeing 737 airplane. 'If you look at the Boeing 737 now compared to when it launched in 1960, it looks pretty much the same but the whole plane has actually been completely changed and reimagined over time. Construction processes, materials and electronics have all changed but it's still a Boeing 737. It's been a series of small changes over time.'

This is innovation, he says, building on something with a series of improvements to deliver something valuable and useful.

Distilling innovation down to three core components

As I spoke to innovation experts, pored through journal articles, examined peer-reviewed research and combed through books, I found three commons threads emerging across the definitions of innovation. There are three components that should be present for something to be considered an innovation, whether that's a product, a service, a process or anything else.

These three components are novelty, value and action.

Component 1: Novelty

Across all the understandings of innovation I explored, novelty was a common theme. Innovation is generally about a new or different approach to something (Ridley, 2020).

There must be a newness or a novelty for something to be innovative.

This could mean something brand new that didn't exist before, a new take on something that already exists or a different way of looking at something that's been around for a long time. If we think about our example of Metallica jamming along with cellists and violinists, the songs themselves weren't new, but the classical string music was new. Novelty can transform something ordinary into something extraordinary. Henderson (2017) asserts that innovation doesn't have to be about groundbreaking inventions or entirely new products; it can be as simple as uncovering new ways to do things.

Novelty is key for innovation.

But novelty can be relative to the context. What's new to one company or industry may not be new to another. For example, something that is innovative for a small local business might be a standard way of working for a multinational corporation. Something can be innovative if it's new to *your organization* – it doesn't have to be new to the whole world.

Component 2: Value

The next theme that consistently emerged across the literature was value.

Innovation must produce something useful, something of value. This might be value for your employees, for your stakeholders, for your family, for society... but the innovation must be valuable. Not just innovation for innovation's sake.

The idea of value creation came up in my interview with Dr Lollie Mancey. She tells me unequivocally that 'innovation has to add value'. For something to be counted as innovative, it should solve a problem or be generally useful. Shapiro (2011) agrees with this, arguing that the process of innovation should begin with a problem that needs to be solved. The process ends with value creation. Laurence Knell tells me something very similar, stating clearly, 'innovation is for solving problems'.

Laurence adds a thoughtful caveat that is useful for us to reflect on: 'An innovation has to be applicable and useful in a particular context. But who defines the value? What might be valuable for you might not be valuable to me.' His advice is to be very clear on how value is defined for an innovation – is it value for the user, value for the business, value for your team?

Component 3: Action

The third theme that emerged was action.

A creative idea alone does not constitute innovation. Laurence Knell tells me during the course of our conversation that innovation is fundamentally about more than an idea – you have to go beyond having a bright idea and actually *do* something with it. Everyone has good ideas, but most ideas will remain conceptual and not be put into practice.

Thinking back to the MIT definition of innovation, this focus on action is central to their understanding of what innovation is: it is 'the process of taking ideas from inception to impact'. It's not enough to just have an idea. You have to do something with it.

In this way, we can understand innovation as the practical application of creative ideas. It involves taking creative ideas and turning them into tangible products, services, processes or solutions that address specific problems or needs. Innovation is more than brainstorming or generating ideas; it involves taking action through refining, testing and implementing those ideas in ways that result in meaningful outcomes.

A brief note on uncoupling creativity and innovation

It's worth pausing briefly here to uncouple the words 'creativity' and 'innovation'. They are often used interchangeably but they are not the same. Creativity is about generating new ideas and innovation is about putting those ideas into action.

Creativity is the ability to generate new, interesting and original ideas. It involves thinking beyond conventional boundaries, making connections between seemingly unrelated concepts, and envisioning possibilities that haven't been explored before. Creativity is the initial spark that ignites the innovation process.

As Theodore Levitt (1963) nicely summarizes it, 'Creativity is thinking up new things. Innovation is doing new things.'

A definition of innovation for this book

We can see from the literature and our experts that, at its essence, innovation is about doing something new or different. It could be a new product, a new process, a new way of operating at work, a new workflow, a different way of doing things. But it's not doing something new for the sake of it – it's about solving problems, creating something useful and adding value. Innovation happens by executing a creative idea.

Here's the definition I've settled on for this book, which came out in my insightful conversation with Laurence Knell:

'Innovation is a creative idea brought to application that results in value.'

A checklist for innovation

Let's take that definition and the three components we've explored and create a practical checklist for innovation. You can use this simple checklist and apply it to your own work. Use it in your job and in your team as a way of creating clarity around innovation and how to approach it.

Here's our checklist for innovation:

- Novelty
- Action
- Value

Let's look at some examples of these components in practice.

Example 1: Novelty and value, but no action

Hazel is a creative communicator in a busy government organization. She comes up with a new way of communicating the company strategy to employees after attending an inspirational conference. She thinks this will bring value to the organization because one of the problems they face is misalignment and a lack of understanding of the bigger picture.

Hazel brings the idea to her manager to discuss it, who thinks it's interesting but says they don't have the capacity to do it right now. Hazel brings it up a few weeks later but again is met with a lukewarm response. The idea never gets off the ground and is soon forgotten about.

We can see in this example that Hazel had one key component firmly in place, which was novelty. She saw a way of communicating the organizational strategy in a way that was new for the organization. One point for Hazel. She also had another key component in place: value. She knew that her idea would help to solve one of the organization's pressing problems by aligning people around the business strategy and helping them to all row in the same direction to achieve their common goals. Two points for Hazel. But, unfortunately for Hazel, her idea doesn't count as an innovation because she's missing the third and final component: action. Her idea was just that, an idea. Nothing came of it; no action was taken, nothing was implemented.

The lack of practical application leaves this potential innovation as nothing more than a creative idea.

Example 2: Novelty and action, but no value

Howard attends the same conference as Hazel. He is blown away by the speakers and his head is buzzing with new ideas by the end of the event. He can't wait to get back to work to start implementing some of these ideas.

One of the speakers talked about how she revamped her organization's newsletter to make it a single source of truth for employees that they enjoyed reading. She successfully used design, photography and graphics to create and deliver an aesthetically beautiful product to employees. It has resulted in clarity around processes and procedures and has reduced confusion in the organization thanks to the clear information presented in the newsletter. Howard was really taken by this idea and decides to replicate it in his own organization. He gets a freelance graphic designer on board and launches the newsletter within a matter of weeks.

Howard's organization is very conservative and current employee communications are often long-winded written emails. So Howard gets one point for novelty: adopting an image-led, graphic approach to a newsletter is novel for his organization. Howard gets a second point for taking action. He implemented the idea very quickly by relaunching the newsletter within weeks of attending the conference. However, where Howard fails to meet the criteria for innovation is in the third component, value. What Howard has not considered is that most of his workforce aren't desk-based and do not use email as a primary communication channel. Although the new newsletter is very beautiful to look at, it is rarely opened and it is not delivering any value for the business. This lack of value makes Howard fall short of innovation.

Example 3: Novelty, action and value

Briege is doing an internal communications audit in her new role as Head of Internal Communications in a bank. She has been running focus groups and stakeholder interviews to really understand the communication needs of the business and the communication preferences of employees. One theme that is emerging again and again is that communications are very long-winded and difficult to digest. This leads to many employees losing interest. Employees are frustrated by how boring and difficult to understand company updates are. Leaders are frustrated by the lack of understanding of the strategy among their teams.

Briege has an idea. She helps the senior leaders to make 90-second videos using their smartphones to talk about company updates and the company strategy. These are informal, largely unscripted and casual – a world away from the long-form written content that employees are used to. This is a very new way of communicating in this organization, so there's one point for Briege: novelty. Briege's second point comes from taking action. She recognized the need for a new way of communicating, she came up with an idea, and she implemented that idea. Tick. Briege assessed the efficacy of her idea by measuring employee understanding of the company strategy, reviewing video open rates and assessing employee satisfaction with the new approach. She is blown away – employee understanding of the company strategy has increased from 25 per cent to 60 per cent in only one month and employees tell her that they really enjoy the videos and find them easy to follow and easy to understand. So that's where Briege gets her third point for value: this approach is new, is implemented, and is delivering value for the business by aligning employees around the strategy.

Exploring types of innovation

Now that we understand the components of innovation and have a clear definition for what it is (a creative idea brought to application that results in value), let's look at the different *types* of innovation.

There are endless ways to slice and dice innovation types. Some experts will tell you there are 12 different types of innovation. They make it seemingly deliberately complex. In the interests of simplicity, let's distil innovation down to two broad types: radical innovation and incremental innovation.

Radical innovation

Radical innovation is usually what we all think of first when we hear the word 'innovation'. We think of something big, life-changing, groundbreaking – an invention that disrupts how we live or interact, like the internet or the smartphone. Radical innovations represent a significant departure from the norm – a profound change or a product that could be meaningfully described as 'revolutionary'. This type of innovation is often quite disruptive as it challenges established norms and traditional ways of doing things. In other words, it breaks stuff. It makes the impossible possible.

Radical innovation typically introduces entirely new products, services or processes that disrupt existing markets and industries. It makes headlines. It is the intimidating type of innovation that makes feel us convinced that innovation is the reserve of the creative elite. Radical innovation represents a bold leap into the unknown, and this is its most distinguishing feature.

Examples of radical innovation:

- **The iPhone:** When Apple introduced the first iPhone in 2007, it was the start of a new era of digital communication and easy access to information from anywhere. The interface, design and functionality of the iPhone revolutionized how we communicate and gave rise to a new mobile app economy, creating a raft of new jobs for developers and entrepreneurs.

- **Digital streaming services:** The introduction of digital streaming platforms like Netflix and Spotify are great examples of radical innovation. They completely disrupted existing models of content distribution and entertainment consumption. They provided consumers with unprecedented control over what they consumed and when and how, sparking a fundamental change in the entertainment industry.

Radical innovation is generally a high-risk type of innovation that requires significant investment in research, development and market adoption. It's a long-term approach to innovation; it can take years of testing and prototyping to develop a brand new product or way of doing things. If it's successful, radical innovation can result in competitive advantage, the creation of new markets and even an impact on society and the economy. But if it's not a success it can drain significant resources and create obstacles for a path forward.

Incremental innovation

Incremental innovation, also known as continuous improvement, refers to the process of making small and gradual improvements to existing products, services or processes. It focuses on refining and optimizing what already exists. The objective is to enhance efficiency, quality and overall performance over time.

Shapiro (2011) says that 'innovation must be a continuous, never-ending process'. Laurence Knell echoes this when he tells me that innovations don't have to be major breakthroughs in technology or new business models, they can be as simple as upgrades to a company's customer service or features added to an existing product.

While radical innovation captures headlines with its groundbreaking inventions, incremental innovation quietly but consistently drives progress and improvement on an ongoing basis. It's all about gradual, step-by-step improvements to existing products, services or processes. Incremental innovation builds on the foundation of established systems, rather than trying to disrupt them. It's about tweaks and evolutions rather than the introduction of something entirely new to the whole world.

Examples of incremental innovation:

- **Software updates:** Computer systems, apps and digital platforms regularly release small, incremental updates. These tend to fix bugs, improve security or address customer feedback. These incremental changes enhance the user experience and keep the software competitive in a busy tech landscape.

- **Product iterations:** Consumer electronics manufacturers frequently release new iterations of their products, such as smartphones or laptops. These iterations often include minor design improvements, enhanced performance and updates based on user feedback. While the core product remains the same, these incremental changes attract repeat customers and maintain brand loyalty.

Incremental innovation is low risk as it involves gradual improvements rather than major changes. It is minimally disruptive and allows organizations to maintain stability while evolving. Over time, the cumulative effect of numerous small improvements can result in significant enhancements in organizational outcomes.

Innovation is often incremental and not a 'eureka' moment

Steven Johnson (2011) argues that we need to rethink our idea of innovation as a singular radical 'eureka!' moment. He conceptualizes innovation as a 'slow hunch', or lots of small, good ideas bubbling together in your brain for a long time that eventually connect and give you the innovative idea.

The invention of penicillin is an example of Johnson's slow hunch theory. We think of the invention of penicillin as a singular moment in time, when actually this is not the case.

The year was 1928 and Dr Alexander Fleming had famously returned from a holiday to find mould growing on a Petri dish of bacteria. He noticed that the mould appeared to be preventing the bacteria from growing and soon identified that the mould was actually producing a chemical that could kill bacteria. He named the substance penicillin. This was the discovery of the world's first antibiotic (Gaynes, 2017).

Eureka, right? Well, no, not really. Because nothing actually came of this discovery for more than 10 long years.

When Dr Fleming published his findings, none of his peers were particularly interested, and he had enormous difficulty in making penicillin into something useful. Penicillin was labelled 'a laboratory curiosity' and it wasn't until 1940 that it was developed into a drug ready for animal testing. The first human trial was conducted in 1941 – 13 whole years after Fleming's post-holiday discovery. It took *years* of experiments, tests and incremental innovation to develop penicillin into the life-saving drug we have today.

Levels of innovation in organizations

It's worth a quick look at the different *levels* of innovation, too, as this can help you think about the extent to which you want to incorporate innovation into your internal communication practices. Do you want to be an ad hoc innovator or have innovation as a system?

Shapiro (2011) distinguished between three distinct levels of innovation to illustrate the different approaches you can take. You might recognize your own organization in one of these three levels:

1 Innovation as an *event*. This is when companies hold one-off brainstorming sessions, annual hackathons or contests to come up with new ideas for the business. It's very much a one-off occurrence and innovation is not embedded in regular ways of working. It's pretty ad hoc.

2 Innovation as a *capability*. This level is more sophisticated than ad hoc innovation events. In this level, organizations create structures and processes to define problems, generate ideas to solve those problems, and put those plans into action. This ties in nicely with our three ingredients of innovation – they're coming up with an idea that is valuable to the business and then putting it into action.

3 Innovation as a *system*. This is the most advanced level, in which innovation is embedded in how the organization works and everything it does. Innovation is not separate from the business but is just part of the actual operating system. Employees are continuously improving processes and products to create ongoing value. An example of this is the *kaizen* principle which originated from the car manufacturer Toyota; ideas and innovations from their frontline workers, captured and put into action regularly, consistently improve their products and their business (Salvador and Sting, 2022).

Why should we care about innovation?

Innovation is important and you should care about it. That's me on my soapbox. I really believe that's true. And I say that simply because the world is changing at an incredible pace and it's so easy to get left behind. Think about simple things that seem normal to us today but that would have seemed impossible 20 years ago – for example, going on a city break abroad 20 years ago usually required you to be adept at reading a paper map or being one of those magical people who have a built-in sense of direction, a bit like a homing pigeon. (I am so jealous of those people. How do they *do* that?!) But nowadays when you go on a city break, you don't need the giant fold-out paper map of the city and you don't need to have a good sense of direction, because Google Maps will bring you anywhere you want to go, easily. Being able to visit a new place and navigate unknown streets impeccably using information beamed from space satellites is incredible – but we take it for granted now. It's normal. We quickly adapt to useful innovations and they become part of how we live.

The pace of change doesn't seem to be slowing down. There are new innovations coming to market all the time that change how we live our lives. Think about the impact that the internet and digital social networks and smartphones have had on how we communicate and interact with others. Perhaps innovation and new ways of doing things will be remembered as the hallmark of the 21st century.

Or maybe not, because innovation has shaped human progress throughout all of history, not just in this century. Think of the earliest days of humanity when innovation could literally mean the difference between life and death. Innovations in hunting, agriculture and shelter construction allowed early humans to survive in difficult environments. As time rolled on, innovation continued to be central to the progress of society and civilisation. Early technological developments such as wheels and basic tools were significant innovations that helped people to harness natural resources and build more complex societies. Innovations in transport, such as ships and roads, enabled humans to begin trading between regions which also resulted in cultural exchanges of diverse ideas. The Renaissance saw a surge in scientific innovation, with Leonardo da Vinci making groundbreaking discoveries which laid the foundation for modern science and engineering.

History is punctuated by remarkable milestones of innovations that changed the world. Here are a few examples that serve as a reminder of how important innovation is to our lives:

- In 1440, Johannes Gutenberg invented the printing press. This completely revolutionized how information was disseminated, making books and knowledge more accessible to people than ever before.
- In the late 18th and early 19th century, the Industrial Revolution saw significant innovations, including the steam engine and the factory system.
- In 1903, Orville and Wilbur Wright flew an aeroplane for the first time. This innovation has completely transformed how we travel around the planet today.
- In the late 20th century, the invention of the personal computer and the internet changed how we communicate, how we do business and how we live.
- In 2003, the Human Genome Project mapped and sequenced the human genome for the first time, which created valuable and unprecedented insights into human genetics and medicine.

These examples show the importance of innovation for human society and how we live our lives today.

That's all history, though – does innovation matter in the workplace today?

Yes, I reckon so. Can you find me a CEO today that thinks innovation isn't important? You might be hard-pressed to source one. CEOs and senior leaders would probably agree that innovation isn't a choice, it's an imperative, due to the changing external environment and the need to stay relevant with changing customer needs. Organizations need to constantly find new ways to stand out, to differentiate themselves and gain a competitive edge – and innovation is how they can achieve this.

And this doesn't refer just to tech companies who create software or computer products – innovation is required across all industries and sectors. Remember, innovation doesn't need to be a remarkable new invention or a 'eureka' moment – it can be small, incremental improvements over time that deliver value to the business or to customers. Innovation isn't just important to businesses, it's also championed by national governments, for example The Oireachtas (National Parliament) of Ireland has 'innovation' listed as one of the six core values (Houses of the Oireachtas Service, 2022). The Irish government has also published a research and innovation strategy called 'Impact 2030', highlighting the importance of innovation to address Ireland's social, economic and environmental challenges (Department of Further and Higher Education, Research, Innovation and Science, 2022).

The modern workplace is rightly obsessed with innovation, which is probably why you're all sick of hearing about it. But when you boil it down, innovation is important to modern organizations for reasons like competitive advantage, growth, customer satisfaction and adaptability.

Competitive advantage

As consumers, we've never had more choice of what to buy and where to buy it and who to buy it from. If you want a new laptop, there are literally thousands to pick from. If you're looking to invest in new employee communication software, you have a huge range of vendors to choose from. How can organizations stand out in these crowded markets and make themselves seen when their competitors are offering similar products or services? Well, they do this through innovating. Innovating, experimenting and trying new things can help organizations to create something more unique. They can become more attractive to customers by doing something different, for example by meeting customer needs in a new way or offering new features.

Look at Tesla, for example. If you want to buy a car, you have endless options to choose from. The car industry is a really crowded market and a lot of products are really similar (especially to consumers like me who are really only interested in the functionality of travelling from A to B). How did Tesla cut through this busy market and make such a huge name for themselves with a cult-like following of fans? They did this through innovation. Tesla disrupted the car industry by introducing electric cars with cutting-edge technology and a focus on sustainability. This approach was smart and gave them a distinct advantage: they caught the attention of environmentally conscious customers in a way that other companies simply couldn't compete with.

Growth

Innovation isn't just about standing out and being different. It's also linked to how organizations can fuel long-term growth. Companies that invest in innovation are more likely to find new and better ways to make money from customers, new markets to sell in or ways to reach more customers without an increase in costs.

Amazon is an incredible example of a company that harnessed innovation to fuel growth. It started as a simple online bookshop in 1994 and today it's one of the world's largest e-commerce and technology companies. Amazon has introduced incredible innovations in the shopping experience for consumers. Let me give you a simple example. The other night I was brushing my teeth and noticed that my floss was running out. I opened up the Amazon app, found my previous order of floss and clicked 'buy again'. I was able to place my order quickly and easily, using only one hand, while I was brushing my teeth with my other hand. And to make this experience even more incredible, the floss was delivered the very next day. This new approach to one-click shopping and quick delivery results in huge value for customers. In my case, it saved me having to (a) remember that I needed floss after I left the bathroom, (b) write floss on my shopping list and (c) walk to the shop and buy floss.

This kind of innovative approach to the customer experience is what has made Amazon such a household name and such a giant business. Innovation has fuelled its growth, far beyond its initial scope as an online bookshop. It's now worth billions.

Customer satisfaction

Smart companies will also innovate regularly to keep their customers happy and loyal and coming back for more. Customers can be hard to please. I know this because I myself am notoriously fussy and I expect high-quality service when I pay money to a company. The only way that companies can keep customers happy in a world when our needs, wants and preferences are changing all the time is by innovating. Innovation can keep an organization responsive to customer feedback and able to adapt to it quickly, whether this means tweaking an existing product or introducing an entirely new service.

Apple is a great example of an organization that uses innovation to increase customer satisfaction and loyalty. Apple has customers who are so loyal they will queue outside in the rain for *hours* just to get their hands on the latest product. How do they achieve this?

Well… through a relentless focus on innovation.

Their products are intentionally designed to be user-friendly, intuitive and easy to use. Customers love them because they can just pick them up and use them. You don't need to trawl through a complicated manual to figure it out. And Apple products are never static, are they? There's always something new, whether that's a new feature or improved functionality or a brand new smartphone. Think about how Apple created an entire ecosystem of products that work together – AirPods, iCloud and Apple Music products, for example, are all designed to work seamlessly together to create a great user experience. This didn't exist before and was an innovation built on understanding what customers wanted and what would keep them satisfied.

Adaptability

Being innovative is great for helping organizations to adapt, too. It isn't just about happy customers or growth, it's also about ensuring that organizations can survive and continue to compete in a world that keeps changing. Think about changes in the economy or changes in international markets or changes in your competitors – all of these things could pose a risk to organizations, and they need to innovate to stay in the game. This is central to how Drucker (1984) sees innovation, describing it as an opportunity for businesses to evolve in response to changing circumstances. When an organization understands that innovation is important and has it as part of its culture, it can respond to challenges and seize opportunities much quicker and easier.

Now I'm a big fan of lying on a giant couch watching TV in the evening, so Netflix comes to mind as an example of an organization that used innovation to adapt to changing market conditions. I'm old enough to remember that if you wanted to watch a film on a Friday night in the 1980s, you had to visit the local video rental shop and physically browse through the thousands of video tapes on offer. On a good day, this could take at least an hour – especially if you had to try to get consensus with your friends or family about which video to get. You'd watch the video at home, rewind the tape back to the start (I am REALLY showing my age now) and then make the walk back to the video shop to return it the next day. This seems crazy now, right? Netflix changed everything, but it didn't set out to do that.

Netflix started as a company that rented out DVDs by mail order. Their innovation was sending the DVDs to your house so you didn't have to visit the physical shop. But they noticed the shift in consumer behaviour towards digital streaming and they were quick to recognize the significance of this. They were able to adapt and innovate, and Netflix developed the streaming technology we all know today that allows us to instantly stream films and TV shows online without having to leave the couch.

Netflix has consistently innovated and adapted to changing market dynamics, and this has helped them to transform from a DVD rental company into a global streaming service worth billions of dollars.

What about us in internal communication?

Our definition of innovation doesn't change when we apply it to internal communication:

'Innovation is a creative idea brought to application that results in value.'

But it helps if we put it in context and talk about what it might mean specifically to us as internal communicators. Internal communicators that I spoke to for this book often thought of innovation as synonymous with technology. A new app, a new digital channel, a new analytics platform.

But, as we've explored in this chapter, innovation doesn't require technology. Innovation could be a reimagining of any part of the communicator's role, workload or tasks. We could innovate to solve a problem: how can we drive strategic alignment through communication? We could innovate to generate employee satisfaction: how could we better meet the needs of our employees? We could innovate to become more adaptable: how do we adapt to an influx of video-obsessed Gen Z workers? Innovation could touch any part of internal communication: how we craft and deliver content, how we create workflows, how we create alignment, how we work with senior leaders, how we streamline our processes, how we automate manual work, how we collaborate with others.

Harry Grout from Scarlett Abbott told me that innovation in internal communication is about two things for him: 'doing something that's never been done before and changing something that works okay for the better'. Natasha Plowman, a communications consultant based in London, told me 'the perception that innovation is just about science and tech is not accurate – it is as much about how we do things, how we come together and deliver work.'

And Jessica Roberts, a communications consultant, told me that innovation is about how internal communicators can be creative in how they solve problems. 'Innovation is about finding new and interesting ways to do something.'

Innovation is for everyone

Here's the reassuring message at the end of this chapter: innovation is for everyone. If you can think up a creative idea, put it into action and deliver value then, boom, you're an innovator. You don't need technology or a budget. You don't need a shock of white hair or a lab coat or a polo-necked jumper. Everyone can innovate. *You* can innovate. And if you do it, you'll reap huge rewards for your organization.

KEY TAKEAWAYS

- Definitions of innovation vary widely.

- Innovation is defined by three key components: novelty, action and value.

- Innovation is not about novelty for its own sake; it should aim to solve problems and add value.

- Our definition is this: innovation is a creative idea brought to application that results in value.

- There are two broad types of innovation: radical innovation and incremental innovation.

- Innovation has shaped how we live and has transformed societies and civilisations.

- Innovation gives organizations a competitive edge, helps them grow, keeps customers satisfied and makes organizations adaptable.

- Anyone can innovate.

REFLECTIVE QUESTIONS

1   Have you ever been involved in a project or initiative that lacked one of the key ingredients of innovation (novelty, action, value)? What was the result?

2   How can you apply these three ingredients (novelty, action, value) to your own work or projects?

3   Which level of innovation (event, capability, system) does your organization currently operate at?

4   How might your organization benefit from moving to a higher level of innovation?

5   Can you identify a problem or challenge in your work or personal life that could benefit from an innovative solution?

References

Department of Further and Higher Education, Research, Innovation and Science (2022) *Impact 2030: Ireland's research and innovation strategy*, 18 May, Department of Further and Higher Education, Research, Innovation and Science, Dublin

Drucker, P (1984) *Innovation and Entrepreneurship*, Harper Business, New York

Eurostat (2023) Innovation, Eurostat, ec.europa.eu/eurostat/statistics-explained/index.php?title=Glossary:Innovation (archived at https://perma.cc/CN9X-TFTP)

Gaynes, R (2017) The discovery of penicillin: New insights after more than 75 years of clinical use, *Emerging Infectious Diseases*, May

Henderson, T (2017) Why innovation is crucial to long-term success, Forbes, 8 May

Houses of the Oireachtas Service (2022) *Strategic Plan 2022–2024: A parliament working effectively for the people*, Houses of the Oireachtas Service, Dublin

Johnson, S (2011) *Where Good Ideas Come From: The natural history of innovation*, Penguin, London

Lee, S and Trimi, S (2018) Innovation for creating a smart future, *Journal of Innovation & Knowledge*, 3 (1)

Levitt, T (1963) Creativity is not enough, *Harvard Business Review*

McKinsey (2022) What is innovation? McKinsey & Company, www.mckinsey.com/featured-insights/mckinsey-explainers/what-is-innovation (archived at https://perma.cc/4HLS-RTLN)

Ridley, M (2020) *How Innovation Works*, Harper Collins, London

Salvador, F and Sting, F (2022) Encourage innovation from all employees, *Harvard Business Review*, 19 September

Shapiro, S (2011) *Best Practices Are Stupid*, Penguin, New York

03

Innovation in internal communication

I like trying new things, asking questions and challenging norms. Probably no surprise there, given that I've written a book on innovation.

And I was always like this, even as a kid. Patient parents, remember? I was often experimenting with things, mixing stuff together to see what would happen, having big meaty discussions about the world and the universe and about why we believe the things we do (I was great fun at parties). This curiosity and experimental mindset never left me. In all the in-house internal communications roles I've held, I've always invested time in testing out new ideas, playing around with different tactics and evaluating the results to keep improving. I've delivered great value for organizations as a result. Turns out, I've been innovating in internal communications for years without even knowing it, and I suspect many of you could be in the same boat.

Innovation isn't new to our profession. But the concept of innovation seems alienating for many of us due to the high-volume nature of our work and the exhausting, frenzied days we often endure. Some days we don't even have time to enjoy a hot coffee, let alone deliver an innovative new approach to our work, right? It seems like innovation in our profession is hard and many of us feel it is simply impossible.

In this chapter, let's take a closer look at innovation in internal communication and critically explore the obstacles we face. What's stopping the modern internal communicator from innovating? We learned in the last chapter that innovation is critically important – so why aren't we all doing it?

Innovation isn't new in internal communication

Here's a reassuring message to get us started: innovation is not new to our field. Innovation has been central to internal communication for years. Think about how communication with employees has changed in the course of your lifetime – my Dad would not recognize the digital workplace we now all take for granted as it simply didn't exist when he was employed. When he worked in an office there was no email, no intranet – it was before the internet had even been invented. It was a different world.

Back in his day, internal communication was characterized by verbal and print communication. There was lots of top-down, hierarchical communications cascading from senior management to rank-and-file employees. Communication was often through one-way, broadcast channels such as memos, circulars, printed newsletters or a company magazine. Townhall meetings were often different, too; there were no such thing as 'ask me anything' sessions, there was little expectation of leadership transparency and, as one older colleague once told me, the expectation 30 years ago was that employees should 'put up, shut up and get on with it'.

But, my, how times have changed.

The workplace is a different beast now, isn't it? The invention of email and intranet systems was a huge change for organizations and completely disrupted traditional modes of communication. These technologies allowed the faster dissemination of information, and enabled employees to self-serve the information they need and want. You no longer had to ring Barry in HR every time you needed a query answered – you could probably answer it yourself by checking the FAQ document on the intranet.

Further changes came with the emergence of social media platforms, peer-to-peer social networks and instant messaging tools that enabled greater lateral communication in organizations, outside of the traditional hierarchy. These platforms signified a shift towards more democratized communication where employees could have conversations with anyone, ask questions of leaders, share their own thoughts more easily and contribute to organizational discussions.

This marked a real shift from monologue to dialogue, from one-way to two-way communication. A new internal communication approach was developing in which employees were more active participants than before. Employees demanded more transparency, more voice and more agency, and leaders found themselves open to scrutiny and challenge.

Digital communication has fundamentally changed how people consume information and we now have mere seconds to capture and hold employees' attention. We are competing for their attention in a world of non-stop, entertaining content that sits in the palm of their hand. We need to ensure that messages can reach employees effectively and drive the desired behaviour change amidst the digital noise. The shift from top-down communication to a more collaborative and inclusive approach has introduced complexities that demand innovative solutions.

All of these significant changes have meant that internal communicators have had to innovate by necessity, simply to keep pace with changes in the world. We've had to adapt and adjust enormously as the workplace moved online.

And here's the thing: the pace of change isn't slowing down. The need for us to innovate hasn't lessened. As the world continues to change, innovation in internal communication must continue. It's not an option, it's a necessity.

New challenges demand our attention now. Communicators must innovate to tackle the modern challenges of communicating with a diverse workforce, the rise of hybrid and remote working, the accelerated pace of digital transformation, the rise of video and audio culture and the changing expectations of employees.

Communicating with a diverse workforce

The workforce is becoming increasingly diverse, with employees from a range of different backgrounds, cultures and generations working together. This diversity requires innovative approaches to communication to bridge gaps in understanding, encourage inclusion and cater to the unique needs of particular cohorts. Employees have greater choice of communication channels, tools and tactics than ever before, so we must innovate to keep our system of communication relevant to our employees.

Organizations that once upon a time only employed people in one city to work together in one office may now have employees from multiple countries around the world with different cultural backgrounds, different languages and varying communication styles. For example, an employee in country X may communicate very directly and bluntly in line with their cultural customs, but this may appear extremely rude to an employee in country Y where it is more culturally appropriate to use softer language or to be more diplomatic. These kind of misinterpretations, misunderstandings or language barriers can hinder effective workplace communication.

A diverse workforce may also have different communication preferences. Some employees may prefer asynchronous written communication that they can read in their own time and refer back to later. Others may prefer synchronous verbal updates where they can hear information directly from leaders and have the opportunity to assess the body language, tone of voice and nuances in the communication. Some employees will appreciate receiving bite-sized video updates that they can consume easily on their smartphone, whereas others prefer longer-form content with more detailed information. Internal communication professionals need a deep, rich understanding of their internal audiences to accommodate these diverse preferences and communicate effectively. Innovation can help us keep pace with the changing needs of a diverse workforce.

The rise of hybrid and remote working

The Covid-19 pandemic was awful and left many of us desperately anxious, ill or burned out. It was a dark, bleak, difficult time and it left its mark on the world in many ways. One lasting legacy from the pandemic is the shift to hybrid and remote working.

The pandemic accelerated the trend for employees to work online, a trend that was already in place thanks to the internet and digital collaboration tools. This digitization is what helped so many of us to make the abrupt shift from working in an office to collaborating with others from our kitchen tables. Technology enabled a huge-scale shift to remote working for many office-based roles.

And as the pandemic slowly wound down and we emerged from our houses, shell-shocked and tired and grateful to hug people again, one thing endured: the appeal of flexible working. According to Microsoft's Work Trend Index (2023), 70 per cent of workers now prefer flexible work options. This doesn't mean we don't enjoy seeing each other. Sixty-five per cent of us still opt for some face-to-face time with our colleagues (Microsoft, 2023). The productivity levels maintained throughout the pandemic showed that it *is* possible to work from home in many roles and it *is* possible to communicate and connect with colleagues in dispersed workforces. We used to be told that we absolutely had to be in the office together to do our work, and the pandemic proved for many of us that was simply a lie. Razzetti (2022) sums it up nicely in his book *Remote Not Distant* when he says: 'The pandemic has put the way we do things around here to the test.'

There's no going back now. For many organizations and many employees, remote and hybrid working is here to stay.

This shift has implications for us as internal communicators. We are again required to innovate, to assess our approach to ensure it's effective in meeting the needs of a changing workforce. Perhaps our channels need readjusting. Perhaps our leadership communication needs rethinking. As with any organizational change, a move to remote or hybrid working means we must take stock of how we work and how this may need to be changed or refined.

One of the obvious benefits that emerged from the pandemic was the accelerated growth of digitisation in organizations. What's that joke that went around at the end of the pandemic? It went something like this:

What's been the most powerful driving force behind your organization's digital transformation?

1 Chief technology officer

2 Chief operating officer

3 The Covid-19 pandemic

Even the most successful CTO would probably have to admit that the pandemic put a bit of fire in the belly when it came to finally pushing out old technologies in favour of newer ones that met the needs of employees. New tools were brought into organizations to help them communicate and collaborate more easily, and what an opportunity this was for us as internal communicators. Think of all the organizations that never had video calls pre-Covid. Or that never had instant messaging systems or asynchronous collaboration tools or virtual whiteboarding capabilities. All of these new tools and tech open up opportunities for internal communicators to innovate by exploiting this technology in valuable ways.

The pace of digital transformation

Building on this, it's not just the pandemic that brought along new tools. Digital channels and communication technologies have been completely transforming the way people communicate and consume information for years.

Think about how digital technology has impacted our lives in the last decade or two. We went from a time when smartphones didn't exist to a time when smartphones are an integral part of our daily lives. We carry our phones around the house, we bring them into meetings, they send us reminders of important tasks we need to do.

We are so outrageously enamoured with our phones that we even bring them into the bathroom and to the bedroom, which could be construed as an invasion of our most sacred spaces. This kind of technology in your hand would have been unthinkable when I was a child. I remember being fascinated by Miles O'Brien in *Star Trek: The next generation* whose character spent a lot of time playing around with futuristic, touchscreen technology. He was able to zoom in and out of images on a screen with the touch of a finger and this blew my mind. Surely this could never be possible! And yet here we are – I can do exactly the same thing now, easily and cheaply, from the comfort of my couch.

The pace of change has been fast and the scale has been dramatic.

All of this technology has made it easier than ever for people to create, share and consume digital content. This of course includes employees in the workplace. Gone are the days where it may have been sufficient to communicate to all employees using just one channel. Now employees operate in a sophisticated digital workplace where they can communicate through email, instant messaging, self-service intranets, social networks, virtual or in-person meetings, video calls, asynchronous collaboration tools and employee apps… to name a few.

More tech and tools are coming on the market all the time. So for us, as internal communicators, the need to keep pace and innovate continues.

The rise of audio and video culture

Video content has become increasingly prominent as a way to communicate effectively and to get your audiences' attention. We see this on platforms like TikTok, where creators make engaging 60-second videos that capture the attention of millions. The creativity and skill of these young creators is astounding. (If you've never visited the Reddit page called r/fixedbytheduet then make yourself a coffee and prepare to laugh it out of your nose. This Reddit page showcases some of the most creative combinations of TikTok videos from different creators and it's absolutely hilarious. This gives you a flavour of the content we're competing against for our employees' attention.)

Smartphones democratized access to creating video content. Now we can all be film makers and video editors and creators. This user-generated content is all over popular social platforms like YouTube, TikTok, Instagram and Snapchat. According to Ceci (2023), TikTok reached more than three billion downloads worldwide by July 2021.

The rise of video platforms like TikTok and Instagram also signalled a technological shift from desktop to mobile. People like consuming content on their phones. It's easy, isn't it, because our phones are always in our hands anyway. TikTok indicates a shift towards short-form video, though longer-form content on YouTube continues to be popular, which serves as a reminder of the diversity of communication preferences our employees are likely to have. This rise of video culture pushes us to innovate in internal communication too, to meet the needs and preferences of different internal audiences.

Similarly, audio as a communication medium has risen enormously in popularity. Podcasts have becoming an increasingly important channel to communicate with an audience. According to Gotting (2024), only 22 per cent of the adult population in the USA was aware of podcasting in 2006. But by 2022, this figure had risen to 79 per cent. More than 82 million people listened to podcasts in 2021 in the USA and this is expected to continue to rise to over 100 million listeners in 2024.

A decade ago, Noyes (2014) wrote in the *Harvard Business Review* that podcasting was entering 'a golden age'. There are at least three million podcasts in existence, the majority of which are in the English language (Thorpe, 2023). Creators can easily and cheaply launch their own podcast using equipment they already have to hand and an editing app on their phone, making audio another democratized medium for anyone to access.

The popularity of podcasts can partly be explained by their ease of access for the audience. I think about how I consume podcasts myself, and it's usually while I'm *doing something else*. I'm loading the dishwasher or folding the laundry or driving my daughter to dance class.

So podcasts fit into my life without any extra effort or friction – they don't demand my full attention and I don't need to watch them or read them. This is an easy consumer experience which we can think about in the context of internal communication and whether we can or should explore audio communications for our employees.

The changing expectations of employees

The dynamics between employees and employers are changing too. Fifty years ago, it would have been the norm for an employee to join an organization for life, sometimes even doing the exact same job for life. Employees were often willing to put up with less-than-ideal working conditions in order to keep their jobs and have financial security. But not anymore. Now it's common for people to change jobs, change employers, even change careers. Employers don't command the loyalty they once did from employees, and they must work harder to both attract and retain talented employees as a result.

I remember once when I got a new job offer, I excitedly rang my mum to tell her the news. I had been in the same job for three years by that stage and was hungry for more responsibility and more seniority. Three years in the same job felt like enough. But when I told my mum I was moving to a new company she was just *baffled*! She couldn't understand why I would leave a decent salary in a pension-able job for a new gig. Why would I want to start over again and make new friends when I was already comfortable? It was completely bizarre to her as this simply wasn't the done thing when she was in the workforce. For her, it was normal to join a company at age 20 and then stay there until retirement at age 65, and be grateful for it.

Our expectations as employees are changing. We demand more now, don't we? We want more than a transaction in which we trade our labour for money; we want purpose, meaning, autonomy. We want to feel valued, we demand a work–life balance, we want bound-aries around our personal time. We also want more say in how things are done, we want more ways to speak up and be heard, we want more transparency from leaders. People are now actively seeking out employers with a positive work culture, opportunities for personal and professional development and increased levels of autonomy. These changing expectations from employees keep us on our toes and demand that we innovate and stay curious to stay effective.

The view from internal communication practitioners

I wanted to make sure I wasn't alone in my assessment that innovation is an ongoing need in internal communication. How do other practitioners view it?

I speak with Janet Hitchen, a communication consultant who led internal communication at Apple. Janet is smart as a whip, bright, creative and quick on her feet. She tells me she enjoys solving problems through creative thinking and admits she has a rebellious spirit – she isn't afraid to break the rules to achieve results. I ask Janet about the role of innovation in internal communication today and whether it's important. She tells me that innovation is crucial because of the pace of change we're experiencing in the workplace. 'Change is the new normal. Everything is changing all the time. This idea of change as a constant is crucial for internal communicators. If you do the same thing over and over, and you stick rigidly to that, then you're not going to evolve or develop new ideas. Internal communication professionals need to get used to adapting, changing and innovating on a regular basis.'

Internal communicators who aren't innovating, she tells me, are going to get left behind. 'If you aren't innovating new ways to approach, consider, design, be inspired and deliver then you're standing still. That's okay for a short time, but long-term that leads to becoming obsolete.'

Janet has a theory: communicators are being afraid of brandishing the labels 'innovative' or 'creative', perhaps by virtue of a lack of confidence. She's experienced this herself, most starkly when working in Apple when she was surrounded by some of the most creative, inventive and innovative people on the planet. 'I think I put the words creative and innovative on a pedestal for a while,' she muses. 'I told myself I wasn't a creative. But you know what? I am creative. I'm not an inventor but I innovate. Working in that kind of environment meant I had to innovate – there was no play book, no "best practice", I just had to figure it out myself.' Janet says that internal communicators need to get over our fear of the words 'innovation' and 'creative' and learn to embrace them.

I also speak with Jonas Bladt Hansen, a communications consultant based in Denmark. Jonas is a fascinating communications practitioner who I have been following online for some time. He was the first person I saw talking about using AI to create an internal communications matrix. He is a forward-thinker and wants to push the boundaries of the profession, and he tells me that this all stems from his deep-seated curiosity. Much like Janet, Jonas argues passionately that innovation in internal communication is critical due to way the world is constantly changing. He tells me that innovation in internal communication is important 'because the way internal communication worked 10 years ago is not how internal communication works today'.

Echoing my thoughts earlier in this chapter about how internal communication has changed over the years, Jonas says, 'We started out as journalists, producing information in a newspaper; we'd publish it and send it out. Now today it's completely different.' He references the digital revolution that has disrupted our lives so enormously. The most important medium for internal communicators used to be a printed newspaper, he tells me, but now it's all online. There have been massive changes.

For Jonas, innovation is more than an opt-in for a communicator with extra time on their hands. He says that internal communicators 'have a responsibility to constantly innovate and try things out and be curious'. Time doesn't stand still, he tells me. Things are changing all the time – just look at the digital world and the changes we've experienced in the last few years.

I ask Jonas what would happen if internal communicators decided they didn't want to innovate, or perhaps if they felt they didn't have time to innovate. He laughs at the absurdity of the question. 'We can't just sit there and think our department will never change.

We will become extinct and redundant if we don't innovate and keep up.'

I talk to Merima Baralić de Ramírez, Senior Communications Director with PepsiCo. Merima is based in Barcelona and is a self-described 'cultural chameleon', someone who is well used to change as she moved schools 10 times across two continents and four languages before the age of 18. This lifestyle, she says, fuelled a tireless sense of wonder and it drives her innovative mindset. Merima tells me, 'innovation is continuously asking and reassessing who are we talking to, how are we talking to them, what are we telling them. Are we keeping up with the times (leveraging tech in the right ways) or reaching our audiences where they are (shop floor, manufacturing line, office, remote, in person, etc.)?'

In Merima's view, innovation is critical for internal communicators. We can't be effective or successful without it. Other departments innovate all the time and by necessity, she tells me, so why would we be any different? She states, 'We innovate a lot in our marketing strategy talking to our consumers – why are some companies not doing the same for their internal audiences?'

Lynn Zimmerman, CEO and Chief Strategist of Swing Strategic Communication based in Colorado, agrees. She says innovation is fundamentally important to internal communication and gives this example: 'If there is even one person who hasn't been reached by communication, we need to keep working at finding ways to reach them. Plus, always doing things the same way is a guarantee that your audiences will lose interest.'

I hear a similar sentiment from Veema Shah, former Head of Internal Communications at the National Crime Agency. She tells me that innovation is crucial in internal communication. 'There's so much *noise* in organizations,' she says. 'We need to reduce this or get through this to get the important messages out there, or use internal communication to set up listening forums, or get the important debates going in the right way for those colleagues.' Veema has the same thoughts as Jonas in Copenhagen – the old ways of pushing out one-way content don't work anymore. The world is changing, employees are changing and we must innovate to keep up.

Time and again, internal communication practitioners from around the world told me that innovation is critical for our profession to drive results. Workforces are becoming increasingly diverse, employees are working in distributed ways, digital transformation is continuing unabated, video and audio culture is rising and employee expectations are changing. Traditional approaches to internal communication don't always suffice to effectively engage and connect with internal audiences.

Innovation is not something to bolt-on to internal communications when you've got a bit of spare time; it's an absolute imperative for long-term success. We must embrace innovation to be adaptable, to be able to solve problems, to reach our audiences effectively, to deliver excellent results, to produce work of value.

But innovation is *hard* for us

The views of these practitioners make it plain: innovation is crucial for internal communication. So let's go ahead and innovate.

Right?

Sadly, it doesn't appear to be that straightforward. Although I uncovered consensus when I asked practitioners about the *need* for innovation, translating this belief into practice and action is a different matter entirely. It seems that internal communicators find innovation very hard.

When I began having conversations with internal communication practitioners about innovation, I had expected to unearth a range of interesting case studies. But instead I was met by anecdote after anecdote about the seemingly insurmountable obstacles they face to innovating. Communicators at all different levels of seniority around the world were at pains to share their stories of time pressure, resource constraints, unrealistic stakeholder expectations... as one anonymous practitioner told me, 'I'd love to spend some time on innovation. But as a team of one, I'm drowning. Honestly, I'm just trying to survive the day.'

Intrigued, I began to tug on the thread of obstacles to innovation in internal communication to see how it would unravel. I interviewed internal communicators around the world, I heard their frustrations and I listened to their stories. I adopted the role of an anthropologist; observing, listening, documenting and getting curious about what all of this means. I began to see themes and patterns emerging. I documented three obstacles which quickly became five obstacles which progressed to eight. The hits kept coming as I spoke to more practitioners. Eventually I settled on 10 obstacles to innovation in internal communication.

I'll set out these obstacles here. These are all based on the real, lived experiences of in-house internal communication practitioners today. The quotes used in this section are all anonymized on request; communicators repeatedly told me they didn't feel comfortable putting their name against these exhortations of brutal honesty. Some feared what their manager would think. Others were worried about their reputation. A few told me that they were frankly embarrassed about how they were spending their time but couldn't seem to change it and wanted the comfort of anonymity.

Here are the key themes that emerged when I investigated the obstacles to innovation in internal communication:

1 Tiny teams and budgets.

2 Time pressure.

3 Lack of autonomy.

4 Hierarchical structures with authoritarian leadership.

5 Resistance to change.

6 Fear of failure.

7 Misconceptions.

8 The pressure to be lean.

9 Technological constraints.

10 Adherence to best practices.

Let's explore each of these before we identify how to overcome these barriers and create opportunities to innovate.

Tiny teams and budgets

Internal communication teams are typically under-resourced and scant on people and budget. Many practitioners I spoke to operate as a team of one or as a tiny team of two. This can make it difficult to invest any time or energy in innovative thinking or in testing out new ideas. I talked to Ciaran (not his real name) who runs internal communication for a global organization with more than 5,000 employees and an annual turnover of millions of dollars. Ciaran is an internal communications team of one. 'I'm constantly told there's no money to hire anyone or even to outsource some creative work to an agency or a freelancer,' Ciaran told me. 'I am doing my best to keep up with the work, but on many days I don't have any space to be creative or figure stuff out properly – I'm just focused on ticking things off an endless list of tasks. If you could tell me when and how I'm expected to innovate, I'm all ears.'

Ciaran wasn't the only one who felt this way. Many internal communicators told me they have very limited capacity for experimentation. Innovation requires trial and error; trying things out, gathering feedback, evaluating results, iterating and trying again. This takes time, effort and energy. Many internal communicators today simply don't have this capacity. One internal communicator in the UK told me, 'I'm just about keeping the lights on. I'm exhausted at the end of every day and it feels like my capacity for creative thinking is getting less and less each week.'

An internal communicator in the US told me that the expectations of what she could deliver as a team of one were 'outrageous'. Exasperated, she laid out the long list of tasks she was meant to accomplish in her role which encompassed everything from creating an organizational internal communication strategy to advising leaders on communication to creating content for the channels, running internal events and even doing graphic design and videography. She has made attempts to reduce the workload to no avail, telling me, 'In our organization internal comms reports up to HR, who frankly just don't get it. I feel very stuck and very tired.'

A tiny team also suggests limited diversity and limited access to a range of skills and expertise. Dr Lollie Mancey told me in our interview that it's virtually impossible to innovate alone; you need a team of people, ideally a team with diverse experiences and diverse areas of expertise. Innovation thrives when these different perspectives and experiences collide around a shared goal of solving a complex problem. But in a team of one or two, innovation may be stifled by the team size.

Budgets (or lack of) play a role here too. Internal communicators told me, over and over again, how their limited or non-existent budgets hinder their desire to innovate. If we think back to Ridley's (2020) understanding of innovation, which is the process of discovering different ways of arranging the world into forms that are unlikely to arise by chance, it's reasonable to deduce that this discovery process requires investment in research, experiments and developing new ways of doing things. Budget restrictions can make it difficult for internal communication teams to explore new ideas, new ways of working or new technologies.

Internal communicators with little to no budget to outsource work to agencies or freelancers are often overburdened, overworked and overwhelmed – they are forced to prioritize routine and urgent tasks over important, long-term work like innovation or big picture thinking. This overwork also results in reduced time for creative thinking and quiet reflection, things we know are important for innovation.

Time pressure

This lack of resources can also lead to the creation of our second obstacle: time pressure. Over and over, internal communicators told me the same thing: 'I haven't got time to innovate.' Communicators acting as a team of one feel particularly squeezed, trying to juggle multiple responsibilities and deliver the work of an entire team alone. There is no time for deep thinking or creative problem-solving. One internal communication manager told me, 'I am constantly putting out fires and dealing with urgent tasks. When am I supposed to have the time for innovation when some days I don't even have time to eat my lunch?'

Innovation requires time and focus, precious things that under-resourced teams simply do not have. It also involves taking the time to ask questions and explore ideas. I asked internal communicators in my network to tell me how they spend their time. Many reported spending a significant amount of their time on urgent work and busy-work unrelated to the stated business priorities. Communicators, particularly those in more junior roles, told me they feel powerless to change this due to leadership demands, line management structures and their junior position in the company.

Even people who have titles like head of internal communications or director of communications told me they spend a significant amount of their time on *urgent but not important* tasks, including a lot of tactical delivery work. This poses a challenge – innovation requires time and space to be creative. And here's my hot take: if you're working in this firefighting, tactical, exhausting way then innovation becomes even *more* important for you. You need to find new, innovative ways to automate work, create systems and improve workflows so that you've got some breathing space to think, plan and deliver value.

Lack of autonomy

Many communicators candidly told me how they lack autonomy in their roles and feel micro-managed. For example, a piece of content may have to go through several rounds of approval before they can publish it on internal channels – and by the time it's approved, it has morphed into a jargon-filled, nonsensical piece of corporate speak that no one will understand or engage with. A director of internal communications in the US told me how his new internal communication strategy got 'absolutely mangled in the approval process' because it had to get approved by multiple senior leaders, none of whom were communication professionals. 'If I just had the autonomy I need to run this the way I want, I could solve all their problems,' he says. 'But the micro-managing culture throttles me, all my plans get changed by others and this stops me delivering great work.'

A poll conducted by communication consultant Mike Klein in 2023 showed the depth of this issue for internal communication professionals. He asked this question: 'Would you prefer unlimited budget or unlimited permission?' Within 48 hours, more than 300 people had voted and the overwhelming consensus is that 'unlimited permission' is what communicators desire most. This signals that micro-management, decision-making and freedom are crucially important to internal communicators today.

Interestingly, the idea of permission-seeking and micro-manage-ment seems more of a pain point for senior internal communicators. One senior leader I spoke to, let's call her Kate, was hired as head of internal communications on the explicit understanding that she would spend her time on strategy, not tactics. In reality, she was closely micro-managed and her role consisted of non-stop tactical execution and firefighting. Her biggest wish, she told me, was 'to have time to stop and think and come up with better ways of doing things rather than the endless pattern of urgent jobs that need doing. I've tried pushing back and I've discussed this with my boss but I get a "that's just the way things are done here" answer and because I'm on probation I don't feel confident enough to push it further.'

Kate and I talked about how her level of permission impacts her ability to innovate. She's nervous about rocking the boat while on probation and doesn't want to be 'too counter-culture' in her approach for fear of upsetting her boss. She's hoping that once she builds up some credibility in the role and gets off probation that things may change, though she admits this might be 'slightly magical thinking'.

Hierarchical structures with authoritarian leadership

Similarly, in organizations where leaders exercise strict control and authority, communicators may feel hesitant to propose new ideas or innovate on existing processes. Rigid hierarchical structures and top-down decision-making can stifle innovation because creative ideas have to navigate through multiple layers of bureaucracy and approval procedures that create bottlenecks. This process can be painfully slow and discouraging, leading innovators to abandon their ideas in frustration. This hierarchy creates an obstacle for innovative ideas to gain traction quickly and successfully.

A friend of mine worked in an organization where the hierarchy was so strict that employees were not permitted to communicate directly with senior leaders who outranked their boss. This organization actually had a documented communication protocol that said you weren't allowed to contact certain people in the organization because of your lowly status as a mere employee – imagine! (And of course, they prided themselves on being innovative and the word 'innovation' was littered all over their website. Go figure.) In that same organization, senior leaders were shocked when they asked employees for ideas to improve how the organization worked and got hardly any volunteers. Quelle surprise.

I spoke to an internal communication manager who is responsible for managing all the communication channels and content in her organization. She told me about the bottlenecks that the hierarchy has created for her and how it reduces her willingness to try new things. 'I came up with a fun, creative campaign for St Patricks Day last year,' she told me. 'I showed it to my boss two weeks before St Patricks Day and she said a few people needed to approve it. I followed up several times but it didn't get approved for three weeks... by that time, St. Patricks Day was well over. I wouldn't bother trying another creative campaign here after that because what's the point?'

Resistance to change

Resistance to change came up again and again in my conversations with communication professionals. Which isn't entirely surprising, as organizations are 'inhospitable environments for innovation' (Levitt, 2002) and are often designed to promote order, stability and routine.

Here's an example. An internal communication specialist in a large UK organization attended one of my training workshops. Afterwards, she was brimming with new ideas and solid proposals for tangible change. She had ideas for how she could innovate in her role. But when she spoke with her manager, her ideas were dismissed. She was told that everything was fine the way it is and there was no requirement to change anything. In her own words, 'The strangest part was that my manager paid for me to go on this course, despite the fact that she didn't want anything to change as a result. It seemed like a tick-box exercise to keep me happy rather than any commitment to identifying improvements or making things better for our employees. The experience would make me think twice about suggesting changes again.'

This attitude is symptomatic of an organizational culture that stifles innovation. A culture that is resistant to change can make it hard for us to introduce innovative ideas and translate them into action. And remember – innovation requires *action*. It's not sufficient to simply have a good idea.

Managers, leaders and employees may be comfortable with existing methods of communication and this may manifest as a reluctance to try new things. Organizational cultures that value stability and consistency may discourage employees from testing new ideas that challenge prevailing norms. Change inevitably brings uncertainty, and people may resist what they don't understand or can't predict. This resistance to change can act as an obstacle to an ambitious internal communicator who wants to experiment and innovate.

Fear of failure

Organizations that innovate well tend to have a healthy approach to failure. Employees are encouraged to try new things and experiment – and if it doesn't succeed, that's okay. An experiment isn't a failure if your hypothesis is proved incorrect, that's actually a very successful experiment that results in valuable learning.

In researching this book, I heard from many internal communicators who said that their organizational culture discourages failure and this makes it hard to try new things. An internal communication manager told me there is a strong unspoken culture of 'failure is not an option' in her workplace. In this kind of culture, innovation is unlikely. If you fear shame, retaliation and discipline then why would you ever try something new or remotely risky? The fear of failure stifles attempts at innovation. There's no guarantee that new ideas will succeed. But we must be allowed to at least *try*.

Fear of failure can be seen most commonly in organizations that are highly risk averse. They may favour the status quo because it feels safer. This can result in a reluctance to change how things are done, even when there are more efficient or effective alternatives available. Innovation requires a willingness to challenge existing norms and embrace change, even when it might not be successful.

I discussed this topic with an internal communication professional in the USA. She accepted a new role last year and was excited to join the team and make a difference. In her first couple of months on the job, she offered up a range of new ideas and suggestions for positive change. Although her manager accepted that her ideas were good, he didn't agree to implement any of them 'in case they don't work out'. She soon came to realize that the organizational culture valued the status quo and there was a fear of trying new things in case they failed. Her enthusiasm for new ideas and innovative suggestions quickly waned.

Misconceptions

Common misconceptions about internal communication can hinder innovation, too. For example, the belief that internal communication is merely about conveying information from top to bottom can limit the exploration of new approaches. I spoke to many internal communicators who were frustrated with the range of misconceptions or misunderstandings of their role and their team. One practitioner told me, 'Despite my best efforts, many of my stakeholders remain clueless about what I'm actually here to do or the value I bring. They just ask me to send stuff out and get annoyed when I start to ask them questions about objectives or audiences.'

Many people I spoke to had similar stories. A Germany-based communicator told me, 'I try to carve out space to think up new solutions or try out new ideas but I'm always getting pulled into last-minute nonsense or things that really shouldn't be part of my job. I try to say no but I'm usually faced with a senior leader who pulls rank on me and I end up spending hours making PowerPoint slides or editing reports that no one will read. They think I'm a performing monkey or something and they give me all their grunt work to do under the guise of it being a comms job.'

This misunderstanding of our role can act as an obstacle to innovation in internal communication, because if your stakeholders don't know what you're there to do or what value you bring the business then innovating in your role won't seem particularly business critical. If this is you, don't panic. It's not hopeless. I've got a solution for you in Chapter 5.

The pressure to be lean

In 2023 there were massive layoffs by companies around the world, particularly technology companies. The tech industry laid off nearly a quarter of a million people, which was 50 per cent higher than the previous year (Stringer and Corrall, 2024). In January 2023 alone, more than 89,000 people were laid off from their jobs in tech. Huge companies like Google, Amazon and Meta reduced headcount, tightening their belts amongst whispers of a looming recession. In early 2023 many economists predicted that a downturn in the economy was coming and that it would hurt; inflation was high and they expected it would only fall with an increase in unemployment (Smialek and Casselman, 2024).

Against this backdrop of layoffs and predictions of economic misery, the words 'Do more with less' began to emerge as a way for teams to somehow deliver their current workload with fewer resources. Top execs across Silicon Valley were touting 'Do more with less' as the key theme for investors (Field, 2023). And I began hearing this mantra in the world of internal communication too. A blog from Unily (2023) states 'the reality is that communicators are being asked to do lots more with the same level of budget and resource'.

Internal communicators feel under pressure to deliver more and better work with less support and fewer resources. This 'do more with less' mentality prioritizes efficiency at the expense of innovation. The constant pressure to cut costs, streamline operations and deliver work with little to no investment prevents internal communicators from dedicating time and energy to innovation.

Technological constraints

Outdated hardware or software, limited access to technology and restrictive IT policies can act as obstacles to innovation for internal communicators. It can hinder our ability to make changes or experiment with new approaches. It also reduces our efficiency, which in turn reduces the time we have available for experimenting with new approaches. I've spoken with communicators who work in wildly inefficient organizations due to the workflows and processes they have to follow on outdated in-house software systems. They have to spend significant time on manual tasks or workarounds, leaving less time for creative or innovative activities.

Many practitioners are operating without the basic technologies or tools they need to succeed in their roles. I spoke with an internal communication professional in Dublin whose request for a digital employee communication tool was denied. 'We are still sending our employee newsletter as a PDF attached to an email,' he tells me. 'It's like we are stuck in a time warp. We would never dream of communicating with our customers like this but somehow for employees it's not seen as important. A lack of tech keeps us trapped and there's very little innovation to be done on our channels and content when I can't even get basic metrics like open rates or click rates.'

This internal communicator was keen to experiment with features like A/B testing to improve open rates, to send targeted messages for different segments of employees, to test out new types of content and measure what works, to trial video or audio content in the newsletter... he had endless ideas for experiments. But with the limited technology available, he felt stuck. He was still sending out the newsletter blind, with little data to show its efficacy for the audience or the organization.

Adherence to best practices

In my humble view, there is an unhealthy obsession with 'best practice' in the world of internal communication. These two words appear again and again, in training courses, webinars, blogs, websites, social media. But a belief in standardized best practices can act as an obstacle to innovation; why would you feel the need to deviate from established norms if you accept that they are the 'best'? Our acceptance of best practice stifles creativity.

Best practice in internal communication refers to widely accepted methods or approaches that are deemed to deliver the best optimal outcomes based on past experiences and industry standards. These practices are often seen as benchmarks for achieving effective communication within organizations. But I'd argue that the idea of 'best practice' can be misleading; it assumes there is a one-size-fits-all solution for diverse situations. In reality, organizational contexts, goals and challenges vary widely from one company to another. This variety makes it difficult to universally define a single 'best' approach to anything.

Call me a contrarian, but if someone tells me there's a 'best' way to do *anything* then you'd better believe I will invest time and effort into interrogating that assumption and finding other (and potentially better) ways to do that thing. Because what you consider best for you might not be best for me. It might be completely irrelevant to me. That is the beauty of our work – it's a nuanced and contextual craft and the word 'best' has no place in it. There's a lot more to unpack around the idea of best practice in internal communication, so the next chapter will dive into that more deeply.

This chapter looked at the relationship between internal communication and innovation. I showed that innovation has been part-and-parcel of internal communication for years and this is set to continue due to the continued pace of change in the workplace. But internal communicators are struggling to innovate. I documented 10 obstacles to innovation through conversations with in-house practitioners. But don't worry, Chapter 5 will give you some practical suggestions on how to overcome these obstacles and free yourself up to innovate.

KEY TAKEAWAYS

- Internal communicators have been innovating for years, particularly in response to the rise of digital communication technologies.

- Communicators must continue to innovate to tackle the modern challenges of communicating with a diverse workforce, the rise of hybrid and remote working, the accelerated pace of digital transformation, the rise of video and audio culture and the changing expectations of employees.

- Internal communication practitioners believe that innovation is crucial for our profession.

- This book documents 10 obstacles to innovation in internal communication: tiny teams and budgets, time pressure, lack of autonomy, hierarchical structures with authoritarian leadership, resistance to change, fear of failure, misconceptions, the pressure to be lean, technological constraints and adherence to best practices.

REFLECTIVE QUESTIONS

1 Do you believe that innovation is crucial for the field of internal communication? Why or why not?

2 Among the 10 obstacles to innovation listed, which ones resonate most with you?

3 In the context of a diverse workforce, how do you currently address communication preferences and cultural differences? Are there innovative approaches you can adopt to bridge communication gaps further?

4 The shift to remote and hybrid work is a lasting legacy of the pandemic. How has this shift affected your organization's internal communication, and what innovations have been necessary to adapt to this change?

5 How do you currently embrace innovation in your role?

6 If you were to identify one area in your internal communication strategy that requires innovation, what would it be, and what steps could you take to introduce innovative solutions?

7 In what ways does a lack of autonomy affect the creativity and innovative thinking of internal communicators? Have you witnessed or experienced situations where autonomy was restricted?

8 How does fear of failure affect the willingness to try new things in your workplace?

9 How do misconceptions about the role of internal communication act as obstacles to innovation? Can you recall instances where misunderstandings affected the innovation potential of internal communication teams?

10 Reflect on the time constraints mentioned by internal communicators. How does the lack of time for deep thinking and creative problem-solving impact the ability to innovate? Have you faced similar time pressures in your role?

References

Ceci, L (2023) TikTok statistics and facts, Statista

Field, H (2023) Tech's new business model: 'Do more with less', CNBC, 11 May

Fitzpatrick, L and Dewhurst, S (2019) *Successful Employee Communications: A practitioner's guide to tools, models and best practice for internal communication*, Kogan Page, London

Gotting, M (2024) US podcasting industry – statistics and facts, Statista, 12 January

Levitt, T (2002) Creativity is not enough, *Harvard Business Review*, August

Microsoft (2023) Work Trend Index, Microsoft, www.microsoft.com/en-us/worklab/work-trend-index (archived at https://perma.cc/8FGV-5QTU)

Noyes, J (2014) Should your company start a podcast? *Harvard Business Review*, 9 December

Razzetti, G (2022) *Remote Not Distant: design a company culture that will help you thrive in a hybrid workplace*, Liberationist Press, Highland Park, IL

Ridley, M (2020) *How Innovation Works*, Harper Collins, London

Smialek, J and Casselman, B (2024) Economists predicted a recession. So far they've been wrong, *The New York Times*, 26 January

Stringer, A and Corrall, C (2024) A comprehensive list of 2023 and 2024 tech layoffs, Tech Crunch, 25 January

Thorpe, V (2023) Podcasts in pivotal moment as number of new shows drops by 80%, *The Guardian*, 4 February

Unily (2023) Do more with less: How internal comms is combating scope creep, Unily

04

Best practice stifles innovation

It's September 2023 on a bright, cold day in Manchester. Communication professionals have gathered together for a conference. This is potentially a ripe breeding ground for an indulgence of our love affair with 'best practice' – perhaps there will be a raft of speakers presenting on different best practices we must follow to be successful in communication.

But wait. Who's this coming?

It's Helen Reynolds, Founder of Comms Creatives. She sweeps onto the stage wearing a colourful striped dress and her signature red lipstick and you already know this is going to be anything but boring. Above Helen is a big yellow slide with seven words in bold letters:

'There's no such thing as best practice.'

Mic drop.

This is a bold statement, one that will surely rankle the sensibilities of many internal communication practitioners. Because as a professional community, we seem to be very much in love with best practice.

Let's back up a bit. What's a *practice* anyway? And what could possibly be wrong with having some *best* ones?

What's best practice?

A practice is simply a specific way of doing something. It could be a method, an activity, a process or a technique. A practice is something that is established, in other words other people have done it before. Typically, practices are based on the accumulated knowledge and experience of people who have come before us: experts and professionals in a particular field who have figured out what works to attain a goal.

So if a practice is a specific way of doing something, then a best practice is considered the *best* specific way of doing something. Best practices are considered effective in solving a specific problem or achieving a specific goal. They're viewed as reliable as they've stood the test of time and they've been used by others with successful results. Best practices are tried-and-tested ways to get a job done so you don't have to start from scratch and come up with a solution by yourself.

Internal communication best practices are widely accepted methods or approaches that are considered to deliver optimal outcomes for communicating inside organizations. These practices are based on past experiences of other communicators, experts and thoughts leaders who have observed and documented what works to achieve a goal. Best practices are often considered a safe and proven path to success. For example, best practices might outline specific ways to communicate with remote employees or how to communicate in a crisis.

Best practices are considered the most effective and efficient ways to complete these tasks and they often serve as guidelines or roadmaps for internal communicators to follow. They're typically shared as recommendations in our field, offering us a structured framework to solve tricky problems. This structured approach can be reassuring; it can feel like a safe approach in which risk is minimized and uncertainty is reduced.

The proliferation of 'best practice' in internal communication

I started getting curious about best practices in internal communication about a year ago. I noticed a pattern emerging across the students I teach, the comments I was reading on social media, the direct messages I was receiving on online platforms and the content I was reading from internal communication vendors, industry experts and training providers. I began to notice two words cropping up everywhere: 'best practice'.

Once I noticed the trend, it was suddenly everywhere. It reminded me of when I got engaged and began to notice shiny engagement rings everywhere. I had never noticed them before and now they were everywhere I looked. Similarly, when I was pregnant with my daughter it suddenly seemed that there were pregnant women *everywhere*. My husband rightly pointed out that they'd always been there, my brain just hadn't been actively noticing them before. My dalliance with the words 'best practice' followed the same pattern; once I noticed the phrase cropping up in one area of our profession then I spotted it in another, again and again. Those words appeared to be everywhere in the internal communication community.

The Institute of Internal Communication (2023a) produces a range of factsheets and guides for its members, which 'provide practice advice and best practice tips'. The Masters in Internal Communication Management run by Solent University (Institute of Internal Communication, 2023b) is designed to give students 'a deep understanding of theory and translate this into high-impact strategic internal communication that is underpinned by best practice, enabling them to operate at the most senior levels'.

A Google search for 'internal communication best practice' gave me 502,000,000 results. I didn't even know the internet was that big. I found content with headlines like:

'14 internal communication best practices for 2023' (Clear, 2023).

'7 internal communication best practices you should follow' (Sinclair, 2021).

'17 internal communications best practices for a stronger employee engagement' (LumApps, 2023).

I see the fascination with best practice in the students I teach, too. I teach a certificate in strategic internal communication and I always ask new students what they're hoping to learn over the course of the programme. One key phrase keeps appearing in their answers, again and again. Can you guess what it is? Yep, you got it: 'best practice'. Students tell me things like:

'We are bringing in a new intranet next year so I'd be keen to understand the best practice approach to doing this.'

'I'm a team of one and I'm also quite new to internal comms. Helping me to understand best practice for how to do my job would be very useful.'

'We have people who don't sit at desks so I'd like to know best practice for reaching non-wired employees.'

I also see the tendency towards a best practice approach reflected in my work with clients. Now in fairness, most of the clients I work with hire me specifically for my curiosity-based approach. I mean, my business is called The Curious Route, after all. But occasionally a client will want to avoid the hard work of curiosity and take a best practice shortcut instead. They don't want to be told that they need a deep understanding of their people or to create tailored communication solutions to meet their specific audience needs – no. That sounds too much like hard work. Instead, they ask me this: 'What's the industry best practice? What are other companies doing? Let's do that.'

Fitzpatrick and Dewhurst (2022) rightfully note that 'There's a tendency in internal communication to think that you can apply a solution from one place and hope it will work everywhere. People think "Well it worked over there, so it has to work here".'

The appeal of best practice

The lure of best practice in internal communication is obvious. I get it, I do. Everyone wants a simple, efficient solution that has been tried-and-tested already and has proved to be successful elsewhere. Best practices offer a sense of security and structure in what can often be a chaotic and challenging field. I've identified four key reasons why best practice is so alluring to internal communicators.

Efficiency

Best practices are seen as efficient. They provide a clear roadmap for achieving desired outcomes, which means we don't need to figure it out ourselves. It seems possible we can save time, energy and resources by following established methods. I mean, someone else has already used this approach and it worked for them – so why not just do what they did? Won't we get the same positive outcome? This makes particular sense in the context of the ultra-busy internal communicators who are operating in tiny teams with no budgets, who say they simply don't have the time to innovate or experiment due to mounting workloads. Best practice offers these busy communicators welcome shortcuts and roadmaps to help them get their job done quickly with the limited resources they have available.

This sentiment was echoed by Simon Rutter, an independent consultant with 20+ years' experience in the world of internal communication. He tells me 'Internal communication practitioners are so busy that they often haven't the time to stop and think. Creativity needs space and time. In the absence of adequate resources, internal communicators turn to best practice advice in order to get the job done quickly and move on to the next task.'

Reducing risk

The second reason we tend to love best practices is because they feel so safe. Practices that have been tried before with successful results are seen as safe choices that reduce the likelihood of us failing. In Chapter 3, we saw that fear of failure is one of the obstacles to innovation in internal communication. Taking a best practice approach is a way of reducing risk and thereby mitigating the chance of failure. It's bit a like a comfort blanket. We cling to it and we feel safe in the knowledge that other people have tried this practice before and it worked for them.

I've seen this play out first-hand with clients. One client with several large manufacturing plants wanted to come up with new and more effective ways to communicate with their frontline factory workers. We discussed what they know about their employees, how we could deepen this understanding and looked at the current channels they were using. We began to throw around ideas of how to make progress, including deep audience research with groups of employees and some experimental new tactics to engage their attention. But the client got nervous. 'What if it doesn't work? What if these experiments fail? I think we should just play it safe and apply the industry best practices instead,' they told me. 'Can you do some research into what our competitors are doing and we'll roll that out.'

This is not an uncommon approach for organizations that are conservative, traditional and thoroughly risk averse. Best practice approaches are very appealing for their apparent ability to reduce the risk of failure.

Expert consensus

Best practices often emerge from the consensus of experts and thought leaders in internal communication. We can see this in our examples above, where reputable organizations like the Institute of Internal Communication and Solent University actively promote best practices in our field. These practices represent a collective wisdom that has been tested and validated by people we perceive as having more expertise and wisdom than us.

I understand this more and more as I teach more students every year. Many people who work in internal communication have no formal communication training. Some make a lateral move into internal communication from HR or administrative roles and look to industry experts to lead the way. They hungrily consume blogs, newsletters and thought industry articles, thankful for the advice and unquestioning of its validity.

I spoke about this in confidence with one of my younger students. She's early twenties, extremely smart and admirably self-aware. She told me, 'I joined my organization as the assistant to the CEO. I started getting tasks related to communication, it started with an employee newsletter and then came employee events and webinars.

I've now been moved into a full-time internal comms role and from the outside it would probably look like I'm doing a good job. But underneath I'm sort of panicking every day because I don't feel like I know what I'm doing. I spend a lot of time reading internal comms blogs and content on best practice. Its essentially free advice, and my god I need it.'

I hear this sentiment repeated in my interview with Paul Bennun, a very experienced internal communication and people leader. He tells me that the best practice approach is most appealing when you're early in your career or you're not sure of how to get things done. 'Best practices can act as a guidance to people and help them to find the right approach to take,' he says, adding contemplatively, 'but of course there's really no such thing as best practice.'

Predictable outcomes

And, of course, we are drawn to best practices because of the tantalizing promise of a predictable outcome. There's an expectation that if we follow established methods then we can reasonably expect consistent and reliable outcomes that others have had before. It worked for them so it's going to work for us too, right? This predictability gives reassurance and comfort, and of course we all want that.

The predictability of a best practice approach provides reassurance to decision-makers and senior stakeholders in the business. Knowing that established methods are being followed can instil a sense of comfort and ease, due to the belief that by using best practices will lead to success. This is highly attractive to leaders because it creates an environment where outcomes can, in theory, be anticipated with a reasonable degree of accuracy. This enables forward planning and goal setting.

One internal communicator I speak with says he leans on the predictability of best practice as a way to get approval for budgets and resources. 'Where I work,' he tells me, 'everything has to go through multiple layers of approval. The more creative or innovative your idea is, the less likely it is to be approved. I've learned over time that you're more likely to get the green light if you explicitly link the project to a best practice and show how the same approach has worked for companies X, Y and Z before. And if the company is one of our direct competitors you're even more likely to get a yes.'

The limitations of best practice

Now you might be thinking that all of this sounds great. A safe, tried-and-tested approach with a predictable outcome that delivers efficiencies – what's wrong with that? Why on earth would we want to deviate from best practices? What on earth is my *problem*?

Well, simply because best practices limit us. Is it realistic to think we can simply transplant tried-and-tested practices from one organization to another, irrespective of the cultural or situational differences? In my view, no, it's not.

Let me explain in more detail and set out my stall here. Be open-minded and I'll see if I can convince you that we need to fall out of love with best practice and have a love affair with curiosity instead. Let's have a look at the specific reasons why I think best practice limits us:

- Context matters.
- It's unstrategic.
- It looks to the past.
- Because of the language.
- It stifles innovation.

Best practice limits us because context matters

Let's return to Helen Reynolds from the start of this chapter to unpack this with us. I ask her about that big yellow slide that boldly proclaimed, 'There's no such thing as best practice'.

'There's no *best* way to do anything,' Helen tells me. 'Anything we do in work or in life is all a matter of perspective. Sometimes all of these business consultants and time-poor managers are looking for the magical answer. But there is never a single answer. In my point of view, best practice is a matter of taste and perspective. There's a thousand ways to do anything.'

Shapiro (2011) points to the critical nature of context and circumstance as one of the reasons that best practices don't work. And he should know – he wrote a book with the bluntly direct title of *Best Practices Are Stupid* (I'm a bit gutted he got that title before I did, to be honest). He says:

> 'Context matters. We often believe we can take a practice from one organization and bring it to another. But culture, resources, competitive position, industry and other contextual factors matter. Replicating a practice from a different organization makes no sense for most companies.'

Each organization has its own distinct culture, values and dynamics. What constitutes a best practice in one company may not align with the culture and values of another. Trying to force-fit best practices into an organization can lead to friction, ineffectiveness and poor results.

I ask Helen Reynolds for her opinion of transplanting best practice from one organization to another to try to replicate the same positive results. Why wouldn't this work? She becomes passionate and riled up, telling me, 'What works somewhere else isn't necessarily going to work for you or for your organization. There are a hundred thousand variables. It might be the same industry and the same type of business but you may not have the same audience, you may not have the same resources, the same characters and personalities in the place you work, and your brand values might be completely different. Assuming something that worked somewhere else will work for you is very unwise indeed.'

I agree with her. The idea that there could be a one-size-fits-all solution for diverse situations in a creative field like internal communication seems highly unlikely. The variety and differences between organizations make it difficult to universally define a single 'best' approach to communication. Helen's thoughts are echoed by Fitzpatrick and Dewhurst (2022) who emphasize that communicators should not be unduly hung up on what other people are doing.

They say that making comparisons between organizations is like trying to take a dose of another patient's medicine – what is useful for one organization might be completely meaningless in another.

Think about this example: say an industry expert proclaims that the best practice for improving leadership communication is to create short, bite-sized, unscripted videos to share with employees. Maybe this has worked well in several organizations and it then becomes recognized as a 'best' way to improve visibility and trust of the leadership team. But will this work in *all* organizations and across all contexts? How about in an organization where the CEO is painfully and excruciatingly terrible on camera? How about in an organization where the employees prefer written communication to video communication? Or how about an organization where leaders communicate in jargon and acronyms and no one can make any sense of the videos?

So context matters. It matters a lot. My interview with Paul Bennun sparks a similar conversation. He tells me: 'My view on it, which I feel more strongly about as I become more experienced, is that everything is situational. You've got to consider so many different factors. Think about the work you need to do to achieve the result that you want. Look at what goal you're trying to achieve, what factors may influence any work you do towards that and therefore what would you choose to do. You can't get that from a best practice approach.'

Best practice limits us because it is unstrategic

In my conversation with our hero, Helen Reynolds, she tells me bluntly that the concept of best practice is very unstrategic in any communications role. This is because in a best practice approach, your starting point is based on what someone else has done rather than on what your organization needs. This is backwards.

For internal communication to have a meaningful impact in an organization, it must be deeply rooted in and connected to the overall business goals and the mission of the company. 'Any time you want to do anything worthwhile, you have to have a clear set of goals and a really deep understanding of what you're trying to achieve,' Helen tells me.

She emphasizes that to accomplish anything meaningful, we need to set clear goals and have a deep understanding of what we are trying to achieve. This strategic perspective is at odds with best practice, which tends to focus on trying to mimic the outcomes of others without necessarily understanding the underlying goals and rationale. Helen argues that, 'In best practice case studies, you don't get the full story of what happened or what went behind it – to think that you can just look at the outcome of someone else's project and know what went behind it is just not sensible.'

Best practices encourage us to look *outside* the organization as our starting point for coming up with strategies and solutions. Instead of starting with a deep understanding of your organization's specific needs and goals, best practice begins by looking at what has worked for others in the past. What are other people doing, what are our competitors doing, what tactics or channels have they successfully deployed that we could replicate? This approach may result in you choosing an approach that is not aligned with your organization's strategic priorities or your organizational culture.

Our starting point should be *inside* the organization. We need a rich, deep understanding of the business and the people who work in it before we start thinking about the right practices to apply. We must get deeply curious:

- What is the organization trying to achieve?
- How can internal communication help to deliver that?
- Who are our employees and what do they care about?

Best practice limits us because it looks to the past

All best practice is in the past. Best practices are just a collection of things that have worked well in the past for other people. That's literally all they are.

Best practice is telling you that something *has* worked in the past, rather than that something *will* work in the future. And in a world marked by constant change, taking a backwards-facing approach to communication seems counterproductive. Best practices don't and can't provide a roadmap for addressing emerging challenges or opportunities; we need adaptability and innovation for this.

While past successes do provide valuable insights, they shouldn't be the sole determinant of how we do things now or how we create strategies for the future. As Shapiro (2011) notes, 'what someone did last year may be irrelevant to what will work today'. Think about the changing needs and preferences of employees, for example. Once upon a time it was best practice for leaders to hold townhall meetings in person. Now many people are working remotely and teams are dispersed around the globe and this practice simply doesn't work for some organizations anymore. Things change, and best practices don't account for this.

While best practices can be instructive and give us insights into potential avenues to solve problems, we need to strike a balance between learning from the past and preparing for the future. You don't need to discard the accumulated knowledge of other practitioners – just be sure to recognize the limitations of a best practice approach in a changing world.

Best practice limits us because of the language

We are all communicators here. We know the power of language and the impact of words. So when I tell you that I have a huge issue with the word 'best' in 'best practice', I know you will understand.

Oh, the *arrogance* of the word 'best'! Maybe it's a redhead thing, but if someone tells me that they've developed the 'best' way to do something then that is simply going to make me super curious to find other ways to do that thing. Is there really any 'best' way to do anything in our field? I'm sure some consultants will tell you there is, but I'm not one of them.

Labelling something as the 'best' way to get something done is so limiting and counterproductive. When we believe there's a 'best' way to do something, it creates a mindset that completely discourages exploration or curiosity. After all, if something is already the best then why bother searching for alternatives or improvements? Surely there is no 'better' than 'best' – so why bother trying? This can inhibit innovation and the pursuit of more effective methods.

In his book *Think Faster, Talk Smarter* (2023), Stanford University lecturer Matt Abrahams challenges conventional wisdom about communication best practices. He suggests that we need to move away from the idea that there is a 'best' or a 'right' way to operate in the creative world of communication. 'We need to dial back our desire to do it "right", because "right" doesn't even exist,' Matt says.

This idea is echoed loudly by Caitlin Kirwan, an internal communication specialist with many years of experience under her belt. She tells me, 'The phrase "best practice" can be problematic due to making internal communication professionals believe there is a right or wrong way to do things.'

And one more thing... the use of the word 'best' perpetuates an illusion of perfection, doesn't it? It implies that there is a single, ideal solution that can be applied to every situation. But we know this isn't true. What's considered 'best' can vary widely depending on circumstances, goals and contexts. What's best for one organization may not be best for another. What's best for you might be absolutely terrible for me. So there really is no such thing as a 'best' practice in internal communication. Not in the slightest.

Best practice limits us because it stifles innovation

Adhering rigidly to best practices in internal communication can exert a stifling effect on our creativity and curiosity. If we fixate on predetermined solutions packaged neatly as 'best practices', it discourages us from exploring alternative ideas or finding our own path to success. The pressure to conform to established norms and other people's best practices may inhibit our willingness to experiment and take risks, both of which are essential to innovation.

Shapiro (2011) argues that reliance on best practice reduces your ability to lead, stating, 'duplicating what others are already doing relegates you to a continuous game of catch-up. Following in the footsteps of others is the fastest way to irrelevancy.'

Relying on best practices can lead to rigid thinking. Internal communicators or their stakeholders may become fixated on replicating what has worked before or what has worked elsewhere. In this fixed mindset, they may struggle to think creatively or generate new ideas. Innovative solutions often involve disrupting existing norms and challenging the status quo, but a commitment to best practices encourages the opposite. It may make an internal communicator resistant to trying new things or actively disrupting what's already in place. We must remain open to new ideas, be willing to take calculated risks, be prepared to challenge existing practices when they no longer serve our organizations' evolving needs and to be curious about bespoke solutions to business problems.

We are blinded by survivorship bias

Something that irks me about best practices is that the success rate is usually over-inflated. We don't hear about all the times that communicators applied a best practice and it failed. I am struck by this paragraph in Shapiro's book (2011):

> 'We tend to focus on the winners and successes, but we don't take time to track down the times when advice or a best practice didn't work. Companies that were successful in implementing a particular practice are at conferences talking about their experiences. But what about the hundreds or thousands of companies that did exactly the same practice and failed? We don't hear about them.'

Perhaps best practices in internal communication are steeped in survivorship bias. Survivorship bias is a cognitive bias that occurs when we focus on the things or practices that *survived* a particular process, while overlooking those that didn't. So you look at all the successful stuff that worked and ignore the stuff that didn't work. In order words, you pay attention to all the examples of where a best practice delivered a great result, whilst ignoring the examples of where it fell flat.

This survivorship bias leads to a skewed and overly optimistic view of the effectiveness of a practice because it doesn't account for all the failures and shortcomings and the things that went wrong for people using that practice. For example, picture yourself writing a detailed entry for a communication award. It's not going to be the full story, is it? You're going to skew it so it's deliberately positive to position yourself in the best light possible. You aren't going to document all the lows, the fails, the things you tried that didn't work – you just show off the success. So it may completely overlook the fact that you tried to implement a number of internal communication 'best practices' and none of them worked for you at all. Like Shapiro (2011) said about the practices that failed, 'we don't hear about them'.

Survivorship bias can lead to poor decision-making because it ignores the data and experiences of failures. But failures are often just as important as (if not more so than) successes. To avoid survivorship bias, we need to consider the full picture, including both the successful and unsuccessful cases, when analysing data or drawing conclusions about a particular practice or approach. This can provide a more realistic and balanced understanding of the risks and potential rewards involved, rather than a blanket acceptance that someone else's documented success is a best practice that can simply be applied elsewhere.

So when you hear about a best practice that works for everyone, sound the alarms and get curious. It probably *doesn't* work for everyone, you're just not getting the full picture.

Best practice limits us because it can be contradictory

Paul Bennun rightfully points out in our interview that best practices can conflict with and contradict each other. What do you do then? Which is more 'best' than the other?

He gives the example of a big redundancy programme happening in an organization. The best practices of the external communications team are likely to conflict with the best practices of the internal communications team.

For the external communicators, their best practice approach might be to keep the redundancies quiet and keep them out of the news. For their team, the less said the better, which means minimizing how much we communicate internally.

But this is going to be in stark contrast to the best practice approach for the internal communication team. They are likely to say that best practice is that leadership need to be visible, they should be out in front of everybody, they need to communicate regularly to build trust. This regular communication, of course, will massively increase the likelihood of the news leaking outside the organization.

So in this example you've got two best practices there that are at cross purposes and clearly conflict with each other. Paul concludes by saying, 'In reality, the answer is situational – it depends where you're at and what your organization needs'.

I was lucky enough to interview Stephen Shapiro. Much to my surprise, the first thing he told me in the interview is that best practices are *not* stupid.

Wait... what?

'I'm not completely against best practices,' he tells me. 'There might be some simple, standard practices that work. But we need to make sure that we understand "Does it fit our context?" The context really matters.' He tells me that what works for one culture, one environment or one situation doesn't necessarily work for another. 'Being a copycat is rarely a solid strategy.'

Best practice only works for simple problems

David Snowden's work is useful here to explore whether best practice makes sense in internal communication (Snowden and Boone, 2007). He developed a sense-making framework, Cynefin, that helps organizations and individuals understand the nature of the problems they face and from there identify the most suitable way for addressing them. This framework emphasizes that one size does not fit all, and encourages adaptive thinking and decision-making based on the specific context and characteristics of a problem.

It's worth appreciating that Snowden puts the problem first and positions the solution later – sort of the opposite approach of applying best practices where you start with a tried-and-tested solution from another organization.

Snowden categorizes challenges or problems in five domains: simple, complicated, complex, chaotic and disorder. Each domain requires a different approach based on the complexity of the problem. You can plot your problems into the domain it fits best and then determine your approach accordingly.

Snowden's five domains are:

1 **Simple:** Problems are well-defined and there's a clear cause-and-effect relationship. This domain is characterized by predictability.

2 **Complicated:** Problems are a bit more complicated but they can be analysed to determine the best approach. Solutions may not be obvious, so expert knowledge is needed. This domain is characterized by predictability through analysis.

3 **Complex:** Cause-and-effect relationships are not clear and outcomes are unpredictable. Solutions emerge through experimentation and innovation. This domain is characterized by uncertainty and continuous change.

4 **Chaotic:** Situations of extreme volatility and unpredictability, often crises where immediate action is needed to stabilize the situation. Once stability is achieved, the organization can transition to one of the other domains for problem-solving.

5 **Disorder:** A state of confusion where it's unclear which of the other domains applies. It requires reassessing the situation and choosing one of the other domains.

A best practice approach is only suitable for problems that fall into the *simple* domain (Snowden and Boone, 2007). For simple, straightforward problems that are well defined and have a clear cause-and-effect relationship, you can successfully use a best practice approach. In internal communication, this could be very basic, simple communications that are managed through clear, pre-defined templates or documented procedures with a high degree of predictability in terms of outcomes.

Let's look at an example. Say I come home in the evening and my house is dark. In this case:

- The problem is well defined: I can't see anything because my house is dark.
- There's a clear cause and effect: the house is dark because I haven't turned the lights on.
- There's a very predictable outcome: if I hit the button on the light switch, my house won't be dark anymore.

In this example, my house being dark is a very simple problem. I can solve it easily by turning on the lights. I don't need to innovate to solve the problem of darkness every time I come home. I can use a best practice approach: the best practice to lighting up my house is to use the light switch. So in the simple domain with a simple problem like this, best practice is absolutely fine.

Best practice is less suitable for complicated problems

For problems that fall into Snowden's *complicated* domain, best practice is less applicable. Complicated problems require expertise and analysis as there's less of a clear cause-and-effect relationship. Best practice approaches don't work for complicated problems for a number of reasons.

First, solutions for complicated problems are context sensitive. What works as a best practice in one context may not necessarily work in another. The context can include things like the type of problem, the culture of the organization, the industry, the company size and the predominant leadership style. Best practices are typically standardized approaches that may not account for the nuances of different contexts.

Secondly, best practice isn't suitable for complicated problems because of the expertise required. Complicated problems often demand specialized knowledge for diagnosis and solution generation. Best practices, by their nature, tend to be simplified, generalized approaches that may not encompass the depth of knowledge and expertise required.

Thirdly, complicated problems aren't static. They evolve and change over time. What may have been considered a best practice at one point might become outdated or less effective as circumstances change or new information emerges, so relying on a best practice can limit adaptability.

Fourthly, there's huge potential for error when you apply best practices to complicated problems. Applying best practices without a deep understanding of the underlying principles or root cause of the problem can lead to errors. People may follow procedures blindly, assuming they are always the correct solution, and fail to notice when circumstances deviate from the norm or when an unusual but more effective approach is required.

Finally, focusing solely on best practices stifles the potential to develop innovative solutions to complicated problems. Best practice discourages the exploration of new and potentially better approaches because people may feel constrained by existing norms. In the complicated domain, it may be required to go beyond what's considered a best practice to find an effective, creative solution.

AN EXAMPLE

Let's look at an example. Say you are working collaboratively with HR to develop and communicate a comprehensive employee benefits package. In this scenario:

- There's complexity in design. The problem involves designing a comprehensive employee benefits package which may be intricate due to different benefit options, legal requirements and cost considerations.

- There's expertise required. Addressing this problem necessitates expertise in benefits administration, legal compliance and financial analysis.

- There are multiple stakeholders involved, including HR, internal comms, finance, legal and potentially external benefit providers. They must all be coordinated and aligned.

- There's a requirement to customize and tailor benefits to meet the needs and preferences of a diverse employee base spread across different legal jurisdictions.

Communicating the new package is complicated as there are different benefits for different employees, a range of different enrolment procedures, multiple different enrolment deadlines and a need to set up two-way communication to take questions and feedback.

In this example, a best practice approach lifted from another organization won't work. You must rely on expertise, analysis and collaboration among multiple stakeholders to design and effectively communicate the new benefits package to your own unique audiences. Your approach must be tailored to the needs, motivations and preferences of your specific audiences, must be appropriate for the organizational culture, must be created with the resources you have available and disseminated using your own particular communication channels.

Best practices are less effective in the complicated domain because of its context-specific, expertise-dependent and dynamic nature (Snowden and Boone, 2007). In this domain, its often more beneficial to encourage critical thinking, innovative ideas and expert analysis to develop tailored, customized solutions to the specific problem at hand.

Best practice is even less useful for complex problems

In the *complex* domain, the concept of 'best practice' is less relevant and less likely to apply. While some general principles for your problem may exist, they are not universally applicable. Complex problems need an approach based on experimentation, innovation, adaptability and context-specific solutions (Snowden and Boone, 2007).

AN EXAMPLE

Let's look at an example. Say you are the internal communication manager in a large and diverse organization and your objective is to improve employee engagement. In this scenario:

- There's no clear cause-and-effect relationship. Employee engagement is influenced by a multitude of factors, making it difficult to identify specific cause-and-effect relationships.

- Employee engagement does not follow linear patterns. What engages one group of employees may not work for another. The relationship between different factors is complex and often nonlinear.

- Solutions for improving employee engagement are not readily apparent or predictable. Strategies that worked in the past may not be effective in the current context, and new innovative approaches may be needed.

- Achieving sustained engagement requires continuous adaptation and experimentation. There is no single 'best practice' that universally applies because what works can change over time.

- Employee engagement involves a diverse set of stakeholders, including HR, senior leaders, managers and individual employees. Coordinating efforts and gaining buy-in from various groups adds to the complexity.

- Personalization adds complexity too; recognizing that each employee is unique and may have different drivers of engagement complicates the development of standardized engagement strategies.

Complex problems, such as employee engagement, are characterized by uncertainty, unpredictability and the absence of one-size-fits-all solutions. For this type of a complex problem, we would need to use a more adaptive, innovative approach rather than relying on best practices that have previously worked for others. There's a need to experiment with different strategies and tactics, gather data on their effectiveness and adjust the approach based on real-time data and insights. It's an ongoing process of learning and adapting to the unique needs and challenges of the organization and its employees.

Internal communication problems are often complicated or complex

Think about the type of problems or situations we're faced with regularly as internal communicators. Communicating about organizational restructures or layoffs. Upskilling resistant or defensive senior leaders. Reaching a diverse global workforce who work unpredictable shifts or hybrid patterns. None of these can be classified as 'simple'. We rarely operate in an environment with clear cause-and-effort or with predictable outcomes. (Oh, if only!)

Internal communicators are often faced with unpredictable, thorny issues and challenges, making it impossible to rely on established best practices to address them. For complex problems with unpredictable outcomes, innovation and creativity are needed to identify novel solutions to tricky challenges.

Best practices don't work well in internal communication precisely because internal communication often operates within the *complicated* or *complex* domains of Snowden's Cynefin framework.

Let's change the language and call them 'good practices' instead

Relying on 'best practice' can stifle innovation by discouraging the exploration of new ideas or novel approaches. We need to fall out of love with the idea that there is a 'best' way to do something, and instead fall in love with curiosity, recognizing that innovation often emerges from asking questions, challenging existing norms and coming up with new ideas tailored for unique circumstances.

Unfortunately, there's no universal, magical 'best practice' for us all to follow in internal communications. There's no silver bullet. Internal communication is hard work and it requires curiosity, exploration and a willingness to try new things (and fail along the way).

But it doesn't mean we need to throw the baby out with the bathwater.

We can absolutely learn from other practitioners and from the success results achieved in other organizations. Caitlin Kirwan believes there's great benefit in sharing advice and things that work well, and I completely agree with her. Maybe we need to change the language we use. Let's not call them 'best practices' anymore. Stephen Shapiro suggests in our interview that we should rename them 'proven practices' or 'past practices'. Caitlin Kirwan suggests we should simply refer to these practices as 'what has worked for us'. These are great suggestions that move us away from the limiting connotations of the word 'best'.

I'm suggesting we call them 'good practices'.

By viewing good practices as insights or data points rather than rigid roadmaps or blanket recommendations, internal communicators can learn from tried-and-tested methods whilst also embracing a curiosity-driven approach to identify what would work best in their particular context. This, I believe, is the sweet spot to find sustainable and lasting success.

KEY TAKEAWAYS

- Best practices are proven and reliable methods or approaches, but they may not always be the best fit for every organization. Context and cultural differences matter, and best practices may not work universally.

- The appeal of best practices lies in their efficiency, risk reduction, expert consensus and predictability.

- Best practices can be unstrategic because they mimic others without aligning with an organization's specific needs.

- Survivorship bias can lead to an overly optimistic view of best practices.

- Best practices can stifle innovation and discourage critical thinking.

- The suitability of best practices depends on the complexity of the problem, with 'best practice' being more applicable to simple problems and less relevant for complicated and complex issues. Complex internal communication problems often require innovative and adaptive approaches.

- The term 'best' can be limiting and may discourage exploration and curiosity. It's more constructive to refer to them as 'good practices' and view them as data points rather than rigid roadmaps for internal communicators.

REFLECTIVE QUESTIONS

1 Do you recognize instances in your own work where a focus on 'best practices' may have hindered innovation or creative problem-solving?

2 How do you navigate situations where best practices in internal communication contradict each other, and what factors influence your decision-making?

3 How do you balance the use of best practices with the need for innovation and adaptability in your internal communication?

4 Are the communication challenges you face in your organization primarily simple, complicated or complex?

5 Reflect on your current approach to internal communication: are there opportunities for you to view good practices as starting points and embrace a curiosity-driven approach to forge your own path?

References

Abrahams, M (2023) *Think Faster, Talk Smarter*, Simon & Schuster, London

Cleary, A (2023) 14 internal communication best practices for 2023, ContactMonkey.

Fitzpatrick, L and Dewhurst, S (2022) *Successful Employee Communications: A practitioner's guide to tools, models and best practice for internal communication*, Kogan Page, London

Institute of Internal Communication (2023a) Factsheets, guides and resources, IOIC, www.ioic.org.uk/knowledge-hub/resources.html (archived at https://perma.cc/K2T4-75TM)

Institute of Internal Communication (2023b) Masters in Internal Communication Management, IOIC, www.ioic.org.uk/learn-develop/qualifications/masters.html (archived at https://perma.cc/E6XV-MKDG)

LumApps (2023) 17 internal communications best practices for a stronger employee engagement, LumApps

Shapiro, S (2011) *Best Practices Are Stupid*, Penguin, New York

Sinclair, S (2021) 7 internal communication best practices you should follow, Talk Freely

Snowden, D and Boone, M (2007) A leader's framework for decision making, *Harvard Business Review*, November

05

Overcoming the obstacles to innovation

The last two chapters were a bit depressing, weren't they? Sorry about that. I mapped out 10 obstacles to innovation in internal communication and took a deep dive into one of them, our love of best practice.

It makes it sound like innovation in internal communication is impossible. But it's not, I assure you. We just need to create some breathing space. We can do that by getting curious about practical ways to overcome the obstacles that are in our way.

That's what this chapter is all about. I'll give you a range of practical suggestions for how to overcome the obstacles. Consider these a pick-and-mix selection rather than a prescription – try them out, play with them, pick the suggestions that suit you and your context the most. Carry out some experiments, evaluate your results and see what is having an impact. This is the starting point to becoming more innovative in your work – creating the space for it to happen. Your results will depend on your level of commitment, the boundaries you're willing to push and your ability to stick with it. And, honestly, some of these obstacles take time, patience and perseverance to overcome. Be patient, make a plan and put in the hard work.

These suggestions, along with advice on adopting an innovator's mindset in the next chapter, will help you remove that self-limiting belief of 'I'm not an innovator' or 'I don't have time to innovate'. Because we can all be innovators, every single one of us. We first need to find the time and space to make it possible.

Let's go through the obstacles we identified in Chapter 3 and suggest ways you can overcome them to begin your new life as an innovator.

Obstacle: Tiny teams and budgets

Internal communicators regularly report having tiny teams and budgets. This can make it difficult to invest time, energy or resources into experiments or executing creative ideas.

Practical steps: Create a business plan linked to business goals

A lack of resources is not an insurmountable challenge. Don't panic. Organizations have money. There are nearly always budgets available for investments and new staff – you just have to demonstrate that the investment will provide value back to the organization. In my work as a consultant and trainer, I see a lot of internal communication strategies that appear to exist in a vacuum; they have no clear links to the overall goals of the business and there is no explicit value proposition for internal communication. I also see frustrated practitioners ask for money for communication tools and focus entirely on the *features* of the tool rather than the *value* the tool will provide. So here's my advice: stop asking for money for tools and tech and new hires. Instead, create a commercial business case which explicitly links your budget request to the objectives of the business.

As professional communicators, we are experts in creating tailored communications for a target audience, and writing a business case is no different. Your target audience is your chief finance officer (CFO), or whoever is responsible for signing off budget requests in your organization. If they get a proposal from you for a budget to bring in a new digital tool, a graphic design professional or a part-time videographer without any stated returns on that investment, then their answer will mostly likely be no immediately. So try to create the business case with your target audience in mind. What does your CFO care about? What motivates them? Hint: it's probably got to do with value for money, efficiencies in spending and meeting overarching business goals.

Use this audience-centric approach to carefully create a business case that sets out a compelling reason for investment in your team. This will make it more likely to get the budget you want. Ideally, you should have an internal communication strategy linked to the business goals already, so use this to demonstrate how you'll add value.

If you don't have an internal communication strategy linked to business goals yet, then take the organizational strategy as your starting point. Let's say, for example, you work in a software company. One of the business goals is to reduce customer churn. The company is losing millions every year when customers choose not to renew their licence. With this knowledge in mind, you begin to think about how internal communication could play a role in reducing customer churn. You start talking to the customer success managers to understand why customers aren't renewing their contracts. Let's say you identify the biggest reason is poor customer service. Customers aren't happy with the help they get when they phone up for assistance, and many of them state that the customer service agents often don't understand the products enough to actually solve their problem.

So now you talk to the customer service agents, the troubleshooters at the front line who take the calls from customers. They tell you they're trying their best – they're getting through a record number of calls every day and they're hitting all their targets in terms of call volume – but they aren't equipped to answer all the customer queries because they *haven't had enough communication about product updates and feature changes*. Customers are asking them about product features that they've never even *heard* about.

Ah!

You've stumbled upon a communication issue in an area of the business with serious strategic importance to your CEO and CFO. Now you're onto something. Keep leaning into your curiosity now, keeping digging deeper down the rabbit hole. What is causing this poor communication? What can be done to improve it? What role can you play in this?

Get the gist of this approach? There are a zillion ways you can add value to the business through improved internal communication and you can uncover these by getting curious about the business goals and how your work aligns to them. Identify ways you can help to deliver these goals and write a business case based on that. Using the example above, you could try to quantify the contribution you'll make to reducing customer churn through improved internal communication. Say the company is currently losing 20 customers a month due to poor communication between teams. What is the cost of that to the business? If a monthly licence costs €5,000 per customer then you're looking at a figure of €100,000 a month or €1,200,000 a year. That's potentially the money you'll recoup through your communication activities. In this way, you'll demonstrate a clear return on investment and make it easier to get a positive response. Your ask for budget will seem much more reasonable when anchored against the huge sums of money the company may lose *without* your help.

Here's a structure you can use to create your business case:

- **Brief summary:** Outline what you want to do, why it matters, how much it costs.
- **Problem:** Outline what business problem this investment will solve.
- **Solution:** Document what the budget is for and how this will solve the problem.
- **Risks:** What are the risks to the business of *not* investing in this?
- **Cost:** Give precise figures. Outline any analysis you did of competing products/services to show value for money.
- **Timeline:** Outline when you need the money and how long it will take to yield a return on investment.
- **Evaluation:** Explain the metrics you will collect to evaluate success of the investment.
- **Appendix:** Include any relevant supporting information.

Obstacle: Time pressure

Internal communicators told me that a lack of time stops them from innovating. There's no time for creative thinking or experimentation when you are frantically putting out fires all day long.

If you feel like this, if you often reach the end of the day and wonder what you actually achieved despite being crazy busy all day, then first of all *I see you*. I understand you because I used to *be* you.

Practical steps: Map out how you're spending your time

Here's my advice: stop what you're doing and invest a few minutes in mapping out how your time is being spent. You might find yourself surprised with the results. As I listened to the stories and frustrations of internal communication practitioners, I heard them repeatedly mention two distinct aspects of time management: (a) they weren't clear on where all their time is going ('How is it 5pm already? I haven't even *started* my to-do list') and (b) they spent a lot of time on *urgent* work rather than *important* work.

You can't carve out time for important work (like innovation) unless you first know where your time is going. So try this practical tool to map out how you're currently spending your time. It's called the Eisenhower Box. It's a simple but powerful visualization tool that helps you map out how you're spending your time and differentiate your tasks between urgent and important (Clear, 2023). You may see it referred to as the Eisenhower Matrix, the Eisenhower Quadrant or the Urgent–Important Matrix. This can help you to prioritize your work, manage your time more effectively and help you feel under less time pressure by delegating or relegating non-important work. It's a great tool for ditching the firefighting mode and carving out some breathing space.

Here's how it works. Think about all the work you've got on your plate right now. Write it all down. All of it. Everything from 'Write content for the newsletter' to 'Build relationship with head of IT' to

'Evaluate success of internal communication plan' or 'Review slides for CEO townhall'. List it all down in as much granular detail as you possibly can. Trawl back through your diary and inbox to remind yourself of how you spent your time in the last week.

Then categorize each task you've written down into one of four groups:

1 Urgent and important (tasks you need do right away).

2 Important but not urgent (tasks you must schedule to get done).

3 Urgent but not important (tasks you should delegate to someone else).

4 Neither urgent nor important (tasks that you should eliminate completely).

Plot them into a simple quadrant that looks like Figure 5.1.

FIGURE 5.1   A DECISION QUADRANT

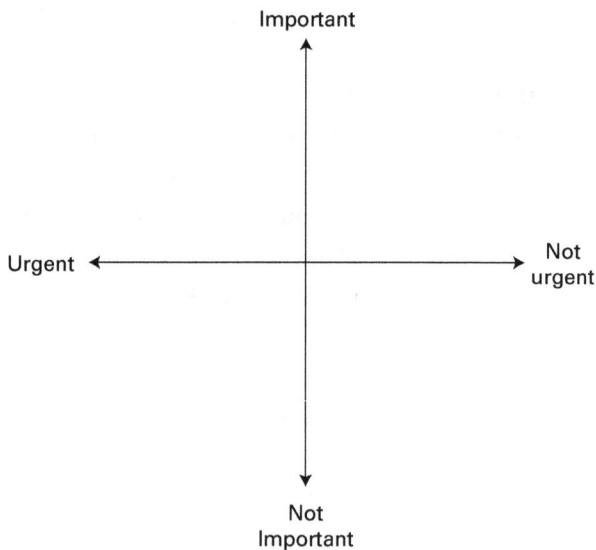

Don't be surprised if you find that much of your work sits in the top left (urgent and important) or the bottom left (urgent but not important) quadrants. Internal communicators who operate as reactive firefighters are often consumed with urgent tasks – which of course leaves the non-urgent important work (such as planning, building relationships, strategy, evaluation or innovation) neglected.

The goal of using a tool like this is to identify how you're spending your time and reflect on how to change it so that you're spending more time on important work (like innovation). If you're working at a senior level in internal communication, then I'd suggest you should be spending most of your time in the top right-hand quadrant: important but not urgent.

Getting yourself out of the 'urgent' zone creates space for planning, reflection and innovation. As Eisenhower himself noted, important work is hardly ever urgent (Clear, 2023). So it's easy to neglect it. Urgent tasks are often short term and things you feel you must react to, such as emails, text messages, phone calls, last-minute requests for work. The non-urgent important tasks 'are things that contribute to our long-term mission, values and goals' (Clear, 2023). You may find that these things are entirely missing from your matrix. Maybe you're not spending any time on important work right now.

Use this to start freeing up your time. For example, look at what you've put into the not urgent and not important quadrant. This could be recurring meetings that you don't need to attend, voluntary committees you don't need to be part of, writing reports that no one reads. Eliminate these tasks completely or bring up a discussion about them with your line manager. Tell your boss that you've gathered some data about how you're spending your time and you'd love to have a conversation about it, because you know you can deliver more value to the organization by reducing the time spent on non-important tasks such as X, Y, Z.

Here's a story about how you can get creative about eliminating busywork. I've a friend who works in marketing. She was fed up with writing a monthly report for the senior team that contained every possible metric she could get her hands on and every detail about every campaign. It took her four days to compile every month, and in her own words 'it was a painful process'. She suspected that none of the senior team were actually reading the report but she had no real way of validating that assumption and she didn't feel comfortable just asking them. So she started adding in funny little lines into the report to see if anyone would notice. For example, on page 4 she wrote 'If you read this, email me and I'll tell you a joke' and on page 5 she added 'Pineapple on pizza is delicious – if you disagree DM me'. She nervously hit 'send' on the report and waited. She was expecting an angry phone call or at least a curious email. But instead there was radio silence. As she suspected, no one was reading this report. This opened up an evidence-based conversation with her bemused manager about her experiment, and they agreed the report could be eliminated.

Smart, right? And brave, too! She started with a fundamental, often-avoided question: Do I actually really need to do this work?

If you ask yourself that question while looking through your task list, would you spot opportunities to eliminate work and relieve the time pressure you feel? The other great question you can ask yourself is 'Does this piece of work help me to reach my goal?' If your time is mostly being occupied with busywork that doesn't make any progress towards your internal communication goal, then you need to stop spending your time in this way.

Using the Eisenhower Box is a practical step towards creating more time for innovation by helping you make decisions about how you're spending your time. Your goal using this tool is to (a) carefully manage the work in the top-left quadrant (urgent and important), (b) intentionally spend more of your time in the top-right quadrant (not urgent and important) and (c) reduce the amount of time you spend in the bottom half (work that is not important) (Clear, 2023).

Obstacles: Lack of autonomy, hierarchical structures with authoritarian leadership

Micro-management and a lack of autonomy can both act as obstacles to innovation for internal communicators. This includes having to wade through layers of permission and several rounds of unnecessary approval to get things done. This can be prevalent in organizations with hierarchical structures and authoritarian leadership.

Practical steps: Improve your influence and negotiation skills

I'm an eternal optimist and I'm here to tell you that there's no obstacle we can't overcome. Even the really tricky ones that involve difficult stakeholders. There's always room to negotiate your position and create more autonomy. You must work hard to gain the trust of your leaders through careful and deliberate negotiation. But how do you actually go about doing that?

I'm suggesting a slightly unorthodox approach to overcoming this obstacle: taking a cue from an FBI hostage negotiator.

Chris Voss is a famous negotiator, well-known for his high-profile career negotiating the release of hostages as an FBI agent. He is now a businessman, advisor and bestselling author. His book, *Never Split the Difference: Negotiate as if your life depended on it* (2016), was an absolute gamechanger for me. His approach reframed how I think about trust, relationships, understanding other people and the importance of negotiation. His primary philosophy is simple and clear: people want to be understood and heard, and empathy is at the heart of any successful negotiation.

Voss puts what he calls 'tactical empathy' at the centre of his negotiation approach. Tactical empathy is centred around understanding the perspective of others, collaboration and active listening – rather than on aggressive, all-or-nothing, forceful negotiation tactics (Voss, 2016). For Voss, empathy is the act of gaining a deep understanding of the other person's perspective and feelings with the aim of making them feel understood.

Voss gives a real-life example of how he deployed tactical empathy in his career. In 1998, he was involved in a lengthy hostage situation where heavily armed fugitives were holding a woman against her will. For six long hours, Voss spoke through the door of the apartment and calmly repeated statements like 'It looks like you don't want to come out' and 'It looks like you don't want to go back to jail'. He used tactical empathy to demonstrate that he understood them and their feelings. Eventually, the fugitives opened the apartment door and gave themselves up, stating, 'We didn't want to get shot, but you calmed us down. We finally believed you wouldn't go away, so we just came out.' When asked later how he managed to de-escalate the situation, Voss explained that he identified the fugitives' emotions, labelled them and used a calm voice to communicate that he understood their feelings and viewpoints. Key to his approach is (a) recognize the other person's perspective, (b) understand their feelings and (c) vocalize that you recognize it so they feel understood.

This approach is in stark contrast to how we typically think of negotiation, isn't it? There's no table thumping here, no forceful arguments or attempts to persuade people with graphs or data. There's just really good active listening and helping people to feel understood and listened to.

> 'Persuasion is not about how bright or smooth or forceful you are. It's about the other party convincing themselves that the solution you want is their own idea. So don't beat them with logic or brute force. Ask them questions that open paths to your goals. It's not about you' (Voss, 2016).

How can we use this approach as internal communicators to negotiate for more autonomy in our roles? Think about your key stakeholders. Who is the cause of your lack of autonomy? Who is creating the layers of permission? Is it your boss, or maybe their boss? Now that you've identified who they are (and it could be more than one person), think about how well you understand them. Do you know *why* they give you so little freedom or require so many layers of sign-off? What is their motivation? Do you understand their perspective? If not, it's time to create some opportunities to get to know them better and deploy some tactical empathy. If you can deeply understand their perspective and make them feel heard, you can gain their trust and be in a stronger position to negotiate. Have a conversation and try using two of Voss's key negotiation tactics: mirroring and labelling. I've used these countless times with great effect – they really work.

TACTIC 1: MIRRORING

Mirroring is repeating the last three or four words of what someone has just said (Voss, 2016). It could look like this:

Your boss: 'We can't finalize this comms plan without the approval of
   HR.'

You: 'The approval of HR?'

It sounds silly but what happens here is (a) your boss feels heard
because you've actively repeated her own words back to her and (b)
you've asked an open-ended question which encourages her to
provide more information and shed light on her position. Mirroring
works by getting your counterpart to reword what they've just said,
often with greater clarity and detail. This gives you more information, which helps you to better understand their perspective.

   Voss (2016) argues that mirroring is effective because it's rooted in
neuroscience. Humans and other animals unconsciously copy each
other as a way of comforting each other. Mirroring insinuates simi-
larity which in turn facilitates bonding and trust. It's a technique
that follows a very basic but powerful biological principle: we fear
what's different and we are drawn to what's similar. You can use
mirroring to encourage someone to bond with you, to keep them
talking and to coax them into revealing their thoughts and feelings.
When we ask someone 'Why did you decide that?' or 'What do you
mean by that?' it makes them get defensive. But, in stark contrast,
when we mirror their words, we signal respect and understanding for
what they're saying.

   I talked about the mirroring tactic at a communications event
once and encouraged the attendees to try it out for themselves. What
I hadn't anticipated is that all the attendees would practice it at the
next coffee break; can you picture the hilarity of 60 eager communicators all trying to mirror each other at the same time!

   I've been using the mirroring technique successfully for a couple of
years and what I would say is this: it feels weird and awkward at first.
You need to practise. You will be convinced that people know what
you're up to, but, seriously, they won't have a clue. My husband once
attended a networking event and was concerned he would find it
difficult to strike up conversations with strangers for hours, so he
actively went in with a plan to mirror people. This is what he told me
when he came home: 'I mirrored people all night. It's literally all I did.

People loved it, one lady told me I was the best listener she'd ever met!'

TACTIC 2: LABELLING

The other tactic you can try alongside mirroring is what Voss (2016) calls 'labelling'. Labelling is identifying the other person's emotions and saying them out loud. This is a negotiation technique that is used to diffuse high emotions by making people feel listened to and understood. You'll see in the hostage example I gave above that he used this successfully with those fugitives: 'It looks like you don't want to come out' and 'It looks like you don't want to go back to jail'.

Voss's labelling technique also comes from behavioural science, from the concept of 'affect labelling'. To deploy this technique effectively, you must identify the emotional state of the person you're negotiating with, label that emotional state out loud, and then stay silent and let the person process the label. Labelling negative emotions helps to diffuse them, whilst labelling positive emotions serves to reinforce them. Ultimately, Voss says, human beings all want to be understood and appreciated, and labelling is a practical way to do that.

Here's how you can use labelling when you're trying to negotiate for more autonomy and freedom in your role as an internal communicator. Say you're having that same conversation with your boss about getting the comms plan approved by HR. Whenever you notice a shift in her facial expression/tone of voice/body language/gestures then use a label to figure out what's going on. Try labels like 'It looks like something just crossed your mind' or 'It seems like you're uncomfortable with that'. Then be quiet, let her process the label and wait out the silence until she speaks. (This bit also takes practice but it's worth it.)

If your boss is adamant that the plan needs to be approved by HR then try to avoid accusatory questions like 'Why are you insisting on that?' or 'Isn't this an inefficient way to do things?' – instead try some more labels. You could try 'It seems like you have a reason for this decision' or 'It sounds like there's good cause for needing to get approval from HR'.

To use labels, use sentences that start with:

'It seems like…'

'It looks like…'

'It sounds like…'

This approach can help your stakeholder to think through their decision without feeling defensive and opens up further dialogue to help you understand and influence their position.

I've had surprisingly good results with this tactic. I say 'surprisingly' because labelling sounds so simple and not particularly exciting – by my goodness, it's powerful. I once had a conversation with a boss who had decided our team would work on a project that I felt was a waste of time and didn't align with our strategic priorities. I used a label and said, 'It seems like you have a good reason for taking on this project' and then I let the silence hang in the air. To my amazement he paused for what seemed like an eternity and said 'Actually, no, I don't'. And the project was dropped. Just like that!

Try out Voss's techniques to improve your influence and negotiation skills. With practice you can deploy tactical empathy to begin carving out the space and freedom you need to become more autonomous and innovative in your role.

Obstacle: Resistance to change

Resistance to change can make it difficult for you to innovate. It can hinder your attempts to try new things or experiment with different approaches. If your manager resists change, or the entire organizational culture resists change, what can you do about that?

Practical steps: Use Kotter's change leadership methodology

You can learn a lot from Kotter's (1996) steps for leading change to overcome resistance to change from stakeholders. Let's have a look at some of Kotter's steps and see how they could help us.

Kotter's first step is to create *urgency*. For any change, you need to develop a sense of urgency for why it needs to happen. So if you want to try new things or experiment with a new approach, you need to create a convincing and compelling case for why it matters. For example, you could develop negative scenarios to show the risks to the organization of *not* trying new things or exploring new approaches. What could happen if we *don't* do this? Balance this by outlining the potential benefits that innovation could bring and link them to the things that your stakeholders care about most. You must make it feel urgent. Make your stakeholders feel that the status quo is not safe and that *not* innovating is risky and may have negative results for the organization (Kotter, 1996).

After you've created a sense of urgency, Kotter recommends forming 'a powerful coalition', in other words a group of people who champion the change and will be your allies. You need this because it's too hard to overcome organizational resistance to change by yourself. You need others on this journey with you. So build yourself a group of influential people in your organization who can work with you to keep championing the innovation agenda. These people don't all have to be senior leaders. Influential people in organizations can have a range of seniority levels, job titles and expertise. Think about who people listen to, who people turn to for advice and who is most likely to influence your greatest resisters. Identify your key stakeholders and see who could help you overcome resistance to change. This could be people who are already doing innovative work in the organization and demonstrating positive results, or people who are at senior levels and are open to doing things differently. Your coalition is the group to spark the change in the organization.

Once your group is created, you need to create a vision for change (Kotter, 1996). If you're an internal communicator who really wants to be let loose to innovate and experiment, then you probably have hundreds of ideas in your head. Start to link your ideas and create an overall vision or story that will be easy for people to understand and remember. What's your vision for innovation in internal communication? What are you ultimately trying to achieve? Remember that innovation is about delivering *value*. Link it back to the business goals and paint a picture of a glorious future.

By developing a really clear vision, you'll help people to understand why you're asking them to do something and why you're seeking change. Once they understand the end game and what you're trying to achieve, it makes more sense. Your vision should be very short and simple – one or two sentences that capture what you see as the future of your team/the organization. It should be easy to remember so that you can literally rattle it off again and again.

But, of course, it's not enough to simply create a vision. You must communicate it. You need to communicate your vision for change frequently to the people that need to hear it – if you feel like a broken record, then you're probably doing it right. You need to be convincing and really embed the vision into everything you're doing. Just as important is the idea that you also role model the behaviour that's aligned with your vision. Your actions will send signals about what's important to you, so make sure that you are deliberately displaying the kind of behaviour that you want from others. For example, if someone else suggests trying something new or running an experiment you should be enthusiastic and supportive. Make visible displays of your support for innovation and doing things differently. Lead by example.

If you can, it will really help you to demonstrate some successful short-term wins. Can you do something to show the value of experimentation and innovation? If you can give your organization a taste of victory in a short time frame, it can drive motivation to continue. Think of some short-term, low-risk initiatives that you could take on without asking permission that would create visible results that your stakeholders can see. These 'quick wins' should be deliberately very achievable, with little room for failure. These will act as proof points that innovation is a positive force and that doing things differently is a good move for the business.

Once you get a win, build on it. It takes a long time for change to really become embedded and for resistance to change to dwindle. Every time you innovate and run a successful experiment, this gives you an opportunity to communicate about your progress. Talk to people about the things you're doing differently and the results you're getting. Make yourself a success story and don't be shy about it. Kotter's (1996) work gives us practical ideas for how to overcome resistance to change.

Obstacle: Fear of failure

Many internal communicators told me they fear being punished or sidelined if they try something new and it fails. So they don't try.

Practical steps: Define boundaries for acceptable failure

I am not suggesting there is a way for you, as an individual, to fix this at an organizational level. If there is a prevailing culture of fear and a pattern of punishing mistakes, then that will only change if the leaders make an intentional and deliberate plan to do so. Innovation is inherently risky and some leadership teams will actively try to avoid failure at all costs.

But at a team level there are things you can do to overcome this obstacle. Sundheim (2013) suggests finding ways to take the sting out of failure to promote innovation. The starting point, he suggests, is by defining a 'smart failure' – the acceptable boundaries within which it is okay to fail. You can do this with your line manager and your team. Work together and have a conversation to discuss and agree on what a smart failure would look like in your team. What are the boundaries you need to set? What level of risk is okay? And how will you recognize and reward smart failures in your team? In Sundheim's (2013) own words, smart failures are 'the thoughtful and well-planned projects that for some reason didn't work'.

Define these together as a team and outline the acceptable boundaries for failure. This makes it clear what kind of experiments or failures are acceptable in your team and gives you freedom to start getting more creative and innovative. Discuss what would make a failure smart in your team, and what would make a failure stupid.

What kind of boundaries or guidelines do we want to create in our team to allow people to fail without getting punished for it? Agree it, document it, talk about it regularly.

It also helps, Sundheim (2013) asserts, to begin rewarding smart failures in the same way that you would reward teammates for succeeding at a task. It rewards the behaviour and signals that failure is acceptable – which in turn signals that innovation is desirable. You could set up a team recognition programme where you recognize people not just for their achievements throughout the year but also for their best *attempts* throughout the year. You could recognize their *behaviour* rather than the *outcome* to signal that failure is acceptable and innovation is encouraged.

Another practical step you can take to overcome the obstacle of fear of failure is to actively talk about failure in your team or with your line manager. Have open, transparent and candid conversations about times you have failed and how those experiences led to growth and learning. Discuss mistakes you've made and what you learned from them. Show how you are able to weigh up the pros and cons in your decision-making process to demonstrate that you can be trusted to experiment safely whilst minimizing organizational risks. Encourage your line manager to discuss their own mistakes and failures. Even just the simple process of sharing and discussing failure takes the sting out of it and makes it more acceptable.

So start small. Start with an immediate colleague or with your boss or with your team. Figure out what an acceptable failure would look like, define smart failures in your team, and go forth and innovate.

Obstacle: Misconceptions

Sometimes, the biggest obstacle to innovation in internal communication is a misconception or misunderstanding about what the internal communications team is there to actually do. If your team is viewed as nothing more than an internal postal service, then innovation won't seem particularly critical – I mean, surely distributing messages from one place to another is very straightforward?

Practical steps: Create a team charter

But there's good news: this is an obstacle you can start overcoming right away. You need to clarify what you do and what your value is in the business, and you can use a team charter to do this. It sounds deceptively simple but I rarely come across internal communication teams who have taken the time to do this. I run workshops with in-house teams around the world to help them create their own team charter for the first time and it's a powerful tool to have in your arsenal. A team charter helps to clarify your team's role in the organization, defines the value you bring and gives you a tool to contract effectively with stakeholders.

Friction can arise when stakeholders have different understandings of what internal communication is for and what your team does. The head of HR, for example, may see internal communication as their mouthpiece to tell all employees about staff benefits or new policies. The CEO might understand internal communication to be all about aligning employees around the new strategy. The director of IT might see internal communication as the distributors of fluffy messages relating to staff parties or well-being events.

Without a common understanding of why the internal communication function exists in your organization, you will constantly be battling with misconceptions and misunderstandings of why your team exists and what you should be spending your time on. You will be pulled in all sorts of different directions. You may find your team operating in a very reactive, firefighting way with lots of time lost to busywork or urgent, non-important tasks.

To tackle this, create a team charter. You can do this whether your team is brand new or if you've been in the organization for years. A team charter will help to position you appropriately in the organization and communicate what your team is all about and how people can expect to work with you. Here's a simple four-step approach to creating your own team charter to reduce any misconceptions about your team:

1 **Create and document a purpose for your team.** Why does your team exist in the organization? What value do you bring? Useful

questions to ask yourself are: Why do they pay my salary? What are they investing in? The definitions of internal communication given in Chapter 1 of this book will be helpful to you in starting this process. Your output here is a sentence that starts with the words 'Our team purpose is...'.

2 **Write down what your team does.** Think about the purpose you documented and then align your activities with that. You should only be spending your time on items that move the needle in your internal communication strategy and align with your team purpose. If an activity is outside of the scope of these then it doesn't go in this section – it goes in the next one. Your output here is a section that starts with the words 'We do...'.

3 **Write down what your team *doesn't* do.** This is so important and something that's often overlooked. For example, perhaps you don't act as the graphic design service for other teams. Perhaps you don't spend time creating PowerPoint presentations for meetings. Maybe you don't buy cupcakes for in-house events. Think about all the busywork you get tasked with and all the meaningless, useless work you do that has no impact. If it's not aligned with your purpose or strategy, you shouldn't be doing it as it's a waste of organizational resources and of your time. Your output here is a section that starts with the words 'We don't do...'.

4 **Scope out ways of working.** Identify and document how you work with other teams and stakeholders. Give outsiders an opportunity to understand how to interact with your team, how to request help, what communication support is available, how decisions are made about what you spend your time on, any templates or guidelines you have and so on. Perhaps you could develop a clear intake process for communication requests, similar to how a creative agency will take a brief. Your output here is a paragraph that starts with the words 'How we work is...'.

You can communicate this charter to your key stakeholders and to anyone who approaches your team looking for assistance. This will help you overcome the obstacle of misconceptions and over time will reduce the number of irrelevant requests that you get, thereby freeing up more of your time to innovate.

Obstacle: The pressure to be lean

Under pressure to 'do more with less', internal communicators can struggle to have time or energy to innovate or experiment. Trying to deliver the workload with fewer resources is difficult enough as it is.

Practical steps: Contract effectively with stakeholders

Perhaps you're in an organization that has gone through layoffs or is cutting costs. Maybe you know that now is not the right time to present a business case or to ask for more support. You've got a lean team and that's that – you've got to make the best of it.

You can overcome this obstacle to innovation by contracting effectively with stakeholders. This is a strategic approach you can take with anyone in your organization to establish mutually agreed ways of working and expectations, for example what is going to be delivered and when. Contracting is essentially a way of negotiating with stakeholders to define roles and responsibilities, objectives, resources, timelines and other parts of the project you're working on together. Your team charter is very helpful in contracting as it gives you a firm starting point in terms of the support you do/do not offer to stakeholders.

Contracting is essentially acting as an internal consultant. When new clients approach me for work, for example, they may ask me for a very specific deliverable, e.g. 'I want you to deliver a workshop' or 'Can you give a talk to our senior leaders?' But I don't say yes immediately. I get curious and I ask lots of questions. I try to understand the problem they are trying to solve before I propose any tactical solutions – because often what they want isn't the same as what they actually need. You can use this same approach internally with your stakeholders.

As an internal consultant, you need to contract effectively not just with your stakeholders but also with your own supervisor (Block, 2023). You need to not only serve the needs of your stakeholders but also fulfil your supervisor's requirements for your role. It's a double whammy and needs to be managed carefully. Here's Block's advice for contracting effectively with your boss:

> 'List the key wants you have of your boss. Then ask your boss to make a list of the key wants they have of you. Exchange lists and meet together to see whether you can agree on a contract that represents a reasonable balance between what your department needs to meet its commitments to the overall organization, and what you need to be responsive to the needs and priorities of your clients.'

This way of working becomes particularly important when you're working in a lean team and expected to magically do more with less. You must invest time contracting with your manager and also with stakeholders to establish clear expectations of what you can/can't deliver, what your role is (and isn't), what the priorities are and so on. Contracting effectively can stop you taking on more work than you can manage and carve out some time for innovation.

Obstacle: Technological constraints

Communicators told me that a lack of access to technology and tools hampers their ability to innovate. Does this completely stop us from innovating?

Practical steps: Reframe how you view constraints

Well first of all, good news. You don't need technology to innovate. You just need a good idea put into action that delivers value. In saying that, having ancient tech can be very frustrating and can absolutely limit your ability to collect data and metrics to drive innovative ideas. If you're an internal communicator working in an organization with outdated hardware or software, limited access to technology and restrictive IT policies, I feel your pain. I understand it and I get it. I've been there. And sometimes a business case isn't the right move, because maybe the tech budget has already been spent or there are cost-cutting initiatives this year.

But there is another route to take to overcoming the obstacle of technological constraints. We could spin these constraints into a *positive* force for driving innovation rather than an obstacle to it. Maybe a mindset shift can help us unlock something here. Let's explore how technological constraints could actually *encourage* or prompt us to innovate.

Acar et al (2019) wrote a piece in the *Harvard Business Review* entitled 'Why constraints are good for innovation'. They noted that people often assume that constraints (such as compliance restrictions or lack of technology) act as obstacles to innovation and that the logical solution then was to eradicate all constraints to allow innovation to flourish. However, their research actually found the opposite to be true: they reviewed 145 empirical studies on the effects of constraints on creativity and innovation and found that a healthy dose of constraints actually helps to *improve* innovation.

This extract from Acar et al (2019) gives a real-life example of how constraints can drive innovation rather than inhibit it:

'Consider GE Healthcare's MAC 400 Electrocardiograph (ECG), which revolutionised rural access to medical care. The product was the outcome of a formidable set of constraints imposed on engineers: develop an ECG device that boasts the latest technology, costs no more than $1 per scan, is ultra-portable to reach rural communities (i.e. should be lightweight and fit into a backpack), and is battery operated. The engineers were given just 18 months and a budget of $500,000 – a very modest budget by GE's standards, given that development of its predecessor cost $5.4 million. Our research suggests that GE engineers were not successful despite these constraints, but *because* of them. Constraints can foster innovation when they represent a motivating challenge and focus efforts on a more narrowly defined way forward.'

This really challenges our assumption that working within a set of technological constraints inhibits our ability to innovate. Perhaps we should consider it an opportunity rather than an obstacle. For some internal communicators, a constraint like lack of technology could be interpreted as a frustrating roadblock. For others, it could be interpreted as a meaty challenge to be tackled. If we frame this constraint as a positive rather than a negative, we can get curious about what we can achieve within the parameters of the constraint and innovate accordingly.

Treat the lack of technology as a creative challenge. What can you do with the technology that you have? How can you innovate to use it more creatively? What can you do without using any technology *at all*? Perhaps the lack of sophisticated technology will spur on greater innovation in your team than you could have expected.

Obstacle: Adherence to best practice

In the last chapter I went into detail about why I think best practice is not the right approach for internal communicators and how it stifles innovation.

Practical step: Get curious about your own organization

If you are still in bed with best practice but want to become an innovator instead, my suggestion is delightfully simple: indulge your curiosity. I see curiosity as the antidote to best practice. In the next chapter I'll explore curiosity more deeply as one of the key components of the innovator's mindset for internal communicators.

Curious communicators are always considering new ideas and examining new ways of working, irrespective of whether they've been proven to work elsewhere or not. More than that, curiosity promotes questioning and rigorous challenge. Internal communicators who lean into their curiosity are more likely to question the status quo and challenge existing norms – in other words, they're more likely to move away from the comfort of best practice in search of something better. These communicators will ask questions like 'Why do we do it this way?' or 'How could this be improved?' or 'Can you explain how this works?' Asking questions is a simple but effective way to reduce your reliance on best practice and embrace innovation.

Curiosity is at the heart of overcoming our inclination to adopt best practice approaches because it drives us to explore, ask questions and change our minds. It encourages us to be creative and to constantly learn and grow. Let's move into the next chapter where I'll unpack curiosity in more detail and explain why I named my business The Curious Route.

KEY TAKEAWAYS

- Despite the many obstacles to innovation in internal communication, it's not impossible to overcome the obstacles and create space for innovation.

- There are a variety of practical steps you can take to overcome these obstacles.

- Try a change management framework to overcome resistance to change.

- Write a commercial business case to get the budget and resources you need.

- Identify and communicate the value you bring as an internal communicator.

- Negotiate with tactical empathy to gain autonomy and freedom in your role.

- View technological constraints as opportunities for innovation.

- Define 'smart failures' to overcome an organizational fear of failure.

- Create an internal communication team charter to clarify any misconceptions about the role of your team.

- Use the Eisenhower Box to manage your time more effectively.

- Indulge your curiosity as a way to move away from a best practice approach.

REFLECTIVE QUESTIONS

1 How do you feel about overcoming the obstacles you face to innovation in internal communication?

2 Which technique in this chapter can you put into action first?

3 Who are the key stakeholders in your organization that you should focus on to deploy tactical empathy to build trust and improve the relationship?

4 Can you think of a time when you failed at something and it led to learning and growth?

5 Have you documented the purpose of your internal communication team in your organization?

6 What tasks do you regularly do that are both non-urgent and non-important, and can you simply stop doing these to free up more of your time?

REFERENCES

Acar, O A, Tarakci, M and van Knippenberg, D (2019) Why constraints are good for innovation, *Harvard Business Review*, November

Block, P (2023) *Flawless Consulting: A guide to getting your expertise used*, Pfeiffer, San Francisco

Clear, J (2023) How to be more productive and eliminate time wasting activities by using the 'Eisenhower Box', James Clear

Kotter, J (1996) *Leading Change: An action plan from the world's foremost expert on business leadership*, Harvard Business Review Press, Boston, MA

Sundheim, D (2013) To increase innovation, take the sting out of failure, *Harvard Business Review*, January

Voss, C (2016) *Never Split the Difference: Negotiate as if your life depending on it*, Random House, London

06

The innovator's mindset

Curiosity has been an enduring theme in my life. I've been curious since a child and am still maddeningly inquisitive to this day. My daughter knows this all too well. When she was five years old, she came home from school brandishing a glittery sticker on her jumper and a happy grin on her face. 'I got a sticker for colouring neatly inside the lines!' she told me excitedly. I paused, then mirrored her words: 'Colouring inside the lines?' She looked puzzled and frankly a bit annoyed. 'My teacher told me that colouring inside the lines is the right way to do it.'

Well. Who would've known that there is a *right* way for a child to put colours on a piece of paper? It seems that the world is full of rigid best practices we are expected to follow, even as children. What does the imposition of these arbitrary rules and norms do to our ability to create, to be curious, to innovate? How does it shape our mindset?

Kids are endlessly curious. Think about the games you used to invent as a child or the imaginative stories you'd create with your toys. You'd be spinning around the garden with nothing but a twig, yet in your childlike imagination you'd have lasers beaming out of your eyes and superpowers to fly through the air and an endless supply of unicorns alongside you.

And then you go to school. You start learning 'the rules'. You're told to colour inside the lines and you're rewarded for colouring the 'right' way. You hear that curiosity killed the cat and that you need to grow up and stop asking silly questions. After more than a decade of formal schooling, most people emerge with the curious side of themselves quite deflated; crushed under the weight of conformity to arbitrary norms and expectations.

As you get older and enter the world of corporate work, your curiosity gets quashed further still. You quickly realize that many business leaders don't like to be questioned. You figure out that it's easier to keep your head down, not make a nuisance of yourself and just do as you're asked. This is the easiest way to escape the ire of a toxic manager or a difficult CEO.

Throughout the course of our life, our curiosity is suppressed. But here's the good news: it never *truly* goes away. And, better yet, you can reignite your curiosity at any time in your life. It's still there. Everyone has it. You can actively practise curiosity like a muscle so you can make it stronger. You can use curiosity as a lever to drive great results.

I'm clearly biased here. I named my business The Curious Route after a light bulb moment of realization about the centrality of curiosity to my life and my work. I'm constantly telling people the benefits of asking more questions and interrogating assumptions. I believe curiosity is a core component of what Couros (2015) has termed 'the innovator's mindset' – the mindset we need to be creative, develop novel ideas and execute them to deliver value.

This chapter will explore the idea of the innovator's mindset and adapt it for the world of internal communication. I'll suggest five core areas you can develop to strengthen your innovative prowess and mindset. This chapter is not a prescription for how to innovate. It couldn't be, as there's no 'one way' or 'right way' or 'best practice' for innovation – just as there's no such thing as best practice in internal communication. Satell (2016) argues that there are as many ways to innovate as there are types of problems to solve and I tend to agree with him. Let's get started by looking at whether innovation can be learned.

Can innovation be learned?

Anyone can innovate with the right mindset. That is my firm belief.

But there are pervasive myths around innovation and creativity, aren't there? Myths that persuade us that innovation is the reserve of tech founders in polo-neck jumpers or scientific inventors with shocking white hair and lab coats. This misconception creates a barrier to entry as it discourages ordinary people like you and me from dabbling in the world of innovation. I'd like to challenge that myth and put it in the bin where it belongs.

I asked Dr Lollie Mancey if innovation is something that can be taught. Can people learn it as a skill, or are some people just naturally better at it than others? She told me, 'There's a perception in the world that innovation is something that special people do, usually to create tech-based products. But innovation is for everyone.'

This sentiment is echoed by Drucker (1984), who argues that innovation is not a natural ability or an innate talent, but rather it's something that can be studied and learned. Innovation and entrepreneurship are not personality traits, he states, but are *behaviours*. It's not a thing that we *are* but it is a thing that we *do*. Isn't that a refreshingly reassuring message? Anyone can innovate.

Innovation is a skill and set of behaviours that can be cultivated and learned by anyone. It can be honed and refined over time as a practice and a discipline. Innovators are made, not born (Roth, 2023).

'If you're not born with it, you can cultivate it' (Gregersen et al, 2009).

There's also no age limit to innovation. Ray Croc was in his 50s when he created McDonalds. Henry Ford was also in his 50s when he set up his first assembly line in a manufacturing plant. It's never too late to start.

Components of the innovator's mindset

Successful innovators don't sit and wait for lightning to strike them with a great idea – they approach innovation as a practice and they work at it. They actively try to create value through executing new ideas. The starting point to becoming more innovative is to understand the innovator's mindset and actively cultivate it in yourself. An innovative mindset stems from a problem-solving approach coupled with curiosity and passion (Marchand, 2022).

But what on earth is an innovator's mindset – and how can you develop one?

Couros (2015) explored the idea of the innovator's mindset and mapped out a series of traits he believed that innovators must possess and cultivate; these include empathy, problem finding, risk taking, observation and resilience.

Others agree that innovators tend to have things in common. According to Roth (2023), innovators all have an insatiable curiosity to learn, tolerance to take risks and an acceptance that they won't always succeed. Gregersen et al (2009) conducted a study over a period of six years to identify what the best innovators have in common and identified core 'discovery skills' such as questioning, observing and experimenting.

I'm suggesting five key traits that comprise an innovator's mindset specifically for internal communicators. These are:

1 Curiosity.

2 Open-mindedness.

3 Resilience.

4 Problem-solving.

5 Observation.

Actively nurturing and practising these five key skills will build your capacity to innovate in your role. This is a practical approach to start your journey as an innovative internal communicator.

Let's look at these five components of an innovator's mindset in more depth.

Curiosity

In my interview with Dr Lollie Mancey, I was struck by how many times she used the words 'curious' and 'curiosity'. I think I lost count when I reached 16 – pretty impressive for a one-hour conversation.

Curiosity came up again and again without prompting. She told me, 'innovation is curiosity at its heart. We have it as children and we start to lose it during the school system and as we grow into adulthood.'

Dr Lollie Mancey argues that curiosity is the core skill we should be encouraging the most in both the school system and in the workplace. In her view, embracing curiosity will result in human flourishing and positive innovations. As adults, she says, 'the freedom to be curious and to experiment isn't something that comes easily to us. We are often told to "stop being childish".'

Curiosity is a skill that all innovators possess. In my opinion, curiosity is a superpower. It is a powerful way of challenging assumptions and norms to explore new and better ways of working and delivering value.

Curiosity is about being deeply inquisitive and interrogating assumptions or asking challenging questions about how things get done. Innovators have a relentless thirst for knowledge and an insatiable appetite for asking questions like 'Why?' and 'What if...?' More than 50 years ago, Peter Drucker described the power of provocative questions. 'The important and difficult job is never to find the right answers, it is to find the right question' (Gregerson et al, 2009). Innovators constantly ask questions. Good questions. Difficult, challenging questions that can sometimes make people feel awkward or uncomfortable. Sometimes the questions will challenge conventional wisdom or widely accepted ideas. Shapiro (2011) says that focusing on questions, rather than answers, will help you find your way to the solution.

Innovators can be a bit childlike in a way, in their tendency to ask so many questions (and questions that some people may think are silly). Think about when you last spent time with a child. How many questions did they fire at you? How many of those questions were outrageous and bonkers and made you stop and think?

Here's a snapshot of some of the questions my daughter has asked me in the last few months:

- What are planets made of?
- How many lungs does an octopus have?
- Where did the first ever kitten come from?

Aren't these questions great? Little kids ask tons of questions like this. Way more than adults do. This is because they are relentlessly curious and they're not afraid of looking silly. By the time we reach adulthood, we often avoid asking questions for fear of looking foolish. Think about it – how many times have you heard a colleague say 'This might be a stupid question but...'. Half the time when people are thinking of a question in work they don't even ask it for fear of looking stupid. Our curiosity gets diminished over time and we don't value it enough.

Innovators go in the other direction – they embrace their childlike sense of curiosity and lean into it, in the understanding that curiosity is key to success. They ask questions like 'What problem are we trying to solve?', 'Why are we doing this now?' and 'What could go wrong?' These kinds of questions are admittedly less entertaining than the questions you'll get from a young child but they're immensely valuable – they get to the root of what you're trying to achieve and why it matters.

Another great question that innovators ask is 'What if... ?' The simple word 'if' can be very powerful. There's a story about Walt Disney that goes like this: when he wanted to build the best theme park in the world, he held a brainstorming session with his team to discuss it. He very deliberately banned the words 'No, because...' from the meeting to prevent anyone shutting down wild ideas or being closed-minded to crazy possibilities. He insisted instead that 'No, because...' should be replaced with 'Yes, if...'. So for example, if someone said 'Could we build a roller coaster that goes 100 feet in the air and then plunges underground and goes through a cave?' no one at the table was allowed to say 'No, because it's too dangerous and it's never been done before'. Instead, they'd be forced into a positive, curious position where they could answer with things like 'Yes, if we hire the best engineers on the planet' or 'Yes, if we can structurally reinforce the cave walls' or 'Yes, if we get the correct planning permission' and so on.

Walt Disney encouraged his team to get curious about what was possible and to innovate beyond what was considered possible. The rest, as we know, is history.

Indulging your curiosity in this way and asking great questions sparks creativity. People who innovate want to explore the unknown and find new or better ways to do things. Curiosity is what fundamentally drives people to identify novel solutions to problems and to uncover interesting opportunities in the unlikeliest of places.

What could curiosity look like in internal communication?

It's not new that internal communicators should be curious. Curiosity is one of the six key skills listed in the Institute of Internal Communication profession map. Let's take a familiar scenario that any internal communication professional will have experienced in one role or another and see how curiosity could play a role.

Steve from HR is launching a new employee well-being policy. He has the policy written and approved and now he comes to you, as the internal communicator, with a request.

'I need a poster,' Steve says. 'The new policy is launching next week and I need you to create a poster to launch it.'

The non-curious communicator might respond like this:

- 'I can have it ready for you by the end of the week.'
- 'I've got a template handy I can use for that.'
- 'No problem, it's on my task list now.'

But the curious communicator doesn't passively take orders like this. The curious communicator asks questions. Good questions that get to the heart of the matter. They might ask things like:

- 'What are you hoping to achieve with this poster?'
- 'What problem are you trying to solve?'
- 'What would success look like for you?'
- 'Who is your target audience?'

Most likely, during this curiosity-fuelled conversation, Steve from HR will realize that a poster probably isn't the most effective communications approach to launch a new policy and you can then have a collaborative conversation where you use your communication expertise to guide Steve to a better solution. You need to dig underneath the request made by your stakeholder (i.e. make me a poster) to find the real reason your help is needed (i.e. effective communication to solve a problem) – your role is to help Steve to find out what he really needs and come up with a plan to achieve it.

Through asking good questions, the curious communicator in this story has avoided undertaking time-wasting work creating a poster and can instead work successfully with the stakeholders to develop an audience-centric, impactful approach to launching the new policy.

Open-mindedness

People who are good at innovation tend to have an open mind. They're able to embrace new information, entertain diverse or conflicting perspectives and listen to new ideas without judgement. They understand that innovation thrives on collaboration and the exchange of ideas. They're willing to listen to information that suggests their opinion is wrong and they're open to being proved wrong.

A good innovator can park their ego and listen to a critique of their ideas, no matter how painful it may be. Shapiro (2011) argues that confirmation bias can hinder innovation. Confirmation bias is when we only look for and listen to evidence that supports our existing beliefs. To be innovative, we must be willing to accept that our idea might frankly be a bit rubbish. He suggests, 'When you view the world through the lens that your idea is good, you only see the evidence that supports your conclusion while subconsciously ignoring all of the points that don't.'

Having an open mind also means being good at taking constructive criticism. In her innovation workshops with students, Dr Lollie Mancey often creates a 'devil's advocate' role in each team to ensure that challenge and feedback will be present. I ask her why this is so important. 'You need a devil's advocate in every innovation team. You need someone to say "Hang on, I don't like this" and who can then completely pull it apart. Some of the most innovative companies in the world have these kind of devil's advocate roles.'

Shapiro (2011) echoes this, saying that a devil's advocate can stop you from getting too attached to your ideas. Having a contrarian person who actively looks for disproving data will help you refine your ideas and make better decisions about which innovations to pursue and which ones to eliminate.

Here is a practical exercise you can try to flex this open mind muscle and cultivate your innovator's mindset. Try to actively take on the role of devil's advocate. The next time you read something in a blog or hear something in a YouTube video, try disagreeing with the content and taking the opposite position. What holes can you make in their arguments? What counter-arguments can you develop? What kind of critical reflection can you make on the content? This process of forcing yourself to imagine an alternative position or a counter-argument can open your mind to a world of alternative possibilities and lead to original insights.

What could open-mindedness look like in internal communication?

Let's look at an example. Olivia is leading internal communication in a large organization. She's developed what she thinks is an absolutely brilliant idea for the next all-employee townhall meeting. She reckons she's on to a winner. But she's developed the idea alone and hasn't had anyone to play devil's advocate, nor has she adopted any critical thoughts about it herself.

At the next team meeting, Olivia announces her idea and says she's going to roll it out the very next week. She's not asking for input, she's just making an announcement. Her team suggest that it might be a bad idea and offer three or four data points that suggest it won't work well in their organizational culture. But Olivia is too far along to stop now. She really loves this idea and KNOWS it will be great. So she ignores the comments and ploughs on regardless.

The next week, Olivia rolls out her great idea and it doesn't go to plan. The CEO is not pleased. Olivia reflects on the team meeting and wonders why she didn't have an open mind about her team's reservations. She was so in love with her own idea that her mind was closed to any criticism or ideas for change. Olivia is doing well in terms of coming up with creative new ideas, but she needs to work on having an open mind, listening to other people's perspectives and being able to fall out of love with her own ideas when needed.

Resilience

Innovation is inherently risky, and innovators understand that not every risk will pay off. You could fail. That's just the nature of it. You might have a brilliant idea that will deliver huge amounts of value, but to get it right you might have to try it several different ways before it works. Because of the risk of failure, the innovator's mindset must also comprise resilience – the ability to bounce back after failure.

Resilience is the ability to bounce back from setbacks (Cross et al, 2021). Being resilient means that you can bounce back from a failure and keep on going. McKinsey (2023) takes it further, suggesting that resilience is not just about bouncing back but bouncing back *better*. Resilient people can deal with adversity and shocks, continuously adapt in response and use this to accelerate and get ahead of competitors.

Innovators tend to be willing to step outside their comfort zones and take risks, on the understanding that playing it safe can stifle creativity and stop them finding new and better ways to do things. Taking risks allows innovators to push boundaries, test ideas with experiments, and challenge or disrupt the status quo. Those who embrace risk-taking and are resilient in the face of failure are more likely to lead the way in pioneering new ideas, products and processes.

Forging your own path is risky, there's no way round that. But it's not chasing needless risks or being reckless; people who are good at innovation take *calculated* risks. They assess the potential rewards of their idea and weigh them against the potential risks, thinking through the obstacles and the chances of success. So, it's a risk-taking approach that is careful, thoughtful and strategic with a deliberate understanding that it *may not work out*. And you're going to try it anyway.

Innovators also understand that failure isn't a dead end; it's a stepping stone to another path or a different solution. Failure is a path to learning and growth rather than something to be avoided or to feel embarrassed about. Innovators can view failure as a valuable learning experience. Failing at something provides insights into what won't or doesn't work and gives you the opportunity to find ways to refine, improve or change your idea. In this way, being resilient means we can not only bounce back from setbacks but also use failure as a stepping stone towards success.

Being resilient can help you to persevere and keep going even when things get tricky. It can help you adapt your approach and keep seeking out innovative solutions to the problems you're facing. Without this resilience as part of your innovator's mindset, you might give up too quickly and never deliver the potential value of your ideas.

To work on cultivating your own resilience, you can actively try to develop a growth mindset. This is a mindset in which you view failures or challenges as opportunities to learn and grow. It can help you to view difficulties as a chance to develop your resilience, rather than something to be avoided. Dweck (2006) proposed two different mindsets: a fixed mindset and a growth mindset. If you have a fixed mindset you try to avoid challenges, you give up easily when faced with obstacles, you ignore negative criticism or feedback and you feel threatened by the success of others. But if you have a growth mindset you embrace challenges, persist in the face of setbacks, learn from negative criticism and find inspiration and lessons in the success of others. Developing a growth mindset will help you become more resilient and in turn help you to develop the innovator's mindset.

What could resilience look like in internal communication?

A friend of mine worked in a company where employee birthdays were a big deal. Employees were accustomed to birthday cards, birthday breakfasts, birthday shout-outs at townhall meetings… you get the idea. It was a *thing*.

When he joined the company, the obsession with birthdays seemed a bit childlike (in a nice way) so he decided to lean into the childishness and hold a kids-style birthday party for everyone who had a birthday in July. He got balloons, music, different types of sweets and he organized party games like Pass the Parcel and Pin the Tail on the Donkey. He thought it would be great. Let me tell you this very truthfully: it was not great. It bombed. It was stilted and awkward and people did *not* enjoy the party games. At all.

He was, of course, terribly embarrassed and he knew it was a whopping failure. But he was also kind of okay with it because he knew this was a huge learning experience. He really learned the danger of assumptions that day. He had assumed that the childlike love of birthdays would translate well into a childish party, but it did not. For next time, he knew he needed to test out any assumptions and get curious about the reality.

After that event disaster, he took it on the chin and actually leaned into it. He talked to colleagues about how he tried a new format but it didn't really work, and he asked questions about what might work better. He forged alliances with people who thought the event was bad and who appreciated his candour; they even offered to help him develop another format and try again. The point is that he didn't let the failure stop him iterating and trying again. He was resilient.

Problem-solving

We learned in Chapter 2 that innovation is about solving problems and delivering value. So it's pretty much essential to include problem-solving in our recipe for an innovator's mindset. Problem-solving involves not just coming up with solutions to problems but also being able to spot the problems in the first place – what Couros (2015) calls 'problem finding'. I speak about this with Dr Lollie Mancey and she tells me, 'There are problems to be solved everywhere. When you have an innovative mindset, you see all these challenges and you're looking for something tangible where you can make a difference.'

People who excel at innovation think about the problem first, rather than the solution or best practice. They get curious and ask questions like 'What is the problem, what do we know about it, how can we break this down into manageable components?' They draw from a diverse toolkit of problem-solving techniques and adapt their approach to different contexts. Their problem-solving ability enables them to dissect complex issues, devise strategies for tackling them and create solutions that drive positive change.

Marchand (2022) talks about the importance of developing *multiple* potential solutions when you're trying to solve a problem. She tells a charming story about how her father, an entrepreneur, used to give her a problem to solve as a child and he insisted that she come up with at least three potential solutions. This forced her to *really* consider the problem and look at it in-depth and from different angles, in order to come up with a few different ways to solve it. Marchand brings this lesson from her childhood into her adult life as an expert in innovation, stating 'One great innovation starts with at least three good ideas. You need to explore multiple solutions before you narrow it down to three, and then one.'

Why not borrow a leaf out of Marchand's book and use this as a practical way to improve your own problem-solving abilities? Let's say in your next employee listening exercise you find out that employees think the quarterly townhall meetings are boring and a waste of time. These meetings are important to your CEO and she will be keen to continue them, despite the feedback that employees aren't paying attention. This is clearly a problem.

Instead of identifying one potential solution and running with it – for example, help the CEO to use storytelling to capture people's attention – why not force yourself to identify a minimum of 10 potential solutions, then whittle them down to a shortlist of three before settling on a final choice. This exercise can be done in an hour, in a group of diverse peers, and will help you think about ways to solve the problem that aren't immediately obvious. Here are a few steps that might help you with this exercise:

1 **Define the problem clearly.** Do you really understand what the issue is and what's causing it? Get clear on what the problem is and write it down.

2 **Analyse information.** Gather together all the information you have and look at it. What is the data telling you? What insights can you glean?

3 **Break the problem into smaller parts.** Complex problems can be overwhelming. Try breaking the problem down into smaller parts to make it easier to analyse and come up with solutions.

4 **Generate multiple solutions.** Write down a list of all the potential ways you could solve this problem. Brainstorm in a group and go nuts – be creative and open-minded to anything, even if it sounds silly. The goal is to explore a wide range of possibilities.

5 **Evaluate solutions.** Assess each of your potential solutions critically. Look at the pros and cons of each one and how feasible it would be to actually do it and think through which would have the biggest impact on solving your specific problem. Give them a score and see which comes out on top.

Doing an exercise like this will help you to improve your problem-solving abilities and analytical skills. It will help you build your innovator's mindset.

What could problem-solving look like in internal communication?

Let's say Jane takes a new job as an internal communicator in a tech company. The leaders are all very enthusiastic about communicating with employees and regularly create verbal, written, video and audio updates for staff. But Jane quickly notices that this enthusiasm is actually causing a problem: information overload. Employees are overwhelmed by the excessive volume of information that's being pushed at them on a regularly basis. They can't keep up and feel confused about what's important and what's not. Employees tell Jane that they have to wade through a range of communication channels to find updates on the business: an internal podcast, weekly townhall meetings on Zoom, CEO emails on a Friday, ad hoc email updates during the week and three different internal newsletters.

In this scenario, problem-solving for Jane will involve finding ways to reduce, streamline and prioritize communication, ensuring that employees receive the information they need without being inundated with irrelevant messages. Jane's first step is to identify and document what the problem is and what's causing it, before beginning to come up with multiple potential solutions to reduce the noise in the organization.

Observation

We've already noted that innovators are curious. But let's push that further and also argue they need to be observant, too. People who are good at innovation often observe, watch and listen more than they speak. They'll observe carefully and begin to link unconnected ideas together. They may carry a notebook with them to record observations or thoughts and this simple practice helps them to become increasingly attuned to their environment.

Why not try this yourself as a way of actively cultivating your observation skills? Carry a notebook with you for the next week and write down anything interesting you observe. (If you're more tech-friendly you may find an app like Google Keep, Evernote or Notion helpful to capture your thoughts on your phone.) These observations could be very simple. It could be things like:

- Three meetings I attended this week did not have any agenda.

- No one seems to be looking at the digital screens in the canteen.

- The number of people attending the townhall meetings is higher than usual.

- When the CEO presents graphs, many employees are scrolling through their phone.

- Mary in IT requested three separate posters last week.

You can use this practice of observation to find new ways of doing things or come up with new ideas. You may observe a longstanding process in an organization, for example, and see it differently to others or see a potential connection with a process in an entirely different part of the business. You may find yourself saying things like 'It looks like we could try something different here' or 'Hang on – this doesn't look quite right – should we change this?' For example, if you observe that there's no agendas for most of the meetings you attend (and in turn, the meetings are generally a waste of time), then this gives you data to have some conversations about meetings as a communication channel and whether they are effective or not. You can suggest evidence-based changes based on the observations you've collected.

Gregersen et al (2009) argued that innovators should act like anthropologists and social scientists: observe people carefully, look at their behaviours, watch out for interesting details about what they do and when and how, and use all of these observations to gain insights about potential new ways of doing things. I love this approach, although admittedly I am biased, as I studied sociology for four years in Trinity College Dublin. Which would explain why I turned into a social scientist in Chapter 3, documenting and telling the stories of internal communicators who struggle with innovation. Here's a story about the power of observation that I remember from my days as a sociology student.

In the late 1980s, Arlie Hochschild, a sociologist at Berkeley University published *The Second Shift: Working parents and the revolution at home*. This book explores the concept that working women engage in a 'second shift' of work at home; they come home from a day of paid work outside the home and then do a second shift of cleaning, cooking, childcare and household tasks inside the home. This book found that women were effectively working an entire month more than their husbands each year. When she was researching the book, Hochschild used an array of research methods. She interviewed 50 married couples about the division of labour in the house. She also used observation as a key research method by observing a dozen homes in order to explore the 'leisure gap' between men and women.

Her time spent directly observing these families was fundamental to her findings. She spent time in the houses, went shopping with the families, watched as the parents read bedtime stories, ate with the families. Hochschild tried to keep her distance and simply observe, noting 'I tried to become as unobtrusive as a family dog.' She observed simple daily occurrences such as who clips the baby's nails, who does the household planning, who notices changes in a child's mood. She documented all her observations.

What she found was fascinating. Her interviews with the families showed an equal division of labour. But her direct observation showed an inescapable contradiction between the family myth (they believed they shared the housework equally) and the actual lived reality of the same families (the women were doing nearly all of the household chores). What they told her in the interviews simply didn't match up with what she observed happening in reality.

If Hochschild hadn't used observation as a key research method, it is likely that her findings would have been very different. If she had relied on interviews alone, she may have concluded that housework is shared equally. (It's a great book by the way and still relevant today – go read it.)

What could observation look like in internal communication?

We can learn a lot from Hochschild and the approach taken by social researchers. Internal communicators talk a lot about listening to employees but speak less about *observing* employees. I'd argue it's just as important. Toyota have a philosophy of *genchi genbutsu*, which translates as 'going to the spot and seeing for yourself'. Direct observation is baked into the Toyota culture – it's how they do things there.

You can take this approach yourself, as an internal communicator. Observation is a particularly useful approach when you start a new job and you're trying to understand the organization and its culture for the first time. A friend of mine tells me about when he took the role of head of internal communication with a large national organization. He didn't know anything about their culture and didn't know how the organization worked. So he spent the first few months observing, listening and asking questions. He tells me about a time he visited one of the regional offices and spent time sitting in the break room, drinking tea and simply observing employees coming and going. He observed a large notice board on the wall by the entrance door, weighed down with endless leaflets and pamphlets and posters. Someone had previously told him 'notice boards are a great communication channel here', but his direct observation suggested quite the opposite. After observing some 20 employees come and go, not a single one of them even *glanced* at the heaving notice board, let alone stopped and paid attention to it. When he examined the notice board up close, he observed that much of the information was out of date and entirely useless.

Another thing he noticed through simply sitting and observing was that when employees sat at a table to have their cup of tea during a break, they nearly always picked up whatever was on the table and thumbed through it. This included a newspaper, a booklet, a pamphlet, a book – it didn't seem to matter what it was, but simply having it there on the table encouraged people to look at it. This was another useful observation to note as he thought about channels and messages and reach in the organization.

Why not try out some participant observation of your own? You could spend a day with a frontline employee or a team and observe them as they work. Spend the day carefully observing the jobs they're trying to get done and how they do it. What kind of communication do they get during the day? What kind of communication do they need that they're not getting? What friction do you observe? Try not to make judgements about what you see: pretend you're a fly on the wall (or an 'unobtrusive family dog' as Hochschild said) and observe as neutrally as possible. Reflect afterwards on this question: What was different than you expected?

The magic happens when these components come together

The five traits above are all crucially important to developing an innovator's mindset. The power of combining them is enormous.

When you are both curious and open-minded, for example, you can become increasingly innovative. Curiosity is the starting point for many innovations, but curiosity alone is limited if it's not coupled with an open mind that allows individuals to embrace the outlandish ideas that curiosity may bring. When curious communicators are open-minded they are more likely to engage with unconventional or conflicting viewpoints, which expands their understanding of a problem and the potential solutions available to them.

Consider the powerful combination of curiosity and problem-solving. Curious individuals tend to ask questions like 'Why?' and 'What if… ?' which are the building blocks of problem-solving. Their relentless curiosity drives them to spot problems, analyse them and begin to think about how to solve them. Curiosity will drive you to come up with five different ways to solve a problem rather than just one. In this way, curiosity and problem-solving complement each other beautifully and it is likely that bolstering one trait will improve the other.

By understanding how these components of the innovator's mindset work together, we can really begin to understand how to drive innovation and become better at breaking away from the safety of best practice.

Adopting the innovator's mindset takes practice and patience

It seems simple now, right? Just get really good at the five traits outlined above and boom, you're a successful innovator!

Easy tiger – these things take time and practice.

Gregersen et al (2009) emphasize that innovative thinking can be developed and strengthened through practice. It takes time. Think of the key traits above as behaviours that you need to rehearse over and over and over again. Display them as traits that will be visible to others. For example, you can start immediately flexing your curiosity muscle by simply asking more questions. This not only indulges your curiosity, it will also help to build your problem-solving abilities.

Here's a practical suggestion to get started. Try writing down five questions that challenge the existing norms or culture in your organization. Do this every day for a month. You'll probably find it really annoying after a couple of days. It's quite hard. But observe yourself and how you feel: notice if it gets easier over time. Are you thinking differently about processes, cultural practices or events? Does it force you think beyond the obvious and examine things more critically? Are you stretching your mind to come up with five questions every day, and is this helping you to become increasingly curious?

The truth is this: if innovation doesn't come naturally to you, then you need to actively work at it. You can do this by adopting the innovator's mindset. This takes practice and patience – it won't happen overnight. It's like learning a musical instrument or mastering a different language: it's doable but challenging. You need to commit and practise.

As you hone your mindset and improve your skills, you may find you become more adaptable as you recognize that innovation often requires stepping outside of your comfort zone and challenging the familiar. As you get more confident with your innovation skills, you can begin to talk about it with others and encourage them to innovate, too. Share your insights and ideas with your team or colleagues. Great innovators inspire and support each other and get curious about what they can learn from each other.

The good news is that anyone can innovate. The bad news is that developing an innovator's mindset is not a quick fix. It's a gradual process of intentional growth and transformation. Over time, you'll become more adept at identifying opportunities for innovation in internal communication and contributing to positive change in your organization. As you practise and hone the five key traits in this chapter, you'll find yourself well on the way to become a truly innovative internal communicator.

(PS If you're anything like me you'll still be thinking 'But *how many* lungs does an octopus have?' The answer, I'm afraid, is zero.)

KEY TAKEAWAYS

- Innovation is for everyone. It's a skillset that can be honed and practised over time.

- I'm suggesting five key traits for innovators in internal communication: curiosity, open-mindedness, observation, resilience and problem-solving.

- These traits complement and support each other. When you strengthen one, it'll have a positive knock-on effect on the others.

- Curiosity is, in my view, the most important component for an internal communicator who wants to innovate.

- Asking questions is one of the simplest ways you can get started with cultivating your innovator's mindset. Try asking 'Why?' and 'What if... ?' and get curious about how things are done and how they could be improved.

- Adopting an innovator's mindset takes patience and practice. Commit to it and stick with it and you'll see improvements over time.

REFLECTIVE QUESTIONS

1 Think about your strengths and weaknesses in relation to the five key traits in the innovator's mindset. Which ones are you pretty good at already? Which do you need to practice?

2 What is your plan for developing these skills over time?

3 How could you measure your progress and success in cultivating these essential traits over the next 12 months?

4 How might you apply the anthropologist or sociologist approach by observing employees in their work environment?

5 How do you respond when you fail at something? Are you open to learning from a failure and using it as a stepping stone for improvement and growth?

6 How well do you define and understand problems before jumping into suggesting solutions?

References

Couros, G (2015) *The Innovator's Mindset: Empower learning, unleash talent, and lead a culture of creativity*, Dave Burgess Consulting, Inc, San Diego, CA

Cross, R, Dillen, K and Greenberg, D (2021) The secret to building resilience, *Harvard Business Review*, January

Drucker, P (1984) *Innovation and Entrepreneurship*, Harper Business, New York

Dweck, C (2006) *Mindset: The new psychology of success*, Random House, New York

Gregersen, H, Dyer, J and Christensen, C M (2009) The innovator's DNA, *Harvard Business Review*, December

Hochschild, A (1989) *The Second Shift: Working parents and the revolution at home*, Viking, New York

Marchand, L (2022) *The Innovation Mindset: Eight essential steps to transform any industry*, Columbia Business School Publishing, New York

McKinsey (2023) What is resilience? MicKinsey & Co, www.mckinsey.com/featured-insights/mckinsey-explainers/what-is-resilience (archived at https://perma.cc/YTJ6-H89Z)

Roth, E (2023) The committed innovator: The core attributes of the innovative mindset, McKinsey & Co, www.mckinsey.com/capabilities/strategy-and-corporate-finance/our-insights/the-committed-innovator-the-core-attributes-of-the-innovative-mindset (archived at https://perma.cc/T4HY-WLYC)

Satell, G (2016) 6 things great innovators do differently, Forbes, 16 September

Shapiro, S (2011) *Best Practices Are Stupid*, Penguin, New York

07

Embracing boredom to drive innovation

Asif Choudry is a bit of a legend in the internal communication world. He is the Founder of CommsHero, a community comprised of more than 13,000 communication and marketing professionals. He hosts a popular podcast with more than 12,000 downloads, he's got an excellent reputation amongst his peers and he loves ironing.

Ironing?

Asif loves ironing because it creates a quiet moment in the day for his mind to wander. He loves ironing because, frankly, it's boring. He tells me that the best ideas he's ever had have come to him in mundane moments when he's doing something dull and boring. And it's hard to think of anything more boring than ironing.

Asif tells me how he intentionally embraced boredom to induce new ideas 10 years ago and CommsHero was founded as a result. 'The whole CommsHero idea was something I brewed up when I wasn't in the office or in work mode,' he tells me. 'I was very much into running at that time and I ran without music or distraction. It was quite boring, on purpose. I came up with the idea around the first CommsHero event, which we held in 2014, and since then all the follow-up ideas for the event come from similar moments when walking in the park or doing the ironing.'

This is refreshingly different to the dominant narrative these days of hustle culture. Our social media feeds are full of influencers and productivity gurus telling us that the only way to be successful is to get up at 5am and work jam-packed schedules to maximize the use of every minute of our time. But this is not conducive to creativity or innovation. Rather, the path to good ideas is quite the opposite.

To drive innovation, you must embrace boredom.

Do you ever get bored?

When's the last time you were bored? I mean really bored, and just sort of… going with it?

Think about a time when you sat at your computer, determined to be creative and come up with a good idea. You set a timer, finish your coffee and… go! You will the good ideas to come. But nothing does. You try the pomodoro technique where you do focused work for 25 minutes, break for five minutes, rinse and repeat until three hours have passed and you've achieved nothing more than a sense of frustration and despair.

Later that same day, when you've given up and completely stopped trying, you're staring aimlessly out the window at a crumpled leaf when all of a sudden a rush of ideas come to you. By Jove, you've got it! You've come up with a great idea when you finally allowed yourself to rest and relax and get a bit bored.

Just like our friend Asif ironing his running shorts.

In this chapter, I argue that this isn't a coincidence. Our best and most creative ideas tend to come when we stop trying to force them and let our brains relax. In other words, innovative ideas can come when we are bored. I acknowledge that this is a somewhat contrarian view in a world obsessed with productivity, but I'm happy to be the lone ranger championing boredom as a catalyst for creative thinking. Let's explore boredom as the breeding ground for innovation and creative ideas.

What is boredom, anyway?

Researchers and authors have been describing boredom in different ways for decades. Phillips (1998) describes it as 'a state of suspended anticipation in which things are started and nothing begins, the mood of diffuse restlessness which contains that most absurd and paradoxical wish, the wish for a desire'. In their book *Out of My Skull: The psychology of boredom*, Danckert and Eastwood (2020) describe boredom as an aversive and uncomfortable state that is similar to the feeling of having something on the tip of your tongue; a feeling that something is missing, though we don't quite know what it is. *Psychology Today* (2023) has an interesting take, describing boredom as a deeply uncomfortable feeling in which you fail to find meaning. Stephen Vodanovich, a psychologist at the University of West Florida, states it far more simply – he says that in Western culture boredom simply means having nothing to do (Gosline, 2007).

The neuroscience of boredom

When we get bored, when we are deprived of stimulation or novelty, a network in our brain called the 'default mode' is ignited (Zomorodi, 2017). In this default mode, we are able to connect the dots between different ideas, find themes in different concepts and solve problems. The default mode is associated with inward-focused thought, self-reflection and the processing of personal experiences (Raichle, 2015).

So, when we are bored and this default mode is activated in the brain, it may seem like the brain is resting. But that's not the case at all. Our brains are busy and engaged in thoughts that lay the groundwork for creative insights. When we're bored, there are two things happening in the brain, according to psychologist John Eastwood (Danckert and Eastwood, 2020). The first is what he calls a 'desire bind' – the feeling that you desperately want to do something, but you don't want to do anything that's currently on offer. The second thing that happens in your brain is that your mental capacity is lying fallow and you're itching to engage your mind in something. For Eastwood, this itchy desire is at the heart of what it means to be bored.

We can actively get our brain into the default mode by allowing it to relax and get a bit bored. Simply creating space for your mind to wander and do nothing can yield remarkable results.

One of the brain's natural responses to boredom is the phenomenon of daydreaming. This is something we are taught is 'bad' – we hear phrases like 'snap out of it' or 'stop daydreaming your life away'. But daydreaming is powerful and should be celebrated. Daydreaming is a cognitive process that allows the brain to make unexpected connections, explore imaginative scenarios and simulate potential future scenarios (Godwin et al, 2017). Daydreaming is more than a mindless distraction – it is a mindful creative process. It can help you to incubate innovative ideas and give rise to potent new ways of working. Science has linked daydreaming with creativity. Boredom makes your mind wander, and this in turn leads to creative thinking.

Research conducted by Godwin et al (2017) yielded reassuring results for those of us prone to daydreaming. They suggest that daydreaming during the workday isn't necessarily a bad thing, and it may actually indicate that you're smart and creative. In their study, the participants who reported more frequent daydreaming scored higher for both intellectual ability and creative ability, and also had more efficient brain systems as measured by an MRI machine. So, the next time you feel guilty for daydreaming on work time, you can turn that guilt into a celebration of your smarts and creative genius.

Boredom is surprisingly good for us

Despite the common perception of boredom or daydreaming as a waste of time or something to be avoided, neuroscience reveals the positive impact of boredom on creativity. Allowing ourselves stimulus-free time enables the brain to process information differently, connect the dots and explore interesting ideas. Boredom has evolved to help us, and we should embrace it as a way of coming up with good ideas and finding motivation (Danckert and Eastwood, 2020). When our brains are relaxed, creativity kicks in and creates opportunities to discover something new.

The author Austin Kleon (2012) understands this well. He is similar to our friend Asif; Austin revels in boring tasks like ironing to brew up some of his best ideas. He never takes his shirts to the cleaners because the mundane process of ironing forces him to get bored and makes his mind wander. Kleon argues that boredom is essential for creative people; we absolutely *must* carve out time to sit around and do nothing.

The famous novelist Anne Enright is equally enamoured with the art of doing nothing. When interviewed about her time in lockdown during the pandemic, she told of her delight at essentially doing nothing all day and suggested that being a bit bored is a great thing. She says, 'Boredom is a productive state so long as you don't let it go sour on you. I wait for boredom to kick in because boredom, for me, is a very good sign' (Allardice, 2020).

Enright is not the only writer to find inspiration in boredom. Neil Gaiman was once asked what advice he would give to aspiring writers. He said you must let your mind wander and drift, and he recommended letting yourself get so bored that your mind has nothing better to do than make up a story (Grady, 2016). And, famously, Kurt Vonnegut said, 'I tell you, we are here on Earth to fart around, and don't let anybody tell you different' (Lezard, 2007).

(I might need to get that printed on a t-shirt.)

I can relate to this; I've experienced what boredom can inspire. True story: I came up with the idea for this book while I was a bit bored walking on the beach. I had forgotten my headphones and I was alone, so I paced the seashore in solitude, listening to the tide and staring into the distance. Seagulls were flying overhead and it was a very peaceful, boring walk where my mind naturally began to wander. I found myself thinking aimlessly about something one of my students had asked me earlier that week, about their desire to learn best practice in internal communication. Then it struck me I'd heard this before somewhere else, in a communications blog I'd read some months prior. But wait, there was more, I had also seen it in a social media post. I began to realize that the phrase 'best practice' was *everywhere* in internal communication, scattered liberally across webinars and workshops and blogs and books and courses. I had just never connected the dots before.

The boredom of the walk allowed me to get curious about the internal communication profession in a new way and I began posing questions about how we work and why. The book proposal flew out of me quickly after that. I found myself talking to a publisher, and before I knew it I had signed a contract and was writing this book.

If I hadn't been beautifully bored that day on the beach, this book wouldn't exist.

Humans try to avoid being bored

Despite the benefits of being bored from time to time, we dedicate a lot of energy to avoiding it. Boredom makes us feel agitated and restless, according to psychologists Danckert and Eastwood (2020), which explains why we'll endlessly scroll on our phones or retie our shoelaces or do *anything* to avoid being bored. Often our first instinct when we feel the unpleasant sensation of boredom is to get rid of it, and to get rid of it fast. It's easy to do this in the digital age with infinite social feeds at our fingertips.

Whitehead (2014) reported on a remarkable study conducted by the University of Virginia that illustrates the lengths people will take to avoid feeling bored. This study found that people would rather administer electric shocks to themselves rather than sit quietly in boredom. Yes, really! Electric shocks! The study put participants into sparsely furnished rooms where they were asked to put away their belongings, including mobile phones. They had to simply sit quietly for 15 minutes and do nothing. But there was a twist: participants had the option to push a button and give themselves an electric shock *if they wanted to*. The results were incredible: even though all participants had been allowed to test out how the shock felt earlier and most said they would pay money not to experience it again, 67 per cent of men and 25 per cent of women chose to shock themselves with electricity rather than sit quietly and endure boredom (Whitehead, 2014).

Timothy Wilson, the social researcher leading the project, was stunned. 'We went into this thinking it wouldn't be that hard for people to entertain themselves,' he said. 'We have this huge brain and it's stuffed full of pleasant memories, and we have the ability to construct fantasies and stories. We really thought this (thinking time) was something people would like.'

There's a kind of social stigma around boredom, too, isn't there? Boredom is viewed as an emotional state to be avoided at all costs, something that's only for lazy, unproductive slobs who lack purpose in their lives. Overcoming this stigma involves challenging ingrained social norms in a radical act to reclaim the importance of inactivity and relaxation.

Boredom shouldn't be seen as something to be avoided. It's a natural and essential part of the human experience, and can be the precursor to something better (Brodsky, 1995). Boredom creates space for thinking, reflecting and daydreaming. I really enjoy this verbatim quote from Nobel prize-winner Brodsky's (1995) work:

> 'When hit by boredom, let yourself be crushed by it; submerge, hit bottom. In general, with things unpleasant, the rule is, the sooner you hit bottom, the faster you surface. The idea here… is to exact a full look at the worst. The reason boredom deserves such scrutiny is that it represents pure, undiluted time in all its repetitive, redundant, monotonous splendor.… Boredom is your window on the properties of time that one tends to ignore to the likely peril of one's mental equilibrium.'

Moments of boredom often precede periods of heightened creativity, introspection and innovative thinking. Rather than trying to escape a sensation of boredom, we should actually move *towards* it and explore what insights or ideas it might lead to (Psychology Today, 2023). Recognizing boredom as an integral part of the human experience encourages us to engage with boredom intentionally, exploring its potential to spark curiosity, encourage self-reflection and cultivate exploration.

Harry Potter was born of boredom

In 1990, Joanne Kathleen Rowling was visiting Manchester with her boyfriend. They were flat-hunting, searching for a place to live together. After visiting several properties, Joanne caught the train back to London by herself. Her train was delayed and she had hours to kill before she would get home. In 1990 there were no smartphones so she had no internet access. She had no book to read either, so she stared out the window, thinking and dreaming, and came up with the idea for a story about a young wizard who goes to wizard school. She didn't have a pen and paper with her, so she spent the time imagining the details and dreaming up the story (Rowling, 2023).

The 'Harry Potter' series by J K Rowling is now world-famous, with seven books translated into more than 80 languages and a massive fanbase all around the world. If J K Rowling had had access to social media and endless videos to scroll through that day, would the idea for Harry Potter have ever come about?

Do internal communicators ever get bored?

I wanted to find out whether internal communicators ever use boredom to spark creativity. Does a bit of boredom help communication professionals come up with good ideas and innovative ways of working?

I speak with Rachael Quinlan, Head of Employee Experience with CluneTech. Rachael has always impressed me with her innovative approach to internal communication; for example, she uses green screen technology and video live streams for internal events and leadership messages with great success. I ask Rachael how she comes up with good ideas. 'Some of my best ideas definitely come from "idle" moments,' she tells me. 'For me it's in the shower, the gym or walking the dogs on my local beach – these are the top three idea-generating spots as they are where my mind wanders.'

She tells me that she's implemented a range of successful new initiatives in work which all came to her when she was mildly bored or actively not working, and that having the flexibility in her working day to accommodate this makes her life much easier. 'I'm definitely someone who needs to step away from the laptop and let myself zone out completely when I need to find a solution for something,' she says. 'Some of my best ideas come from those mundane boring moments. If I was chained to the laptop all day every day, I would probably achieve a lot less.'

Boredom helps to incubate creative ideas

Being bored helps us come up with creative ideas – we've covered that. But it does more than that. It can also help us to *incubate* ideas and grow them into innovations that will generate real, tangible value. Once an idea comes to us, it needs time to percolate and incubate and gestate. Boredom allows this to happen as it creates the mental space for it.

Remember, innovation is more than a good idea – it's a good idea that's been implemented and delivers value. It takes reflection and thinking and pondering and figuring out to be able to do that.

Johnson (2010) argues convincingly that innovations don't occur from 'eureka moments', despite the popular misconception that this is how great ideas are born. Remember this from Chapter 2? On the contrary, Johnson says, good ideas often come from 'slow hunches' – the incubation and evolution of ideas over a long period of time. If you look back through history, he claims, lots of the best ideas have had very long periods of incubation (Johnson, 2010). The development of a good idea is nearly always a long process where someone has just a fragment of an idea and it needs time to churn around subconsciously in their head before forming into something more tangible and concrete. This process can take ages – it could be a year or even 10 years before this nugget turns into a fully formed idea that's actually useful and will deliver value. Allowing ourselves the space to be bored creates the opportunities for these slow hunches to form by switching on our default mode and allowing our brain to connect the dots and explore new possibilities.

Think about Charles Darwin, for example. He had the theory of natural selection noodling around in his head for months and months before his 'eureka' moment where he realized how everything fits together (Johnson, 2010). He had the idea, but it wasn't fully baked and he hadn't connected all the dots yet. His now-famous theory came into view over a long period of time. It was a slow hunch.

So remember: good ideas can take time to grow. If you've never had a 'eureka' moment, then it doesn't mean you're not creative or good at coming up with ideas. It probably just means you're totally normal like the rest of us. Give yourself some space to be a little bit bored now and again so your brain can slowly piece your great idea together, bit by bit.

The decline of boredom in a digital age

Even though boredom is important, it's so easy not to be bored these days. In an era of constant connectivity, there's always something vying for our attention – whether that's another episode of the latest Netflix show, a notification from a social media platform or an endless barrage of emails. The digital age provides us with endless distractions and an infinite scroll of entertainment. Devices like smartphones and smartwatches encroach on our daily lives with increasing frequency, and can gradually erode the moments of stillness or nothingness in our day. We are constantly connected with an ever-present allure of instant information.

This ceaseless connectivity gives rise to a new challenge – a scarcity of moments untouched by external stimulation. This may be diminishing our tolerance for the slower, quieter interludes that lead to boredom and in turn lead to creative thinking. Our constant engagement with digital devices leaves little room for our mind to wander (Zomorodi, 2017). And is all this digital technology having an impact on our attention spans? The easy and constant access to information and entertainment has cultivated a society accustomed to fleeting moments of focus and short attention spans. A decade ago, we shifted our attention at work every three minutes. Now we do it every 45 seconds and we do it all day long. Zomorodi claims that the average person checks email 74 times a day and switches tasks on their computer 566 times a day. If we are always paying attention to something and never have the space to be bored, the default mode in our brain that leads to daydreaming and creative thinking can't be switched on.

The good news is that we don't have to allow this to continue. We can actively resist the pull of constant connectivity and cultivate intentional practices so we can relax and daydream and have space to be bored.

Resisting the cult of productivity

But how can we do that, at a time when we feel under such social pressure to be busy and endlessly productive? It's likely that your social media feeds are brimming with influencers and business leaders who tout the benefits of being relentlessly productive, and who scorn the idea of being idle or bored. Robin Sharna (2018) published a book called *The 5am Club* that evangelizes rising out of bed at 5am in order to be successful in life. Sharna's thesis is that you should get up at this ungodly hour while the rest of your family are still sleeping so that you can focus on distraction-free self-development and productivity. *The Guardian* (2023) newspaper once referred to the 5am Club as 'an exhausting approach to self-improvement' and I'm inclined to agree.

But when we hear stories on social media and in news outlets about famous billionaires who credit their success to early mornings and 16-hour workdays, it makes us feel the pressure to pursue productivity so that we can be successful too, just like them. It makes us feel pressure to avoid being bored at all costs. It stigmatizes boredom.

Lanquist (2018) wrote a feature on early-morning risers where she documented some frankly outrageous morning routines. What was interesting is that her article included *successful* people. These were not the routines of us slobs or regular plebs, but these people were *successful. Better than us.* For example, she documented the routine of Wendy, aged 40, who is a prosecutor, author and university lecturer. Wendy gets up at 3am every morning. (Or should I say every night?)

Yes, 3am! She proudly asserts that she doesn't even need an alarm clock, she naturally wakes at that time. Her terrifying morning routine includes drinking coffee at 3am and working until 6am when she goes to the gym and then straight to the office to do more work. I am tired just reading about it. Another woman featured in the article is Alison, a corporate communications director. Alison gets up at 4am to go to the gym and by 6am she's back home to do the washing up, eat breakfast and prepare her lunch. She takes her children to school at 8.30am and then goes to work. Imagine – she's already been up for 4.5 hours and she's only now going to work! Lanquist's article is called '39 morning people share the extremely productive things they do while you're sleeping' and if you feel guilty when you read it then that was probably the intention.

These kinds of articles showcase what I like to call 'the cult of productivity' – the modern idea that we must become more productive, we must achieve more, we must work harder and longer or else we are a failure. There is a stigma around being idle or being bored and it's time to fight back. I don't *want* to fill my day with endless tasks. I don't want to achieve more or be endlessly productive. I want to be happy and content and interested in things and help others. I want to enjoy just being alive. Isn't that enough?

For people like Wendy or Alison mentioned above, their main priority is *productivity*. Look at all I've achieved, they seem to say, when you're all lazily sleeping in bed. I've written 20 emails before you even brushed your teeth, you idle slob!

But this productivity culture, this hustle culture, just creates endless busyness. If you're constantly ticking off a checklist, following a strict routine or chasing deadlines, when will you have the opportunity to daydream or gaze at a picture or explore new ideas in your head? The pursuit of productivity is detrimental to our ability to innovate. So I'd really encourage a shift in the other direction: how about we become *less* productive in order to be *more* creative? We can do that through indulging our boredom from time to time.

While we're on the topic of endless productivity, let's take a minute to talk about the importance of sleep. Our friend Wendy who gets up at 3am is only getting about six hours of sleep per night – and that's on the nights when she manages to get into bed at the planned time. Six hours of sleep doesn't sound like a lot, and it doesn't sound like a particularly envious existence. We've all heard the old mantra that you need eight hours sleep a day, but is there any truth in this? Does your sleep actually affect how creative or innovative you are?

In short... yes. Sleep is absolutely crucial for coming up with good ideas as it influences cognitive function and our problem-solving abilities. When you have a good night's sleep, you benefit from improved attention, concentration and decision-making abilities. Sleep also helps you with learning and with your memory, both of which you need to cook up some new ideas (Yong, 2018). Scientific studies by Drago et al (2010) show the correlation between sleep and creativity. Getting plenty of sleep helps the brain to form new associations and insights, directly contributing to innovative thinking and imaginative processes. Sleep also helps to recharge and restore the brain, making you feel refreshed and able to think about problems or challenges clearly.

In a world where we are encouraged to do more and more and more, I offer an opposing view: let's do less, be more creative and harness the power of boredom to drive innovation.

Can boredom really be useful for busy internal communicators?

I know what you're thinking right now. You're annoyed with me. You're thinking 'Joanna, I don't have *time* to be bored! You don't understand what it's like! I'm busy *all the time*!'

I get it. I do. I've been like you. I've been the endlessly busy, fire-fighting internal communicator who is exhausted at the end of the day despite the task list being only half finished. Go back and read Chapter 5 again and do the Eisenhower Matrix exercise. Find some of the tasks that fill your day that are a waste of time and put them in the bin immediately. Because what I've realized over the years is this: you'll never get any extra time. Time is finite and there simply isn't extra to go around. You need to be intentional about how you spend your time and what you want from your life, and you need to carve out the time for what's important to you. Time is your most precious asset and you must protect it fiercely.

I'm suggesting here that boredom and space and thinking time are *extremely* important if you want to be creative and innovative. So, you must actively create a 10-minute gap to go for a walk with no music on, or just stare blankly at the grass in the garden while you sip your morning coffee. You don't need hours of free time; you just need to create little cracks in your day to make space for reflection. Of course, there's a balance to be struck here. We need a mixture of focused, goal-oriented work and the essential pauses in between that allow for reflection, idea generation and creative thinking.

You just need to make space in your life for a bit of boredom to let new ideas take shape in your mind.

Creative people value boredom

I want to share a couple more stories of creative professionals who understand the power of boredom in generating creative ideas.

I speak with Nicholas Wardle, co-author of one of my favourite business books, *Monetising the Employee Experience* (Wardle and Sharples, 2021). I asked him about how boredom fits into his life. He tells me that one of the key things he's learned over the years is not to force creativity. 'If I'm not feeling it or am unable to find a solution, I always take a break and do something boring,' he says. He calls these boring things 'displacement activities' – boring little mundane actions he does to allow his brain to relax and his mind to wander. One of his favourite ways to do this is kicking a little sponge football around his sitting room, and this is exactly what he was doing when he came up with the idea for his second book. He was kicking the football around, letting his mind explore old memories of Liverpool Football Club legend Kenny Dalglish and famous football commentaries, when he began to connect seemingly unconnected things and came up with the idea for his book. It's unlikely, he tells me, that he would have dreamed up the concept for the book while staring at a computer screen.

I also speak with a friend of mine who works as a graphic designer in a creative agency. He's not an internal communicator but his industry is creative and complex, as ours is. His job is demanding and he is expected to churn out creative, interesting ideas every single day. How does he do it? He tells me that sometimes when he's really struggling to find a solution or come up with an idea, the worst thing he can do is actively keep trying. Often, he tells me, he'll down tools and go for a roam about the city. He'll grab a takeaway coffee, sit in the park, feed the ducks and do some people-watching. He deliberately leaves his headphones behind and he doesn't scroll on his phone – he just *is*. He allows his mind to rest and some boredom to set in, and more often than not a great idea will strike.

Interestingly, sometimes the idea doesn't come to him until the next day: 'Sometimes my brain needs time for the ideas to roll around before I realize what they are.' He laughs as we wind up our chat, saying, 'It must sound like I'm just sort of mooching about doing nothing all day. But the hour I invest in boredom pays off in enormous value for our clients, who get the best of my creativity when I have the space to think and rest and reflect. So there's an argument to be made about the ROI of boredom.'

Practical ways to embrace boredom

If you have found yourself caught up in the modern cult of productivity and now want to tread a different path, I'm here to help. Resist the pressure to be increasingly more productive. Embrace a bit of idleness and the idea of doing nothing for a while. It's not a waste of time, it's actually time well spent. Any time you are resting or relaxing, you are investing in creativity and idea generation. Why don't we call it 'being actively idle'. Maybe it'll catch on… we might even start a movement of 'idle influencers' who decry a 5am power shower in favour of a 9am slow stroll. How lovely.

Here are some of my very simple, practical and no-cost suggestions for allowing a bit of boredom to seep into your life as a way to spark creative ideas and drive innovation.

Put your phone down

Seriously – that's it. That's the advice. Put your phone down. You probably don't consciously realize it, but your phone is in your hand an awful lot. Zomorodi (2017) ran a challenge called 'bored but brilliant' in which she asked a group of more than 20,000 volunteers from more than a dozen countries worldwide to do various things to create space for boredom in their life. One of her challenges was gloriously simple and yet surprisingly difficult: don't hold your phone in your hand for a full day. Participants quickly realized how much time they spent with their phone in their hand – when they were walking to the shops or they were simply moving from room to room in their house. Participants felt restless and unhappy without their phone to hand. Another challenge she posed for volunteers was to delete their favourite app from their phone for a day. This might be a game or a social media app. During her challenges, 90 per cent of participants reduced their phone time and 70 per cent reported having more time to think.

Zomorodi's ultimate point was this: using your phone less can create space in your day where you can become less distracted, a bit bored and thus more inclined to be creative.

Think about what you can learn from this in your own context. How can you make some time away from your smartphone? Can you leave it in another room overnight while you sleep? How about putting it in another room while you're working on something that requires deep concentration? The next time you're sitting on the train home, think about JK Rowling; put your phone in your pocket and just stare out of the window. Let yourself be bored, even if it feels uncomfortable and annoying, and see where your mind wanders.

You can also do a very simple but effective change to the settings on your phone: make your phone screen turn to greyscale at a certain hour each night, say 7pm or 8pm, whatever time you want to stop looking at the screen. It transforms your social media feed from a colourful, entertaining, eye-grabbing spectacle into a dreadfully dull sight of various greys. This makes it much easier to put the phone down and not feel tempted to continue scrolling. (By the way, when I first started doing this I *hated* it. My brain staged a revolt and I actually switched it back! I tried it again a few days later and still felt annoyed by it, but stuck it out this time. It took me at least two weeks to get used to it, so if you try it and feel uncomfortable then I urge you to keep going, ride out the discomfort and stick it out.)

Disconnect from constant stimulation

When was the last time you took a walk without listening to a podcast or having music playing? What about the last time you drove to the shops – did you have the radio on? Here's a simple way to reduce the constant stimulation in your life: switch off the radio and drive in silence. Sounds boring, doesn't it? That's kind of the point. Lean *into* the boredom rather than trying to escape it.

Here's something you can do right now, after you finish reading this paragraph: go for a walk and don't take your earphones with you. No podcast, no music, no audio book… just walk with your thoughts. Listen to the birds, notice how the sky looks, just walk and be bored and be okay with it. Get curious about where your mind goes and what you find yourself thinking about. If you feel annoyed or irritated, get curious about that, too. Just… be.

(Stick a bookmark here and go for a walk now – you can read the rest of this chapter later. Seriously – go!)

Spend some time alone

These days, it's easy to avoid being alone. Even when we are not in the physical presence of others, we have social media feeds full of our friends and family to keep us company and keep us occupied. For some people, the thought of spending time alone is uncomfortable and unwanted. If you're an introverted person like me, you probably enjoy time alone and would quite happily pass a whole day without interacting with anyone. If you're on the other side and more extroverted, like the one guy in the electric shock experiment who shocked himself an impressive 190 times in 15 minutes, you may find the idea of solitude excruciating.

But solitude can be a great way to create opportunities for bore-dom, daydreaming, creative thinking and introspection. It frees us of our inhibitions, lets us truly be ourselves and gives the brain a chance to relax. If you don't naturally like being alone, then start small. Go for a walk in nature by yourself or block off an hour in your diary for quiet, uninterrupted focused work alone. Practise until you feel more comfortable with solitude. It is a great way to create space for boredom and fresh thinking.

Conclusion

Boredom is seen as something we should avoid at all costs. But in this chapter we've explored the idea that boredom is a powerful catalyst for creative thinking and innovative ideas. Contrary to the recom-mendations of productivity gurus that dominate the narrative today, I suggest that we spend more time doing *nothing*. This will help us to become our most creative and innovative selves.

KEY TAKEAWAYS

- Boredom, often viewed negatively, is a catalyst for creative thinking and innovative ideas.

- When we are bored, the brain activates the default mode network, facilitating connections between ideas, finding themes and problem-solving. Boredom is not a state of rest but an engaged mental process that sets the stage for creative insights.

- Boredom is a natural and essential part of the human experience.

- Despite its benefits, people often go to great lengths to avoid boredom.

- Boredom helps with more than just generating ideas; it helps with incubating them.

- The prevailing culture of productivity and the glorification of busy schedules may inhibit creativity through stigmatizing boredom or rest.

- Putting your phone down, disconnecting from constant stimulation and spending time alone can create space for boredom in your life.

REFLECTIVE QUESTIONS

1 Reflect on a time when you found yourself in a boring situation. Did it lead to any unexpected insights or creative ideas?

2 Does the concept of embracing boredom for creativity challenge your beliefs about productivity and success, especially in a culture that glorifies constant activity?

3 How comfortable are you with the idea of actively resisting the pressure to be constantly productive in your personal and professional life?

4 Consider instances when you daydreamed during work hours. Were these moments counterproductive, or did daydreaming lead to creative solutions or ideas?

5 Examine your attitude towards boredom. Do you see it as a negative state to be avoided, or are you open to viewing it as a path to creativity and innovation?

References

Allardice, L (2020) Tiger King and a bloody Mary: Hilary Mantel, Simon Armitage and other writers on lockdown life, *Guardian*, 3 April

Brodsky, J (1995) In praise of boredom, *On Grief and Reason: Essays*, Penguin, Harmondsworth

Danckert, J and Eastwood, J (2020) *Out of My Skull: The psychology of boredom*, Harvard University Press, Cambridge, MA

Drago, V, Arico, D, Heilman, K, Foster, P, Williamson, J, Montagna, P and Ferri, R (2010) The correlation between sleep and creativity, *Nature Proceedings*, 9 March

Godwin, C, Hunter, M, Bezdek, M, Lieberman, G, Elkin-Frankston, S, Romero, V, Witkiewitz, K, Clark, V and Schumacher, E (2017) Functional connectivity within and between intrinsic brain networks correlates with trait mind wandering, *Neuropsychologia*, August, 103, 140–53

Gosline, A (2007) Bored? *Scientific American*, 1 December

Grady, C (2016) Neil Gaiman: Boredom is a writer's best friend, *Vox*, 24 June

Guardian (2023) The morning routine backlash: You can get up at 5am – but it won't make you popular, 25 April

Johnson, S (2010) *Where Good Ideas Come From: The natural history of innovation*, Allen Lane, London

Kleon, A (2012) *Steal Like an Artist: 10 things nobody told you about being creative*, Workman, New York

Lanquist, L (2018) 39 morning people share the extremely productive things they do while you're sleeping, *Self Magazine*, 20 April

Lezard, N (2007) Farewell to a master of farting around, *Guardian*, 12 April

Phillips, A (1998) *On Kissing, Tickling, and Being Bored: Psychoanalytic essays on the unexamined life*, Harvard University Press, Cambridge, MA

Psychology Today (2023) Boredom, *Psychology Today*, www.psychologytoday.com/ie/basics/boredom (archived at https://perma.cc/69RF-8A9A)

Raichle, M (2015) The brain's default mode network, *Annual Review of Neuroscience*, 38 (1), 433–47

Rowling, J K (2023) My story, J K Rowling, https://stories.jkrowling.com/my-story/ (archived at https://perma.cc/66SB-6FVC)

Sharna, R (2018) *The 5am Club: Own your morning. Elevate your life*, Thorsons, London

Wardle, N and Sharples, M (2021) *Monetising the Employee Experience: How to prove the ROI for investing in your people and unlock lost productivity*, Brand Experiences

Whitehead, N (2014) People would rather be electrically shocked than left alone with their thoughts, *Science Magazine*, 3 July

Yong, E (2018) A new theory linking sleep and creativity, *The Atlantic*, 15 May

Zomorodi, M (2017) *Bored and Brilliant: How spacing out can unlock your most productive and creative self*, St Martins Press, New York

08

Fuelling innovation through cross-disciplinary learning

Have you ever been reading something online when you stumble across a nugget of scientific research or a new study that just blows you away? And you begin to think Hmm... I could apply this in internal comms....

I had that feeling the first time I read psychology books like *The Chimp Paradox* (2012) by Steve Peters and *Influence: The psychology of persuasion* (1984) by Robert Cialdini, or when I bought my first subscription to the *Harvard Business Review* and starting nosing around non-communication business articles. This curiosity and hunger for knowledge expanded my horizons and helped to improve my thinking and my approach to internal communication. It helped me to innovate.

In this chapter I aim to whet your appetite for stepping outside the internal communication world and getting curious about other disciplines. In my experience, exploring other disciplines fuels creativity and innovative ideas through the collision of unrelated ideas. You'll start to connect previously unconnected dots and think about how to apply ideas from other industries into internal communication.

This chapter is not an exhaustive prescription for *what* to learn from other fields, rather it gives you a flavour of *how* you can begin to learn from other fields. It will give you what I hope is a tantalizing taste of what's beyond our own profession and show you how this cross-disciplinary learning can help us to become more innovative in our approach to internal communication.

Why look beyond internal communication?

Surrounding yourself with people who think differently than you do and have studied different fields than you is really helpful for innovation. Cross-disciplinary learning encourages breaking down the traditional siloes that confine knowledge to one industry or another. Integrating insights from diverse disciplines can help you innovate and think creatively. In essence, this is all about my favourite word: curiosity. Getting curious about what's happening in other industries can be great for innovation.

Stepping outside our usual learning zone and drawing inspiration from diverse disciplines can help us to think differently about what we do and how we do it. I suggest this because innovation often emerges at the intersection of different areas of expertise, where different perspectives collide. Intentionally cross-pollinating your mind with learning from different sectors and disciplines will do wonders for your creativity.

Here I'll give you a flavour of the value of getting curious about psychology, science and marketing.

Learning from… psychology

Psychology is the discipline of understanding human behaviour. Sounds like something kind of important for internal communicators, right? We tackle the complexities of human behaviour every day in our job, given that our work is so fundamentally about influencing employee behaviour and sentiment. Getting curious about psychology can help us get a better understanding of the people we are trying to reach and how best we can positively influence them.

A great place to start learning about psychology is with Dr Robert Cialdini, the American psychologist I mentioned at the start of this chapter. He has spent decades studying human behaviour and figuring out what makes people tick. Based on his research over the years, he argues that there are six fundamental principles that influence people. His book, *Influence*, was written in the 1980s and has since sold more than 7 million copies worldwide in 44 different languages. (Yes, it's *that* good.) According to Cialdini, influencing people is a science and not an art; there are proven ways to influence people that can help to make you more successful in roles like marketing or communication.

Let's dive into some of Cialdini's psychological principles to see what we can learn about human behaviour and how we can apply his research to our work in internal communication. We'll unpack three of his principles: reciprocity, social proof and scarcity.

Reciprocity

Picture the scene: it's Friday afternoon and you're in work, getting ready to wind down for the weekend. You've a few bits to check off your to-do list before you can finish up and head home. Unexpectedly, your colleague Sandra appears at your desk with a box of delicious-looking blueberry muffins. 'Hey, want one?' she says, smiling widely. You accept (of course) and chat for a moment before she casually says, 'Could you help me finish off my speaking notes for the big presentation on Monday? I could use an outside perspective.' Now this was *not* on your pre-weekend to-do list, but before you know it you're in the conference room with her going through her notes.

How did she manage that?

Well, according to Cialdini, it's simple really – people feel obligated to return favours and feel indebted to people who give us a present. It's that old chestnut of 'I'll scratch your back if you scratch mine.' This is the reciprocity principle. When Sandra offered you that tasty muffin, she probably knew exactly what she was doing: you were far more likely to help her on a Friday afternoon after a free muffin than if she came to your desk empty-handed. Clever Sandra.

A 1996 study on gift-giving found that the reciprocity principle is alive and well; their findings revealed that when people give gifts, they are followed by return gifts most of the time. The study found that people who give loads of gifts will receive loads of gifts back – and those who don't give many won't receive many (Komter, 1996). The phenomenon of reciprocity has been documented for a long time. In the 1920s, the anthropologist Malinowski (1926) observed the principle in action in villagers in Papua New Guinea. The villagers who lived by the coast delivered fish to the inland village and in return they received vegetables from the inland harvest. He concluded that their social system was based on a give-and-take approach in which favours were reciprocated.

So we know that this principle works. Can we apply it in our work in internal communication?

In short, yes. A very simple way you can use this principle at work is go out of your way to help others without the expectation of anything in return. This builds up positive relationships, positions you as helpful and builds up a bank of reciprocity. Say, for example, that Helen, the IT Manager, is holding a department townhall meeting next week. Each department looks after their own local meetings and you don't officially have a role to play in it. But you overhear Helen talking about the meeting in the canteen, where she says the townhall plan feels very dry and she is worried people might get bored. So you offer to help her brainstorm some ideas, or you straight up offer her a few tactics that may help based on what you know about her audience and her topics. In short, you go out of your way to do a good deed. Now fast forward a few weeks when you need some help from IT whitelisting a new comms channel that you've having trouble with. It's more likely that Helen will help you get it sorted because you've already helped her first. This is reciprocity in action. It can be particularly powerful when you go out of your way at work to help others achieve *their* goals (Cialdini, 1984).

So the takeaway is this: help people. Find simple ways you can do people favours, in the knowledge that it may well pay off in the long run through reciprocity. This can help you immensely in your attempts with innovation as you will build up increasingly good relationships across the business and find it easier to get things unblocked as you try new approaches. It's also just a nice way to operate and live your life, isn't it? Helping others is a nice vibe.

Social proof

Have you ever gone to a fancy restaurant for a tasting menu and felt baffled by the sheer volume of cutlery in front of you? Four forks –

really? What on earth are they for? When the first course comes out, you're not sure which fork to use. Think about what you do next. Most likely, you'll look at the other people around the table to see what they do, and you'll copy their behaviour.

This is the essence of Cialdini's principle of social proof. It's about conforming to socially acceptable behaviour through copying the actions of those around us, and trying to find the 'correct' way to behave or fit in. Cialdini argues that humans are driven by a deep desire to conform and belong (Cialdini, 1984).

This idea can be seen in research that predates Cialdini's work. In the 1950s, Asch designed a lab experiment to study the idea of conformity (McLeod, 2023). Fifty participants took part. The research was delightfully simple: two cards were presented to the participants. On one card was a straight line. On the second card were three straight lines of different lengths, marked A, B and C. The participants had to select which of the three lines was the same as the first card – and the lines were deliberately very different lengths to make it quite obvious that C was the correct answer. But here's the twist: many of the participants were 'stooges' who were in on the experiment and were deliberately giving the wrong answer. Eight participants lined up in the room and had to state out loud whether A, B or C was the correct answer, with the real participant always going last. Would the real participant give the correct answer, or would they go along with what the others in the group said?

The results were fascinating. On average, a third of participants went along with the others in the group and gave the clearly wrong answer. Across all the rounds of experiments, 75 per cent of participants conformed to the wrong answer at least once, with only 25 per cent of them never conforming. Even more interesting is the results of the control group; with no pressure to conform to a group answer, less than 1 per cent of participants ever gave the wrong answer, which indicates that it was indeed easy to see that C was the correct answer.

What on earth is going on here? This is Cialdini's idea of social proof in action; people are heavily influenced by the actions and behaviours of others. When Asch's participants were interviewed after the study and asked why they gave the wrong answer, most of them stated that they knew the answer was wrong but went along with what the group said as they didn't want to be ridiculed or seen as strange.

People tend to look to those around them to guide their decisions and actions. They want to know what everyone else is doing. (Doesn't that sound like our own obsession with 'best practice'? Where we desperately want to know what other companies and other communicators are doing?)

We can use this principle in our work in internal communication. Say you are running a communication campaign about a series of learning seminars available to employees. Your objective is to get as many people to voluntarily sign up as possible. Why not use the concept of social proof to help influence them? Get testimonials and quotes from people who have done the seminars before. Get them to give the seminars star ratings. Use their headshots, testimonials and star rating front and centre of your campaign as social proof that the seminars are worthwhile, and to demonstrate that many employees have already done the seminars *and so should you*. You can use lines like '84 per cent of your colleagues said this course helped them succeed' or 'Rated 4.5 per cent stars by employees across the company'. You see this kind of approach in marketing all the time, for example on the sales page of a learning course you'll find testimonials from previous students to create a feeling of social proof to influence your decision to buy the course.

Using employee testimonials, success stories of employees who have benefited from a particular course or initiative, and data around previous sign-up numbers can serve as powerful social proof and can encourage others to sign up and participate. Try it out – it will cost you nothing but some time and effort and can reap huge rewards in terms of influencing employee behaviour and achieving your objectives.

Scarcity

I was shopping online for a dress once and I fell prey to a clever use of the scarcity principle. I found a dress I liked but wasn't totally committed to and I put it into my shopping basket so I could come back to it later. But when I put it into the basket, I got a message that said 'hurry – only two left in stock' and before you know it, I had paid for the dress. Even though I wasn't sure it was right yet. This is Cialdini's principle of scarcity in action; the idea that when there's less of something, it makes us want it more. It creates a sense of urgency and makes us act.

This will seem intuitively correct to you when you think about how often we encounter this principle in our day-to-day lives. Think about the frenzied attempts at getting a ticket when Taylor Swift announces a concert ('There's only a limited number of tickets available!') or the madness of Black Friday sales in the US ('Only available while stocks last!'). When items or opportunities are perceived as rare, limited or in short supply then they're perceived as more valuable. People then become motivated to act quickly or seize the opportunity, for example they'll make a purchasing decision faster than they usually would. Like I did with the dress I didn't even really want.

This is the essence of what the kids these days call FOMO: fear of missing out.

Thinking about our own world of internal communication, consider the example of our communications campaign for the learning seminars again. When you're designing the campaign, you may initially assume that employees will determine whether to sign up or not based on the usefulness of the seminars. But what if you considered instead the idea that the appeal of the seminars might not lie in their content, but in their *availability*? Inoue and Ariga (2015) suggest the water-diamond paradox as a way of understanding the scarcity principle. We need water to survive as humans and we buy it very cheaply, yet we pay much higher prices for diamonds even though we don't actually need them at all. The paradox is that the value of each object doesn't lie solely in its usefulness, but in its availability.

Scarcity drives a perception of value.

Cadbury Creme Eggs strike me as a real-life example of the scarcity principle in action. (If you live in a country where you don't get Creme Eggs, you have my sympathy.) Creme Eggs are small chocolate eggs (about the size of a chicken's egg) filled with soft, sugary goo that are available to buy *only* around Easter time each year. You simply cannot buy them in November or in July or whenever you want – only at a predetermined time of year and for a limited time only. The effect this has on people is hilarious; people go *nuts* for them. They buy loads of them, and they buy them frequently while they're available. I once had a boss who ate five of them in one afternoon simply because she knew they were going to disappear soon. (She told me later it was an extraordinary mistake never to be repeated, in case you get any ideas.)

Organizations use the scarcity principle all the time in marketing to drive sign-ups for events, increase sales or get people on their email list. For example, they might run flash sales where items are on sale for 48 hours only, or they might advertise an event and say 'Sign up quick – only five spots left!'

So why not apply these same ideas to internal communication? Thinking about our communication campaign on the learning seminars, couldn't we communicate that the seminars are available for a limited time only, or that there are a limited number of spaces available? We could say that it's first-come, first-served to create a sense of urgency. Highlighting the scarcity of the learning opportunity can motivate employees to sign up quickly instead of prolonging the decision. Using the scarcity principle can help you influence employee behaviour and create a sense of urgency around specific initiatives or opportunities in the company.

Now, a brief word of caution here – be careful with applying these psychological principles. Use them wisely, ethically and fairly. You want to influence people, not manipulate them. You need to balance the use of psychological influencing with your ability to maintain trust and credibility with other employees.

Learning from... science

We can also look to the broader world of science and scientific research to fuel our learning. I quite like reading science journals and research studies to see what insights I can glean for my communication work. Here are a few nuggets I've picked up from reading scientific research that will give you a flavour of the kind of learning you can get when you step outside the internal communication world.

Brain scans reveal that reading fiction improves your empathy

There's some really interesting scientific research on how reading improves our empathy, through putting us in other people's shoes as we follow characters through a story. Dodell-Feder and Temir (2018) undertook a meta-analysis of 14 scientific studies that looked at whether reading fiction made us more empathetic, and they concluded that yes, reading fiction books does in fact have that effect. Stillman (2021) summarizes this nicely, saying, 'reading is basically an empathy workout'.

How does this work? Well imagine you're reading a great novel and you're completely engrossed in the story. You feel that you know the main characters so well that they're practically friends of yours. Reading fiction puts us into the shoes of another person, i.e. the characters in the book, who can be very different from ourselves. This pushes us to see things from another perspective and helps to boost our emotional intelligence.

This isn't guesswork – this is scientific research and it's backed up by brain scans. When we are engrossed in a good novel, our brains are highly engaged. Our brains are doing more than processing the language but are actually mirroring the actions and feelings of the characters in the book (Stillman, 2018). For example, if you're deeply immersed in a book where a character is going for a swim, parts of your brain will light up as if you were actually physically swimming yourself. Isn't this incredible?

What does this mean for us in internal communication? Well we know that empathy is a crucial skill for communication; we learned this from our FBI hostage negotiator Chris Voss in Chapter 5, and now we know from neuroscience research that reading fiction books is a proven way to increase our empathy. So this is your cue to join your local library and indulge yourself in some gorgeous fiction. You can enjoy your time reading fiction guilt-free, safe in the knowledge that it's proven to be good for your brain and will help you to become a better communicator through increased empathy.

Clear writing makes you sound smart

In 2005, Daniel Oppenheimer of Princeton University was struck by the academic, long-winded language that all his students used. He developed a hypothesis that they were deliberately using complex language in an attempt to appear more intelligent.

He designed an experiment to test his hypothesis. He asked participants to rate a number of writing samples. Some writing samples used complex vocabulary, some had simpler words. He ran five different experiments to test how readers responded to the different writing types.

His finding was striking. When writing is clear and in simpler language, the author is rated as more intelligent. His conclusion was this: readers are likely to rate an author as more intelligent when they can clearly and easily understand what is being communicated.

Oppenheimer's research title is itself a great example of using complex language versus simple language to convey the same idea: 'Consequences of erudite vernacular utilized irrespective of necessity: Problems with using long words needlessly'.

The key message from Oppenheimer's study is that long, complex words that make an article hard to read or understand will lower readers' evaluation of the author. This is really useful ammunition for us in the world of internal communication, where we are regularly battling against a barrage of jargon and convoluted language with stakeholders. The next time one of your stakeholders is absolutely insisting that their newsletter article must be in complex language, you can show them the study by Oppenheimer. You might just convince them that using clear language will help to make them be perceived as more intelligent in the organization.

Great writing lights up the human brain

There's more good news from the world of science research: effective writing has an incredible impact on our brains. Scientists have discovered neurons in the brain that light up as people respond to great writing. If you can make you reader enjoy your writing, their brain releases pleasure chemicals in their brains and they'll keep reading (Birchard, 2021). This neurology research actually shows *how* the brain responds to words and stories. If you write something *good*, the reader's dopamine will start flowing in the part of the brain known as 'the reward circuit'. If you write something *great*, opioids will be released to turn on the reward hot spots. It's surprisingly like the effects of a good meal or a big hug; great writing makes us feel pleasure. Scientists can now see this happening using MRI and PET machines. Reward regions in the brain light up when people read certain types of writing or hear it spoken out loud. Your own writing has the potential to light up the brain of your readers.

Birchard (2021) summarizes some of the characteristics of strong writing that are most likely to induce this response in the brain. You'll see immediately why I love diving into scientific research when you see how immediately applicable and actionable this research is:

- **Simplicity:** Keeping your writing simple increases the brain's 'processing fluency', which means the speed at which people can understand things. We can deliberately make our writing simpler by ruthlessly deleting any unnecessary words (what Stephen King (2000) calls 'kill your darlings'). We can use short sentences and reduce the amount of information so that we only give the reader the important information that they really need.

- **Specificity:** When language is specific, circuits in the human brain respond. Researchers have found that when specific words are used, more neurons are activated in the brain than when general words are used (Birchard, 2021). This means that more specific words cause the brain to understand things more easily – for example, the specific term 'magpie' instead of the general term 'bird'. The takeaway here is that using more specific, vivid language will appeal to your readers and help them understand your message more easily.

- **Surprise:** The human brain is wired to constantly make predictions. This includes trying to guess the next word in a sentence. Giving your readers an unpredictable surprise will help them learn and retain information. People have an appetite for the unexpected and the unpredictable. We see this in the film industry all the time – some of the best movies ever made have a shock twist at the end that keeps us guessing. The human brain rewards surprise. For example, a study in the Wharton School found that newspaper articles rated as 'surprising' were more likely to appear on the 'most emailed' list (Birchard, 2021). Think about your own writing – how can you include a surprise to keep employees interested?

- **Emotional language:** People in business often fall into the trap of thinking that logic and data will persuade everyone to their way of thinking. But science shows that brains process the emotional meaning of words within 200 milliseconds of reading it – much faster than we understand it's logical meaning (Birchard, 2021). So when we read emotional material, we reflexively react with feelings first. Joy, disgust, pride, anger, fear... our brains are hardwired to respond with emotion *first*, and reason second. Use this scientific knowledge to your advantage. Use emotionally charged words in your writing. Go back to the age-old communications question of 'What do you want your reader to *feel*?' There's good science to show how important it is.

- **Anticipation:** Human beings love anticipation. One study showed that people are often happier planning a holiday than they are actually taking one. Scientists call this 'anticipatory utility' (Birchard, 2021). We can use this knowledge to appeal to our reader by driving curiosity for what's coming next. Here's an example of Steve Jobs doing this when he addressed Stanford University in 2005. He said that he was there to simply tell the crowd three stories from his life. No big life-changing advice, just stories. As you can imagine, the audience were hanging on his every word as they were so curious to know what the three stories were. You can do this in your writing too. Start a report with a question or use a customer problem as a hook.

These effective writing tips from neuroscience research can help us to directly understand how to reward our readers and keep them coming back for more.

Rhyming words help us remember information

In 2017, a doctor called Tapas Mukherjee was working in an English hospital. He was dismayed by the findings of a survey that showed 55 per cent of nurses and doctors in his hospital weren't following guidelines on the management of asthma. Even worse, 38 per cent of them didn't even know these guidelines existed (Murphy, 2013).

Mukherjee created a communication to fix this and astonishingly only two months later 100 per cent of doctors and nurses were now aware of the guidelines. Compliance rates had shot up remarkably. Doctors aren't exactly known for their top-notch communication skills, so how on earth did he do this?

The secret is surprisingly simple: he used rhymes.

Rhymes are surprisingly powerful. They help us to remember things. Rhymes increase processing fluency, in other words they help us to understand messages more easily. We can process them in our brains and make sense of them more easily. This makes us more able to remember the key message (Murphy, 2013).

Not only that, but rhymes are very persuasive. Scientists have identified a cognitive bias known as 'the rhyme-and-reason effect'. This shows that people are more likely to believe statements that contain a rhyme compared to statements that don't. Rhyming actually influences our perception of accuracy. In a study published in the *Journal of Psychological Science*, researchers found that participants who were given rhymes found the message more accurate and more insightful (McGlone and Tofighbaksh, 2000).

Another study by the same researchers the year before had similar findings – people rated rhyming phrases as more accurate than non-rhyming ones even when the message was exactly the same. For example: 'Anger restrained is wisdom gained' was more believable than 'Anger held back is wisdom gained' (McGlone and Tofighbaksh, 1999). You were probably told as a kid: 'An apple a day keeps the doctor away'. And you will probably remember that phrase for your whole life. Would it have been as memorable or believable if the phrase was 'An apple a day keeps you healthy'? Probably not.

This science explains why marketing teams around the world use rhymes to advertise their company's products. They know what they're doing and they know it's a good commercial investment to produce slogans like 'A Mars a day helps you work, rest and play' or 'Once you pop, you can't stop'. So what's to stop you from taking this nugget of scientific research and using it in your work in internal communication?

How about adding a rhyme to key statements that you want to make more convincing or memorable to employees? This can apply, for example, to something that is traditionally very boring and you need to capture people's attention. Crafting catchy and concise rhymes can make messages more compelling and help employees to remember crucial information, and this is all backed up by scientific research.

Learning from... marketing

Returning to a field slightly closer to home, it's worth learning about marketing to fuel our innovative ideas in the world of internal communication. Marketing is about influencing and persuading prospective customers to buy your product or like your brand. People who are great marketers tend to do certain things very well: they understand their customers deeply, they understand their customers' journey, they map their results to business outcomes and they produce content that is useful to their audience.

The importance of understanding your customers

Marketing 101 is this: know your customer. Marketing professionals understand the need to adopt an audience-centric approach and they develop deep understandings of their target audiences in order to make campaigns successful. We intuitively know that this is also important in internal communication, but how many of us have actually carved out the time to develop and document deep understandings of our internal audiences? It takes time, energy and resources to conduct the research and analyse the data, and often this is pushed to the bottom of an endless to-do list and communications are just sent to all employees instead.

For years, marketing teams have created personas of their target audiences; detailed profiles that represent the people they are trying to reach and influence. This is a practice that is sometimes used in internal communication but could be adopted more widely. This would allow us to gain valuable insights into the motivations, preferences and needs of distinct employee groups – instead of the dreaded 'all staff email for everything' approach.

Having personas or any sort of documented way to understand your employees enables you to tailor messages and select the right channels to reach each segment effectively. This approach acknowledges the diversity within the workforce and can help to make internal communications more relevant to each audience group. Yes, it's a lot more work, but it can increase your impact and help ensure content is relevant to employees.

Customer journey mapping

Taking this a step further, we could also borrow from the journey mapping that marketing teams do. Customer journey mapping is a way of visualizing the end-to-end experience that a customer has with a company by mapping out all their interactions with the company.

This could include the marketing emails they receive or the customer service they get on the phone or the content they read on the website. Mapping out how and when a customer interacts with the company helps the marketing team to gain better insights into the behaviours, needs and frustrations of customers at each stage so they can serve the customers better and improve the overall level of customer satisfaction. The idea behind customer journey mapping is to take control of every touchpoint along the journey so it is all well-designed to meet the customer's needs, instead of just hoping that things work out.

We can take this idea of customer journey mapping and apply it to internal communication by mapping out our employees' journey. Many practitioners who work in employee experience have adopted this as a practice to identify parts of the employee experience that need more attention, for example onboarding or offboarding. As internal communicators, we can learn from this approach to create maps that illustrate the various touchpoints and experiences that our internal audiences have throughout their time in the organization. This can help us to identify critical communication moments and create opportunities to communicate more effectively.

For example, an internal communicator working in a retail environment might invest some time in mapping out the employee journey of frontline workers. You could map out what their day looks like and note where they're spending their time and how they're getting their information. You might notice and document touchpoints such as:

- The employee clocks in at the clocking station at the start of their shift.
- Next they go to the locker room to get changed and leave their belongings in their lockers.
- They have a pre-shift briefing with their team supervisor before they hit the shop floor.
- Any updates needed during their shift are done through word of mouth.
- At the end of their shift they return to the clocking station to clock out.

In each stage of this employee journey, you'll notice opportunities for communicating with employees that meet them where they are. For example, if there's an important announcement that everyone needs to know then you could post it by the clock-in station as you know that all employees have to go there before and after their shift. You could look at putting a digital screen in that area as you know it will have a good reach. You also know that each team will have a pre-shift briefing with their supervisor and this could be a key channel for communicating operational priorities. You get the idea.

Borrowing the idea of a customer journey from marketing and translating it into a way of identifying communication touchpoints for our employee audiences is very useful.

Mapping activity to business outcomes

Another lesson we can learn from the world of marketing is their ability to map their activity to business outcomes and demonstrate their position as commercially necessary to the success of the organization. Savvy marketing teams are positioning themselves as revenue drivers in the business rather than cost centres (Balis, 2022) and perhaps we should be learning from this. Previously, marketing teams would often find themselves at the brunt of cuts to discretionary spending as their work wasn't directly tied to profit creation (sounds familiar, doesn't it?). But now, with highly measurable communication channels and campaigns, marketing teams are showing the tangible impact of their work on bottom-line results such as sales and profits. This enables marketers to gain more respect and status in the organization as their work become less fluffy and more tangible in terms of driving revenue.

Marketing teams do this by setting clear, measurable objectives that are directly tied to business outcomes. We know that we should be doing this in internal communication – we've been told it a thousand times. But how many of us are actually doing it? Can you look at your calendar for the week and clearly see links between your work activity and the objectives of the business? (If you can say 'yes' to that question, then I commend you immensely – well done.) Marketers develop clear key performance indicators for their campaigns and initiatives and are expected to explain the return on investment of their work. I see internal communication teams as no different – we should also be able to account for our work and clearly demonstrate the value we bring to the organization. We cannot do this without establishing specific objectives that align with broader organizational goals and having measurements in place to show progress.

We can learn from our peers in marketing on this. For instance, our internal communication objectives could contribute to increased productivity, higher level of profits or reduced employee attrition – whatever your organization is trying to achieve at the macro level. This alignment to the overall goals of the business ensures that internal communication efforts are purposeful and measurable, and directly contribute to the organization's overarching goals, making internal communicators command more respect for their work and leaving them less prone to layoffs when times are hard.

Part of this work requires us to become more comfortable with data and measurement, and I know that many communicators will readily admit that they struggle with metrics and proving results. I'll explore this in more depth in the next chapter and give you a scientific framework to help you.

The need for content to be relevant and useful

Marketers often use the phrase 'content is king'. For some companies, the content they create is so good that they can use it to attract paying customers without investing any money in advertising. (Spoiler alert: I run one of those companies.) This is called 'content marketing'.

Content marketing works because it is audience centric. A content marketer is creating content that provides the audience with genuine value. Maybe the content is helping to solve a problem for the audience, for example, or helping them to get unstuck on a thorny challenge or get inspired with a new idea related to their work. Whatever the angle, content marketing aims to deliver great content that the audience will find useful and interesting, thereby capturing and holding their attention.

This is a great way for internal communicators to think about content, too. How often do we get told to send stuff out without questioning whether the audience needs that information or not? It shouldn't be about what the most senior person in the room wants to be included in your newsletter, or who's shouting the loudest to get a big button on the front of your intranet. What does the audience need, what problems are they struggling with and how can our content help with that? How can our content help people to do their jobs and to feel connected to the business? And how can we make this content engaging and interesting for the audience?

Adopting the approach of a content marketer may spur on innovations in your content creation process that are easy to implement but will make a big difference.

Practical steps to fuel innovation through cross-disciplinary learning

I argue in this chapter that a great way to get new breakthrough ideas or different insights is to expose yourself to different ways of thinking and different disciplines. Here is a practical, action-oriented list of suggestions of how you can go about doing this.

- Attend a conference from an entirely different field.
- Read a book you think you will disagree with.
- Read a book about a topic that intimidates you.
- Listen to a podcast from someone with a different worldview than you.
- Pick up a science magazine the next time you're in an airport.
- Book a contrarian speaker for an event in work that will ruffle some feathers.
- Follow blogs or publications from fields like psychology, marketing or science.
- Join online groups comprised of professionals outside of internal communication.
- Take a course in an unrelated field.
- Listen to a podcast from a discipline you know nothing about.
- Seek out a mentor from another industry.
- Engage in conversations with individuals who challenge your viewpoints.
- Pick up a magazine you've never read before.
- Put 30 minutes in your diary each week to read a non-fiction, non-communication book.

These are very simple, practical steps you can take to incorporate learning into your routine and ensure that you're regularly exposing yourself to diverse perspectives and different ways of thinking.

The importance of looking beyond internal communication is clear. Exploring other disciplines and exposing ourselves to new ideas can fuel our creativity and spark innovative ideas. Cross-disciplinary learning is a way for internal communicators to step outside their comfort zones and draw inspiration from diverse disciples and alternative thinkers.

Spending time learning about psychology and psychological principles can help us understand more about human behaviour and how to positively influence it through communication tactics. We can build positive relationships through reciprocity, leverage social proof in our campaigns and use the scarcity principle to create a sense of urgency for employees. Delving into the world of scientific research opens up a world of ideas we can draw on to innovate in our field. Insights from brain imaging studies tell us about ways to improve empathy, the importance of effective writing and how to make messages memorable. These studies show the actionable value of scientific research for internal communicators. Learning from the discipline of marketing reminds us of the importance of high-value content and having a deep understanding of our audience, as well as the need to measure our work and relate it back to commercial business outcomes.

Ultimately, I'm advocating for a curious approach, one in which we are constantly poking our noses into other disciplines and other fields and asking, 'What's this? What's that? What can I learn from these?' If we renegotiate the boundaries of where we learn and who we learn from, we can integrate insights from psychology, science and marketing and beyond. This diversity of learning can help us to fuel our innovator's mindset and cultivate an environment in which we can connect the dots and spark new ideas.

KEY TAKEAWAYS

- Diversity breeds innovation, so explore ideas beyond the internal communication field for inspiration.

- Learn about behavioural psychology from people like Dr Robert Cialdini to recognize how to understand and influence your stakeholders and employees.

- Read about scientific research and published studies to glean insights you can use in your work in internal communication.

- Study marketing for ideas around positioning your team internally, making your content valuable and segmenting your audience.

- There is a whole world of knowledge out there – get curious about it and don't stay siloed in internal communication.

REFLECTIVE QUESTIONS

1 How comfortable are you with stepping outside the internal communication world to explore ideas from diverse disciplines?

2 In what ways can you apply the principles of reciprocity, social proof, and scarcity from psychology to innovate in your approach to internal communication?

3 How might incorporating insights from scientific research, such as the impact of fiction reading on empathy or the neuroscience of effective writing, influence how you do your work?

4 Have you considered positioning your internal communication efforts as revenue drivers, similar to marketing teams? What metrics could demonstrate the tangible impact of your work on business outcomes?

5 How well do you understand the specific needs and frustrations of different segments within your internal audience? What steps can you take to improve audience segmentation for more targeted communication?

References

Balis, J (2022) 5 ways marketing leaders can drive more value in 2022, *Harvard Business Review*, 23 February

Birchard, B (2021) The science of strong business writing, *Harvard Business Review*, July–August

Cialdini, R (1984) *Influence: The psychology of persuasion*, William Morrow & Company, New York

Dodell-Feder, D and Tamir, D (2018) Fiction reading has a small positive impact on social cognition: A meta-analysis, *Journal of Experimental Psychology*, 147 (11), 1713–27

Inoue, A and Ariga, A (2015) How scarce objects attract people: The effects of temporal and social contexts of the scarcity on object value, International Marketing Trends Conference, Paris

King, S (2000) *On Writing: A memoir of the craft*, Simon & Schuster, New York

Komter, E (1996) Reciprocity as a principle of exclusion: Gift giving in the Netherlands, *Sociology*, 30 (2)

Malinowski, B (1926) *Crime and Custom in Savage Society*, Harcourt Brace, New York

McGlone, M and Tofighbakhsh, J (1999) The Keats heuristic: Rhyme as reason in aphorism interpretation, *Poetics*, 26 (4), 235–44

McGlone, M and Tofighbakhsh, J (2000) Birds of a feather flock conjointly (?): Rhyme as reason in aphorisms, *Journal of Psychological Science*, 11 (5)

McLeod, S (2023) Solomon Asch conformity line experiment study, *Simply Psychology*, 24 October

Murphy, A (2013) Need to remember something? Make it rhyme, *Time*, 17 September

Oppenheimer, D (2005) Consequences of erudite vernacular utilized irrespective of necessity: Problems with using long words needlessly, *Applied Cognitive Psychology*, 20 (2), 139–56

Peters, S (2012) *The Chimp Paradox*, Vermilion, London

Stillman, J (2018) This is what a great book does to your brain, Inc.com, www.inc.com/jessica-stillman/this-is-what-a-great-book-does-to-your-brain.html (archived at https://perma.cc/6W54-6B7Z)

Stillman, J (2021) This is how reading rewires your brain, according to neuroscience, Inc.com, www.inc.com/jessica-stillman/reading-books-brain-chemistry.html (archived at https://perma.cc/K67R-SAAM)

09

Measurable experiments using the scientific method

Ah, the chapter you've all been dreading: the one where we talk about *measurement*. The bane of every communicator's life. In this chapter I want to talk about it in a different way. I want to introduce you to the scientific method and show you how to start using measurable experiments to drive innovation in your work as an internal communicator.

Here's a generalization that is largely true in my experience: internal communication professionals struggle with data and measurement and numbers. We were probably pretty good with words at school but not as good with maths. Certainly, for me, my experience of maths in school was one where I felt intimidated, overwhelmed and frankly a bit stupid. I didn't *get* maths. Algebra was beyond me. Once letters got introduced into equations that was it for me, I was hopelessly lost. This experience carried over into my adult life where my fear of maths was reignited during my university degree in sociology. Diving into lectures on quantitative data collection, I struggled with independent variables, using data analysis software and getting to grips with complex multi-variate data structures.

But a subject I really enjoyed in school, and still love as an adult, was science. Science is the ultimate indulgence of curiosity, isn't it? Looking at things, poking at them, asking endless questions, testing out ideas, sharing results, trying again, failing, figure out why it failed, trying again... I love everything about the way scientists approach their work. I think internal communicators could learn a lot from scientists and the rigour they apply to their thinking and decision-making.

In this chapter I suggest that we do just that: internal communicators can adopt the scientific method as a framework to run measurable experiments to drive innovation. The scientific method is immensely useful for internal communicators who want to find new ways to add value, and it's a simple framework that anyone can use. Maybe you're really bad at maths like me and that has instilled a limiting self-belief in your head of 'I can't do measurement'. Let's hush that voice once and for all as I'll show you how you can use the scientific method to get comfortable with testing, measuring and innovating on a regular basis.

Why do we need measurable experiments in internal communication?

I talk to a lot of internal communicators in the course of my job as a consultant and trainer and I hear a lot of things like this:

'I *feel* like that campaign was really successful.'

'I *think* that message landed really well.'

'My *gut* is telling me that we should use a new channel.'

While gut instinct and intuition are powerful and shouldn't be ignored, they are not a great way to make decisions in work, especially ones where resources or money are involved. This over-reliance on gut instinct rather than data is not an issue confined to us as internal communicators – it is rife right across the business world. Thomke and Loveman (2022) state that 'despite decades of admonitions about the dangers of gut instinct, many managers continue to over-rely on intuition and personal experience in decision-making, even when the evidence contradicts them'.

Making decisions on gut instinct is easier than making decisions on data. It's easier and it's quicker and you can tick things off the list and move on to the next thing. But good decisions really need to be based on evidence and data – because maybe our instincts are wrong.

Maybe we are biased or our perspective is skewed or we are making flawed assumptions. That's where science can help us. If we begin to think and act more like scientists, we become aware of flaws in our perspective and become more likely to interrogate assumptions before we act on them (Thomke and Loveman, 2022).

We need an expert here

This chapter is so fundamentally important and so close to my heart that I wanted to bring in an expert to explain the key concepts and get us on the same page. Now I'm not easily intimidated but when I introduce our expert, you'll understand why I was quite nervous doing this interview.

Our expert is Professor Patricia Maguire of University College Dublin (UCD). She is the Director of the UCD Institute for Discovery, a Professor of Biochemistry and a Fellow of the Conway Institute of UCD. Professor Maguire is a biomedical scientist with an exceptional record of high-performance research. She's been published in a variety of leading international journals, been awarded more than €5 million in competitive research funding and she has led on several global research collaborations with institutions like Harvard Medical School and Cambridge University. Most recently, Professor Maguire has led on a revolution in pre-eclampsia care using artificial intelligence. Professor Maguire and her team are using cutting-edge biomedical, clinical and machine-learning research to develop a prototype risk stratification tool to identify women with pre-eclampsia and how they will progress through the remainder of their pregnancy. This project has been rated as excellent in the UNESCO Global Top 100 AI projects addressing the UN sustainable goals.

Now can you see why I was nervous doing this interview?

Lucky for me, Professor Maguire is incredibly friendly and generous and great to speak with. She kindly took time out of her day to answer my questions on the scientific method and to outline why it's not just for scientists – it's for everyone. Let's start at the beginning: what is the scientific method?

What is the scientific method?

The scientific method is a simple, structured framework for solving problems and driving innovations based on data and evidence. Successful innovation often emerges from experiments, trial and error and learning from failures (Ridley, 2020) and this is no different for the world of internal communication. The scientific method relies on objectivity and evidence rather than personal insight or experience to make decisions (Thomke and Loveman, 2022).

Professor Maguire tells me that the scientific method is a way to explore ideas and observations through experiments. It's a process of objectively establishing evidence and facts though experiments and tests. The method is comprised of five key steps in this order:

1 Observation

2 Hypothesis

3 Experiment

4 Analysis

5 Conclusion

Let's look at each of them and get a clear understanding of what they all mean.

Observation

The first step of the scientific method is observation. Observe something about the world that intrigues you and makes you want to learn more. Here are some sample observations that an internal communicator could make:

- Our organization sends a lot of all-staff emails.
- The newsletter articles that focus on our core values get the fewest clicks.

- Employees were scrolling through their smartphones during the last CEO townhall meeting.

These are simple observations about something you've noticed. You don't know *why* these things are happening. You're simply observing them at this point and writing them down.

A simple way to make this a regular practice is to write down your observations in a notebook as they pop into your head. You'll forget them otherwise. Jot them down. Don't put any limits around what your observations could be. A fundamental principle of the scientific method is that everything is open to investigation and testing. Everything you see and observe is open to scrutiny and all the assumptions we have are open to challenge. If you'd like to start thinking like a scientist, then this is how you start: capture observations.

Your observations can have multiple sources. They can come from employee insights gathered through quantitative data collection (surveys or net promoter scores, for example) or qualitative data collection (focus groups, listening sessions, interviews and so on). Your observations might come from overhearing a conversation in the office, noticing a conversation in an online chat channel or simply seeing something that you find interesting.

One thing that's worth remembering here is that innovation should result in value. So, you might gather 100 observations but not all of them will be valuable or worth investigating. Critically scrutinize them and consider how they may relate to the overall goals of the business or to your own communication strategy. Try to think objectively and identify which observations could be potentially important to the business – rather than what is just personally interesting to you.

Hypothesis

The next step is to formulate a hypothesis based on your observation. Professor Maguire pauses here and says, 'Sometimes people get a bit confused when they hear the word "hypothesis" because it's not really a word we use in everyday life. It's something I have to explain to people a lot, even people in the lab or doing a PhD.'

A hypothesis is simply a *statement*. It's a statement based on the observation you made. A hypothesis must be testable – it's either correct or it isn't and you can test it through experiments. For example, Professor Maguire says, a hypothesis could be 'The sky is blue'. It's a clear statement and you can go about proving whether it's true or not.

Here are the key ingredients for a hypothesis:

- A statement.
- It's binary.
- You can test it.

Here are some internal communication hypotheses we could create based on the sample observations made above:

- **Observation:** Our organization sends a lot of all-staff emails.
- **Hypothesis:** Email is a noisy communication channel in which messages get lost.

- **Observation:** The newsletter articles that focus on our core values get the fewest clicks.
- **Hypothesis:** The way we communicate our core values is boring to employees.

- **Observation:** Employees were scrolling through their smartphones during the last CEO townhall meeting.
- **Hypothesis:** The content of the CEO townhall meetings does not meet the needs of attendees.

Here's an example of how a company developed a testable hypothesis to improve customer satisfaction in a bank from Thomke and Loveman (2022). Research found that customers waiting in line at the bank experienced a gap between their *actual* waiting time and their *perceived* waiting time. People waiting in line for two minutes felt like they were waiting in line for two minutes. But people who waited for five minutes felt like it was much longer, as much as 100 per cent longer.

The bank thought about various ways to fix this, with the end goal of improving customer satisfaction, and they came across studies that suggested that time seems to pass faster when people are distracted. Armed with this knowledge, they decided to run a measurable experiment in just one branch which was based on a testable hypothesis: distracting people will reduce their perceived waiting time. For this experiment, they put TV screens above the row of bank tellers and showed a news channel to keep people distracted as they waited in line. After a few weeks, the team measured customers estimates of wait times and found that in the experimental branch with the TV screens, over-estimation of waiting times had dropped from 32 per cent to 15 per cent.

I like this example because it shows that the team collected an observation (people feel like they are waiting longer than they really are), then developed a clear and measurable hypothesis based on that observation (distracting people will reduce their perceived waiting time) and were able to run an experiment in one branch to test it out and compare it to the other bank branches. This experiment was clever and simple, and delivered quantifiable results.

This example also reinforces what we discussed in the previous chapter about reading widely and learning knowledge outside of your field – the bank experiment was prompted by someone on the team having some knowledge from the world of psychology on the power of distraction.

Experiment

Now you've made your observation and you've developed a hypothesis, it's time to design and run an experiment to determine whether your hypothesis is correct or not. The whole point of the experiment is to test your hypothesis. You need to design your experiment carefully, measure the right things and collect the results. Think about the bank example above – they designed the experiment based on their observations (putting TV screens in view of waiting customers), they deliberately made the experiment measurable (they put the TV screens only in one bank branch) and they had a clear plan for data collection (they ran the same survey after the experiment that had run before so they could compare the results).

Scientists in the lab can spend a long time in the experiment stage. Professor Maguire tells me that some experiments will run for *years* trying to test just one hypothesis. Luckily for us, experiments don't need to be as in-depth or as long term as that. They can be quick and simple and easy to execute.

Let's look at one of our examples to see how we could run an experiment to test our hypothesis:

- **Observation:** Employees were scrolling through their smartphones during the last CEO townhall meeting.

- **Hypothesis:** The content of the CEO townhall meetings does not meet the needs of attendees.

- **Experiment:** In the next CEO townhall meeting, design the content around what your attendees need to know rather than what your CEO wants to tell them. For this experiment, you could collect data from your employees about (a) their satisfaction rating with the current townhall meeting content and (b) the topics they'd like the CEO to discuss at the next meeting. You can use that data to create a baseline satisfaction rating and also to create the new employee-led agenda for the next meeting. After the next meeting is completed, ask the employees the same question about their satisfaction rating with the townhall meeting content and gather that data.

In the example above you'll see that running an experiment can be quite simple. In this example, you're just gathering some information from employees and repositioning an existing townhall meeting. It doesn't require budget and it won't take weeks of your life. It's quick and simple and you'll be able to measure and test whether it works.

Analysis

The next step of the scientific method is to analyse your results. Look at the data you've collected and the results you've found. What do they mean? What can we learn from this? For example, maybe you found that the satisfaction rating for the CEO townhall jumped from an average of 4/10 up to 8/10. Maybe you also observed during the new townhall format that people were less likely to be scrolling on their phones and were paying more attention to the content. These are good signals that your hypothesis was correct. And this is great data to present to your CEO and senior leaders.

When you're combing through your results, keep your eyes open for anomalies or things that look strange. Did you get any unexpected results? If so, don't ignore them – interrogate them further. An anomaly is generally noticeable because it doesn't fit with what we expected to find or it doesn't align with what we are seeking.

Conclusion

The final step of the scientific method is to draw a conclusion based on your analysis. Professor Maguire is quick to point out that you might not just make one conclusion – you might, for example, make three conclusions. The conclusions are the results of your experiment that you can share with others and should show whether you proved or disproved your hypothesis.

In our example of the CEO townhall meeting, you might conclude something like:

- Satisfaction ratings for the CEO townhall meetings increased by 100 per cent when employees had the opportunity to contribute to the agenda.
- Employee input is crucial to designing the CEO townhall meeting.
- Employees are more likely to listen to the CEO when she discusses topics they care about.

Now what's critical here is that data must trump opinion or ego. Maybe your CEO thinks they are wonderful and can do no wrong. That doesn't (or shouldn't) override the evidence showing that the townhall they've designed is ineffective. The empirical evidence gathered in the experiment and the conclusions drawn from that must prevail even when they clash with strong opinions, including those of leaders (Thomke, 2020). It's normal and expected that people will easily accept 'good results' (the ones that confirm their own personal assumptions or opinions) of our experiments but may challenge or refute 'bad results' (the ones that show their assumptions are wrong).

I have a friend that works in marketing. He reports directly to a CEO who operates on ego, not data, and it leads to a lot of frustration and bad business decisions. The marketing team were gearing up to launch a new website for the company and poured months of their life into extensive customer research, testing ideas and running experiments to get the launch just right. Armed with all the data and empirical evidence, they brought the proposal to the CEO for sign-off. But, guess what, the CEO didn't like the selected font or the shade of blue or the style of images. So, despite the evidence and data to show that this would all be effective with their customers, the CEO insisted on changing the whole design and layout to be more in line with *what he felt* would work. (Guess what – it didn't work – and naturally it was all the fault of the marketing team.) Booking. com seem to be an opposite case study, as their internal culture is deeply committed to following data over ego, with one director quoted as saying, 'If the test tells you that the header of the website should be pink, then it should be pink. You always follow the test' (Thomke, 2020).

The scientific method for internal communication professionals

I ask Professor Maguire if she thinks the scientific method is a good framework for non-scientists, such as internal communicators. She is absolutely emphatic in her answer of *yes*. 'It's a good framework for outside the lab,' she tells me. 'It's so valuable. You can pretty much use it in any part of your life where you want to be more systematic in your approach.'

The core value of using the scientific method in internal communication is about making data-driven decisions. For too long we have relied on instinct, intuition and gut feelings about what's working and why. But taking a scientific approach helps us to go beyond this and actually *prove* what's working and why, through developing and testing hypotheses.

Professor Maguire emphasizes the importance of the scientific method for people in any industry, in any job, at any level of seniority. 'I always tell my students that this approach should make them really good problem solvers and really good decision-makers. Whether they work in the lab or they go and get a corporate job, their training in scientific rigour will always be of benefit to them.'

She also emphasizes the importance of empirical evidence. This is information that you've gathered to prove or disprove your hypothesis, through experiments or observation. You need this evidence to stand over your results and to make reliable and true conclusions. It's a fact-based approach rather than an intuition-based approach.

I'm a communicator, get me out of here!

Now maybe you're reading this and you're thinking, 'Yeah, I get it, the scientific method makes sense' and yet you still feel a bit intimidated about the approach. We are communicators, not scientists, right?

Well, honestly, I'd love us to be both. I ask Professor Maguire what she would say to someone reading this book who feels intimidated by the scientific method but would like an easy way to get started. What initial steps could we take to dabble in science? Her advice is great and makes science accessible for all of us. She advises this: start small. Start with something small that's not critical in your work and carries no risk. Pick something you can experiment with safely and not feel nervous about. Don't make your first experiment really complex –

deliberately pick something straightforward, simple and easy to execute.

For example, maybe you've got loads of data from your last employee engagement survey. You could pick one specific item from that and try to gather more facts around it and gain insights. What hypothesis can you create based on the information you have? What experiment can you run to test this out? When you have some results, look and see if your hypothesis has been proved correct or incorrect. What is the empirical evidence telling you and what can you conclude from that? What actions are you going to take based on the findings?

You can use this approach to ensure that you're regularly thinking critically and evaluating what you're observing and the data you're collecting. You're not trusting any assumptions but rather you're taking a dispassionate look at the data and trying to understand what it's telling you.

This is the crux of what we can learn from scientists like Professor Maguire: scientists are always learning. Their mind is always open to being proved wrong. They're always looking to improve and to learn more. They are endlessly, relentlessly curious and they're trained to be open-minded. Professor Maguire tells me, 'The more experienced you become, the more you actually realize how little you know. I know that sounds nuts, but over time you realize, my goodness, there's so much to know and the world is constantly changing. So the best thing you can do is train your mind to be open so you can keep learning and improving in an ever-changing world.'

I love this advice because it so beautifully encapsulates everything we need to remember about an over-reliance on best practices. The world is changing and best practices become obsolete and irrelevant very easily. Curiosity, experiments and an open mind can help keep you successful even when everything around you is changing.

An example from a non-scientist in the real world

I wanted to speak with a non-scientist who is using the scientific method and running experiments in real life, to show how practical and easy and valuable it can be. I reached out to Gary Fox, who runs a successful podcast called The Entrepreneur Experiment. This podcast reveals the secrets and systems world-class founders use to build their business, their body and their brain. The podcast is a mix of interviews with founders and solo episodes where Gary discusses the experiments he's running and the results he's found. The latter episodes are titled 'Idea Lab' and I was fascinated by Gary's commitment to experiments, measuring results and using the data to iterate and improve his business.

Gary tells me that he noticed a pattern across the many successful business founders he was interviewing for the podcast – they were all successful as a result of a deep commitment to experiments. They were willing to experiment again and again and again, and weren't daunted by the prospect of failure. Instead, he said, they seemed to view failure as fuel – it propelled them towards better products, improved services and ultimately successful businesses.

Gary has adopted an experimental approach to his own work. The first lesson he shares with me is that running experiments is a deliberate, intentional act and you need to put in the effort. 'I got really busy earlier this year and didn't do any experiments for a while, simply because I didn't make a deliberate effort to do it if I'm being totally honest,' he tells me. 'Life got busy and I didn't make time for experiments. You have to schedule them and make them a priority.' This is a good lesson for us – we must actively make time for experiments. They won't happen by chance.

In July 2023, Gary ran a few different experiments. Let's look at one of these so I can walk you through his hypothesis, his data collection and his results to show you how simple this can be and how anyone can start using the scientific method.

One of Gary's experiments was related to his podcast. Gary has huge ambitions for his podcast and is focused on growing the number of downloads every single month. Here's how he used the scientific method to run an experiment to increase podcast listeners:

- **Observation:** Gary observed that short-form video was exploding all over social media. TikTok, Instagram and YouTube were bursting with videos of 60 seconds or less.

- **Hypothesis:** Could this video culture be harnessed to drive more listeners to the audio podcast? Gary decided to run an experiment. Here's the hypothesis he developed:

  > Posting short-form videos on TikTok, YouTube, LinkedIn and Instagram every single day for a month will drive an increase in podcast downloads.

  (You'll note that his hypothesis is in line with Professor Maguire's guidance earlier in the chapter – it is a clear statement and is in binary yes/no terms. It is measurable and testable.)

- **Experiment:** And so, the experiment began. Gary and his team filmed, edited and posted a huge number of short videos and distributed them across various social media channels. On Instagram alone he posted 100 reels in just one month. He consistently posted video content on all four social channels every single day for the whole month.

- **Analysis:** The results of Gary's experiment were impressive. For the month he ran the experiment, he totalled 760,730 impressions across all four social media platforms. On Instagram he gained 2,000 more followers as a result of the short-form video content. This tells us that his content was viewed a lot and he gained more followers, so let's look at his hypothesis: did this experiment drive an increase in his podcast downloads? The answer is a resounding yes: his podcast downloads increased by 106 per cent.

- **Conclusion:** The conclusion Gary was able to draw is this: posting short-form video content regularly across a range of social channels is an effective way for him to build his audience, drive listeners to his podcast and ultimately drive success in his business. As a result of his experiment, Gary has the data and evidence to show that investing his time, energy and money into short-form video content is a wise business move.

Jay Clouse on developing an 'experimentality'

Let's look at another real-life example of a non-scientist adopting the scientific method. Because there are creative people like you and me using the scientific method all the time. They're not in a lab and they're not wearing a white coat, but they are harnessing the power of measurable experiments on a regular basis to drive spectacular results.

One of these people is Jay Clouse. Jay is the founder of Creator Science, a business that helps people to become professional creators. His mission is 'to help you break through the noise and earn a living as a professional creator' and he touts his newsletter and podcast as 'evidence-backed advice to help you succeed'. It's immediately apparent that measurement, evidence and data is important to him.

Jay has invented a word that I want you all to know about. I love a portmanteau myself so I was particularly delighted to find Jay's fusion of the word 'experiment' with 'mentality': *Experimentality*.

An experimentality is an experiment mentality, and one that Jay argues is absolutely crucial for success. 'Instead of relying on best practices or assumptions, an experimentality pushes you to run small, controlled experiments to find the truth in the data,' he tells me. 'An experimentality is what makes you a creator scientist.'

He gives the example of someone posting on social media. You could make assumptions about why some of your posts get a lot of engagement or you could rely on what other people tell you is best practice – or you could get curious and run some experiments to test out what's actually happening. For example, you could look at some of your top-performing posts and analyse them. Look at the word count, look at the topics, look at the writing style, look at the images or videos used. Really look at the data and then use it make evidence-based decisions on how to create great posts. Jay sums it up: 'We publish, we gauge the response and we use that information to inform the next iteration.'

The best creators, Jay says, don't just rely on their intuition – they rely on data. Data enables you to run experiments to drive improvements in your content and ultimately get better outcomes.

What advice would Jay give to readers of this book who want to run experiments but aren't sure where to start? 'Start by understanding the idea of controlled experiments,' he suggests. 'Controlled experiments mean changing one variable at a time in order to determine what variables actually influence the outcome.' For example, you could change the thumbnail image that accompanies a video but not change the title. Or you could add a new section to your website to see if it influences other areas. The idea is to change just one thing at a time and then measure the impact of it. What's driving positive changes? What can you leverage further to influence the results you want? The impact of this approach is hard to overstate. In Jay's own words, 'This bias for experimentation is what allows top creators to achieve extraordinary outcomes.'

Jay has developed his own take on the scientific method that he uses on a regular basis. It looks like this:

- goal
- hypothesis
- experiment
- results

He says that using this framework allows him to start with a goal in mind and then deliberately design the experiment to find ways to influence that goal. You form a hypothesis for how you can influence the goal, then run an experiment to test it and measure your results.

Here's an example experiment he has shared with members of his online community, The Lab:

- **Goal:** Get people to listen to/care about re-aired, past podcast episodes as much as new episodes.
- **Hypothesis:** As a listener, I don't like when a podcast re-airs an episode but doesn't make that clear from the title or intro. There have been times that I listen to an episode and quickly realize, 'Wait is this the same episode with this guest I listened to years ago?' So in the past when I've re-aired episodes, I tag the title with (REPLAY). I wondered if I could use literally just a different word/

tag to signal that this is worth listening to. Maybe 'Replay' makes it seem not new *and* not exciting?

- **Experiment:** I re-aired my episode with Codie Sanchez. The reality is, there are a lot of weeks where playing a past episode is a *better* listener experience than me pulling together some off-the-cuff solo episode. Instead of (REPLAY) I started the title with (GREATEST HITS). I was hoping this would signal to folks that this was a *popular, high-quality* episode, and even though it's not 'new', if it's new to you then you should listen.

- **Results:** We're only 48 hours in, but this episode is performing 100 per cent better than past re-aired episodes. It seems (so far) that it's performing on par with a *new* episode and I've had several listeners talk about it on social media. Very good signals! If this type of performance is repeatable, not only will I publish a Greatest Hits episode at least once a month, I may publish two to four each month. With 140+ episodes, this would resurface episodes consistently while also giving me extra ad inventory to increase sponsorship revenue on the podcast (with little extra work).

Jay's take-home advice is this: run experiments where you keep it simple and only change one variable at a time. Try using his four-part framework above to design and run some of your own experiments.

The benefits of adopting the scientific method in internal communication

Adopting a bit of scientific rigour can be a gamechanger for internal communicators. It can help us make better decisions, improve how we work and drive innovations in our communication. For me, the biggest advantage lies in the shift to evidence-based decision-making. By embracing a systematic approach to capturing observations, creating a hypothesis and then testing it through measurable experiments, we can move beyond relying on instincts or intuition. We can make quality decisions grounded in empirical evidence. This will not only drive internal communication success but also help you position yourself as a data-driven problem solver in the business. The scientific method can reduce errors in our judgement, eliminate bias from our decision-making, ground our approach in evidence and find unlimited sources of innovation and improvement.

The scientific method can help you to become more innovative, which of course is the entire point of this book. Successful innovation often comes from trial and error. Try new things, test new ideas, run an experiment. What worked, what didn't, what can we learn? Lean into your curiosity and pair it with the scientific method to formulate hypotheses, experiment and try to prove or disprove your ideas.

Be willing to be objective with the data: if your hypothesis is proved wrong it doesn't mean the experiment was a failure. It doesn't mean that *you* are a failure. It means your experiment was a success, you found out something interesting and the data is giving you useful information to learn from. The joy of the scientific method is that it frees us from a reliance on other people's best practices. It gives us a structured way to observe our own context and circumstances, and then build out our own solutions and practices based on the data and evidence we uncover.

Dr Maguire leaves me with these words of wisdom she heard recently at an event: 'Decisions or actions based on incomplete data is guesswork.' Let's actually repeat that because it's so powerful:

'Decisions or actions based on incomplete data is guesswork.'

Do you want to run your career on guesswork? I sure don't. By embracing the scientific method you can make the shift from guesswork to empirical evidence and use your data to create a long-lasting impact in your organization. But remember – experiments won't happen by accident. You must make the deliberate and intentional choice to invest your time, effort and energy into running measurable experiments and analysing the results.

A parting thought: The language of measurement can be difficult

Before I close out this chapter, I want to explain some of the key terms you're likely to encounter in the world of communication measurement. The language we use to talk about measurement is tricky and almost seems deliberately obtuse and non-inclusive. It can put you off diving into data and metrics because it just seems so *complicated*. It can feed into your negative self-belief of 'I can't do this'. So let's knock that on the head right now. Table 9.1 lists some of the key terms you'll come across, and what they mean in simple terms.

TABLE 9.1   Key terms in communication measurement

Term	Explainer
A/B testing	A/B testing, sometimes called split testing, is a measurable way of experimenting with communication activities. It involves comparing two versions (A and B) to determine which one performs better – for example you could write two different subject lines for your email newsletter and use an A/B test to determine which one is more appealing to your audience.
Engagement	This is a misunderstood word as it can be used to refer to employee engagement (see Chapter 2) or to engagement with content. For the latter, engagement refers to the level of interaction and involvement your audience has with your content. It includes actions such as comments, likes, shares and clicks.
KPIs	Key performance indicators (KPIs) are specific metrics that can help you measure the success of your communication efforts. They indicate whether you are performing in the way you hoped. These will vary depending on your objectives but can be things like intranet traffic, click-rates, attendance numbers, satisfaction scores and open rates.
NPS	Net promoter score (NPS) is a quantitative measure between –100 and +100. It measures how likely employees are to recommend the organization as a place to work and is generally gathered through surveys. It's debatable whether it's a meaningful measure or not but I'll let you make up your own mind about that.
Objectives	Objectives are things that you aim to achieve through your communication activities. These give you direction and focus and help you ensure that all your activities are leading to a specific outcome.
Outcomes	Outcomes aren't about the things you're producing, they're about the changes that occur as a result of the things you're producing. Unlike outputs, outcomes focus on the impact your efforts have on the audience or organization, such as reduced employee attrition or improved employee satisfaction.

(continued)

TABLE 9.1   (*continued*)

Term	Explainer
Outputs	These are your communication products or deliverables. In other words, the things that you do or create or produce. For example, newsletters, blog posts, townhall meetings, videos and infographics are all outputs.
Reach	You may hear people talk about the 'reach' of our communication. This simply means how many people were exposed to a particular communication message or campaign (how many people it reached). It helps you to understand whether your channels are effective at reaching all of your employees or not.
ROI	Return on investment (ROI) essentially looks at the balance between the investment made into internal communication versus the results achieved. In other words, is internal communication good value for money in the business? It's an attempt to quantify the return from the money, time and resources spent. Having SMART objectives and clearly defined outcomes will help you enormously to demonstrate your ROI.
Sentiment analysis	Sentiment analysis goes beyond click rates or open rates and instead evaluates the emotional tone or attitude expressed by the audience. It might look at the sentiment expressed in comments on the latest CEO blog, for example, to help gauge employee perception.
SMART objectives	SMART objectives are a really helpful way to set objectives to make them useful and practical for you. SMART stands for specific, measurable, achievable, relevant and time-bound. This framework can be tricky at first but it will help you create well-defined communication objectives at the outset which in turn makes it much easier to capture the right measurements, track progress and evaluate your progress.

If you want to learn more about communication measurement, I'd recommending reading about the Barcelona Principles. These are a set of voluntary measurement guidelines established by the PR industry more than a decade ago and give a helpful framework for communications measurement. Although some of the principles are more relevant to external rather than internal communication, I do find their emphasis on outcomes and goal setting very helpful and perhaps you will too.

KEY TAKEAWAYS

- Many professional communicators, even those operating at the most senior levels, are intimidated by measurement and data. But it doesn't need to feel so overwhelming.

- The scientific method is a powerful tool for innovation. It offers us a structured framework for testing, measuring and driving innovation in our work.

- There are five key steps in the scientific method: observation, hypothesis, experiment, analysis and conclusion.

- The scientific method is valuable not just for scientists but for professionals across all industries, offering a systematic and evidence-based approach to problem-solving and decision-making.

- Non-scientists like Gary Fox and Jay Clouse are embracing measurable experiments to fuel innovation and success.

- The iterative nature of the scientific method will help you to continuously improve and grow.

- Empirical evidence is essential for decision-making. It's not enough to rely on gut instincts. Use the scientific method to make a transformative shift from guesswork to empirical evidence.

- Start small. Begin experimenting by selecting a non-critical aspect of your work to test assumptions and evaluate your observations and data.

- The language used to talk about communications measurement can be off-putting and complicated. Use the simple explainers in Table 9.1 to understand the words and what they mean.

REFLECTIVE QUESTIONS

1 How do you feel about the topic of measurement, data and experiments in internal communication?

2 Do you agree with my suggestion that the scientific method is not exclusive to scientists but applicable to various fields, including internal communication?

3 Can you identify observations in your current role that might lead to hypotheses about improving internal communication?

4 Reflect on Gary Fox's podcast experiment. How might a similar experimental mindset be applied to your work in internal communication?

5 Can you recall instances where small, deliberate experiments could have been conducted to test assumptions and improve outcomes?

6 How open are you to starting small experiments in your work, as suggested by Professor Maguire? Can you identify a non-critical aspect of your role where you could initiate a simple experiment to gain insights?

7 Reflect on the idea that scientists are always learning and have an open mindset. How open are you to being proved wrong or adapting to new information?

8 Consider the quote 'Decisions or actions based on incomplete data is guesswork.' How can adopting the scientific method help you move away from guesswork in your decision-making processes?

References

Ridley, M (2020) *How Innovation Works*, Harper Collins, London

Thomke, S (2020) Building a culture of experimentation, *Harvard Business Review*, March–April

Thomke, S and Loveman, G (2022) Act like a scientist, *Harvard Business Review*, May–June

10

Do you embrace or resist technology?

Last year I was in the market for a new set of headshots. I wanted to update my profile pictures on social media and on my website, but I was facing an obstacle: I really, *really* hate getting my photo taken. I find the whole process excruciating.

I'm not quite Chandler-from-*Friends* bad, but I find posing and fake smiling and the interminable *waiting for it to end* just does me in. (My husband will attest that this was even the case on our wedding day.) I don't particularly enjoy having to do my hair and makeup, commute into the city and invest hours of my life just to get a few pictures.

If only there was another way. An easier way for photo-phobic, homebody people like me.

Enter AI.

I had heard about a new artificial intelligence tool on the market that could potentially solve this problem for me. This tool claimed it could generate 400 professional-looking headshots in an hour, and all I'd have to do is upload 25 selfies taken with my smartphone. It kind of sounded too good to be true, but I was curious so I went for it. An hour later, I was honestly amazed at the results. I had at least 10 really good headshots that I could happily use on my socials and website, and a wealth of genuinely hilarious bloopers that would serve me well for laughter-inducing slides at events about AI. So, a win–win all round for me, really.

This, for me, was a genuinely innovative technology. It solved a problem for me (I didn't want to pose for a set of headshots) and delivered value (I got great photos for my social media and website). Remember our definition of innovation – it must add value. It should solve a problem. For me, this ticked all the boxes and I was so pleased I had followed my curiosity to explore the tool.

But what happened next was the really interesting bit.

I posted about my AI headshots on social media. I showed the photographs and explained the process and how easy it was. People's reactions were fascinating. The majority of comments I got could be broadly categorized as 'curious'. People were interested and asked lots of questions; they'd never seen anything like this before and it captured their attention. Some people went on to invest in their own AI headshots using the same tool and sent me their pictures after-wards, and I noticed some of them using the new photos on their social media feeds.

But a small and vocal majority were *horrified* at my experiment. Some people were surprisingly *angry* with me. They said my photos were not authentic. They claimed that these new technologies were the antithesis of the creative field we work in. They said I was at risk of losing the trust of my audience because the photos weren't the 'real' me. Interestingly, some of these technology resistors had profile photos that were clearly digitally retouched under heavy layers of make-up, which made me more curious still: what's the threshold for 'realness' in a photo? Photoshop is okay but AI is not? Is it the 'newness' of the technology that people are railing against?

The comments were emotional and raw, and it was a fascinating experience to read them and see people react. It made me reflect on how we, as a creative profession, react to emerging technologies. Do we adopt the innovator's mindset and approach new technology with curiosity and an open mind? Or do we react with fear and anger and resist what we see as an intrusion into our usual way of doing things?

That's what I will explore in this chapter. Why do we sometimes resist technology, even if it can help us, and what can we learn about that? How can we embrace technology as a driving force for innovation in internal communication, even if it may make us feel uncomfortable?

This chapter on technology is very deliberately put at the end of this book. When I first started exploring the topic of innovation in internal communication, everyone assumed I was referred to innovation through technology. People thought I was going to write a book on employee apps or intranet platforms or digital tools, but this was never my intent. I wanted to uncouple the concept of innovation from the world of technology and show that innovation doesn't necessarily *require* technology. I hope this has been covered well in the previous chapters. In saying that, technology can be immensely useful for innovation. You just don't *need* it, so if you're a zero-budget communicator with dinosaur technology reading this then don't fret.

In this chapter we'll explore ideas around resistance to technology and the risks we face as internal communicators if we refuse to embrace technological advances. I'll tell a story of an internal communicator who is leading the way in embracing tech and using it to innovate. Let's dive in.

The impact of technology on internal communication

Technology has already fundamentally changed our profession. Once upon a time we may have been pinning a paper memo to a noticeboard in a physical office, now we often work in paperless digital workplaces with the ability to send targeted messages in complex global organizations. Technology has opened up a world of two-way communication, multi-media content and measurement dashboards. We have a vast array of digital tools and platforms at our disposal. This has changed the way that organizations communicate with employees and has also transformed the way that we, as internal communicators, work.

Changes in the world of external communication have also had a significant impact on our industry. The internet and social media democratized the sharing of information, which has consequences for internal communication. Employee audiences have expectations of consumer-grade communication inside organizations, where they can self-serve information quickly, get bite-sized content as they need it and get fast responses to their queries.

And now, in the wake of a worldwide pandemic that acted as a catalyst for remote work, technology has acted as the great enabler of new ways of connecting, communicating and collaborating across geographically dispersed employees. We can collaborate asynchronously across locations and time zones and communicate easily with colleagues anywhere in the world without ever meeting in person. This has required us as internal communicators to keep pace with the technologies that enable this way of working; there simply is no alternative to adopting and learning the technologies needed for remote and hybrid work.

Use technology to solve a problem and add value

Remember our definition of innovation in Chapter 2?

'Innovation is a creative idea brought to application that results in value.'

Innovation via technology in internal communication must deliver value. It can't simply be tech for tech's sake. It should address a pain point or help to deliver a business goal or deliver something genuinely useful for the organization. Technology should *solve a problem or add value*. All the software companies that make employee communication technology will tell you in their marketing material that you *need* their product to be an effective internal communicator. But maybe you don't. What you do need is an ability to solve problems, and that may or may not involve technology.

There are so many new tools on the market these days, but truth be told you probably don't need most of them. You might only need one and you must get curious to find out what that is, based on the specific needs of your organization and the audiences you serve. And beware of anyone who tells you that you must use Technology X, Y or Z because it's 'best practice'. Just because a tool has worked for someone else in another organization, it doesn't necessarily mean it's going to work for you. Bringing in new technology without a clear understanding of the problem it will solve or the value it will create will be a pointless and unrewarding process.

You may work in an organization where you can be innovative in your internal communication without any shiny new tech at all. You may not need a tech stack. But you definitely need an 'ability stack' – the ability to listen, be curious, observe, ask questions and solve problems. Focus on this first, and then see if technology can assist you second.

People resist new technologies... even if they are useful

Here's the thing about technological change – it is never done. It's a bit like the laundry at home; just when you think you've finally finished, you discover something else that needs your attention. Just as my family creates a never-ending pile of socks, T-shirts and jumpers to be washed, software companies are unleashing new tools, platforms and technologies onto the market all the time. It is never *done*. We must be constantly learning and listening and leaning in to keep up.

And yet, despite the need for us to keep pace with new tech and try new things, resistance to emerging technologies is rife. We saw that in the reactions of some communicators to my AI headshots. But this reaction is actually to be expected. It's downright *normal*. History teaches us that anytime a disruptive new technology is introduced, people will actively resist it.

I spent many pleasant and howl-inducing hours exploring the Pessimists Archive, an online collection of media clippings and stories of technophobia throughout history. This archive sets out a chronology of resistance to new technologies stretching back to the 1800s, with photographs of newspapers from the times and hysterical headlines warning of the dangers of technology. The website argues that we need to understand the history of technological resistance because:

'Only by looking back at fears of old things when they were new, can we have rational constructive debates about emerging technologies today that avoids the pitfalls of moral panic and incumbent protectionism' (Pessimists Archive, 2023).

Here are some of the stories that caught my eye in this archive that illustrate clearly that resistance to disruptive technology is pretty common.

The telephone was invented in 1876. We take phones for granted now, we have grown up with them and they don't seem like a big deal. But when the telephone was first introduced, it caused quite a stir. And guess what, people resisted this new technology. The telephone was branded a nuisance, with *The Times-Democrat* newspaper angrily declaring it 'an aggravation of so monstrous a character as to merit public denunciation' (Pessimists Archive, 2023). People said the telephone would upset our nervous systems. Pearl-clutching parents denounced the telephone for its ability to let young lovers have private conversations across a geographical distance. People even wondered whether telephones would be used to communicate with the dead (LaFrance, 2015).

Technology resistors claimed angrily that people working as telephone operators were suffering from a painful new disease called 'the telephone ear' which induces headaches and buzzing sounds in the ear and can lead to an abscess forming in the ear requiring a dangerous operation to cure it. The first newspaper clipping listed in the archive about the telephone is from 1876, but the hysteria and resistance to telephones endured for *years*. Twenty years later there was still headlines about 'telephone ear', warning people that if they used a telephone three or four times a day then it is likely that they would fall prey to this terrible affliction (Pessimists Archive, 2023). Even more than three decades after the telephone had been introduced, newspapers still decried the technology as a nuisance and a tyranny. The resistance was enormous.

New technologies that disrupt society will always meet resistance. But what I want you to think about as you work your way through this chapter is this: do you want to be a technology resister who rejects new inventions based on an emotional reaction? Or do you want to be one of the curious explorers, willing to try out new tech and assess its merits for yourself?

Let's look at another couple of examples from the archive to demonstrate that the resistance to new technology isn't a one-off confined to the invention of the telephone.

The first motor car was invented in 1886 by Carl Benz. Again, this is a piece of technology that we completely take for granted today and it's become an essential part of how we live and work. But when the car first came on the market, pessimists and technology resistors didn't see it as a welcome addition to their lives. They called it 'the devil wagon' (Pessimists Archive, 2023) and argued vehemently that it would destroy the world. Newspapers proclaimed that people riding in motor cars would suffer greatly from the affliction of 'motor face' due to the speed of travel, which led to passengers having a wrinkled brow, pursed lips, half-closed eyes and a set jaw. Not just that, but it was claimed that driving a car is debilitating to the human nervous system due to the immense dangers involved. The invention of the car was even blamed for a couple's divorce in 1928, more than 40 years after the car had been invented.

The invention of the television in the 1920s wrought similar hysteria and technophobia. Today, TVs are commonplace in homes around the world, with some homes having multiple televisions in the same household. It's no big deal. But it was when it first appeared. Syvertsen (2017) argues that 'no modern medium has been detested as much as television'. The television was blamed for a range of social problems for decades, including the decay of moral values, impaired physical health and a fall in social culture. Newspaper clippings illustrate a moral panic about the addictive quality of television, declaring the technology to be as dangerous as drugs (Pessimists Archive, 2023).

And, in the 1970s, along came the home computer and guess what – people resisted it! (Do you see the theme emerging here?) Home computers became widely available in the 1980s and 'computerphobia' became widespread (LaFrance, 2015). People were afraid of the home computer for a myriad of reasons. They had fears of being replaced by a machine or of becoming addicted to it, they were afraid of the complexity of the machine and their own lack of knowledge of how to use it or how it worked, they had fears about losing control or looking stupid. Computerphobia continued for years.

My own story about AI headshots makes more sense now, doesn't it? People throughout history have always had an emotional resistance to new and disruptive technologies.

But why?

Why would people reject new technologies if they have benefits and can add value?

Why we resist new technologies

We can understand people's resistance in a few different ways: fear of the unknown, fear of loss, perceived complexity and job insecurity. Let's have a look at each of these and you can reflect on which ones you may recognize in yourself.

Fear of the unknown

Human beings don't like uncertainty. It feels uncomfortable and even threatening. Uncertainty and the unknown seem to spark heightened brain activity in areas of the brain related to vigilance and anticipation of consequences, according to neuroscientists (Robson, 2021). It makes intuitive sense that we fear the unknown. Our brains are always trying to predict what's coming next so that we can be prepared for it, but this is a lot harder or nearly impossible if you're faced with uncertainty. So we simply avoid the uncertainty altogether by resisting the unknown.

Juma (2016) examined why people resist potentially useful technologies and found that familiarity was a key reason. People like what is familiar to them and they want to stick with what they know. A study on American consumers found that 52 per cent of adults say they feel more comfortable using brands and products that they are familiar with (Kennedy and Funk, 2016). That same study found that more than one in three consumers prefer to wait until they hear about other people's experiences before trying something new themselves, with only 15 per cent saying they usually try technology products before other people do. This has all the hallmarks of Cialdini's principle of social proof, doesn't it?

People may make bold claims to argue against the introduction of new products or new technologies. People once claimed that coffee could drive you into a state of hysteria or could make you sterile (Juma, 2016). Driving these kind of sensationalist arguments, Juma claims, is an instinctive fear of the unknown. People may have an emotional reaction to a new technology because it challenges their view of the world or disrupts their familiar environment. Sounds like how people reacted to the invention of the telephone or the television, doesn't it? This helps us to understand why people may be more cautious in their approach to new technology or may actively resist it entirely. The unknown or the unfamiliar can make us feel uncomfortable and sometimes it's easier to just avoid it.

Raub (2021) argues that fear of the unknown often comes down to a lack of knowledge, suggesting that the important factor is whether it motivates you to learn more or causes you to resist. If you allow the fear of the unknown to rule your responses, it can hinder your ability to learn. The famous astronaut Chris Hadfield once said that the best antidote for fear is competence (Powell, 2018), so as internal communicators we should actively learn about technologies as a way of decreasing our level of discomfort and our fear of the unknown.

Fear of loss

People don't fear technology itself, argues Juma (2016); rather, they fear the loss it may bring. This loss could relate to their identity, their way of working, their way of living or how they earn money. For example, many people who grew crops for a living resisted the adoption of mechanical farm equipment – even though the equipment could make their lives easier. The machinery represented a loss to their connection to the land and to their traditional ways of life.

Understanding this deep fear can help us to reduce resistance to technology.

The concept of loss aversion as a psychological phenomenon is well documented. Prospect theory argues that people are inherently loss averse and don't always make rational decisions (Tversky and Kahneman, 1979). In other words, people may make decisions on their assessment of how much they could possibly *lose* rather than how much they stand to *gain*. This theory stands in stark contrast to our assumptions that people make rational choices. We see this in real life all the time. Say you introduce a brand new intranet platform that helps people find helpful information in real time, personalizes their digital experience and guides them to all the tools they need to do their job... and yet some employees will simply refuse to use it. Rational decision-making models tell us *of course* they will use it. But prospect theory enables us to think about their decision-making in terms of their perception of *loss*. Are they resisting the technology because they fear a loss of the familiar, a loss of power, a loss of control, a loss of the way they've always done things, a loss of the company culture they've become accustomed to?

According to Tversky and Kahneman (1979), we value losses and gains differently. We are more afraid of losing something than we are excited about gaining something. For example, if we lose €1,000 on a bet, we'll feel this pain more deeply than the excitement we may feel about winning €1,000. So when we think about people's reaction to technology, we can apply this same theory. When the television was invented, people feared the loss of moral values in society and a decline in people's mental and physical health. This perceived loss greatly outweighed the potential gain of having a television in your house for entertainment or education.

So remember: humans don't always react rationally. Think about the reaction to my AI headshots. It was a moral panic and perhaps it was grounded in a perception of loss for some people; a loss of our traditional ways of producing photographs or a loss of the creativity we pride ourselves on. We need to understand that people will often have emotional and not rational reactions, and we must consider the losses people are feeling when faced with new technologies.

Perceived complexity

The perception that new technologies are complex or difficult to use can deter individuals from embracing them. This is related to the fear of the unknown but it goes deeper than that. It's about the fear of looking stupid or feeling out of your depth. People may feel that new technology brings a steep learning curve or that the technology is beyond their ability – this can lead to resistance.

I see this in real life all the time. A friend of mine moved to the US and wanted to make sure she could stay in contact with her ageing parents easily. She bought her mother a smartphone with the hopes they could video call each other regularly. In her mind, this was a generous, thoughtful gift that would ensure they could stay connected despite the geographic distance between them – but to her mother, this was an enormously complicated piece of technology and she *hated* it. She completely refused to use it and wouldn't even try. This was, of course, enormously frustrating to my friend, but also completely understandable on the part of her mother. Sometimes the idea of learning a new piece of technology can be totally overwhelming and we need to understand that when thinking about our employee audiences, and indeed ourselves too.

PR Newswire (2023) found that that 47 per cent of employees are concerned about their own lack of technological skills in an age of technological change. The same report noted that a staggering 74 per cent of employees say there is a gap in expertise on how to adopt digital transformation in their business. This is very useful data for us to have. If employees resist a new piece of technology, get curious about it. Do they feel overwhelmed about the complexity of the tool? Are they worried about looking stupid? Do they need more training and support? Once you identify the source of the resistance, you can create a plan for how to overcome it.

Job insecurity

People may resist new technologies if they fear it could displace them from their jobs. Automation, robotics and artificial intelligence gives rise to anxiety, as people worry about the prospect of becoming obsolete in the workplace. People fear being displaced by new technologies that are capable of performing a range of tasks with increased speed, efficiency and precision. As machines become more advanced and can begin to do things like generate content drafts or write speeches or create blog posts, there is a legitimate fear on the part of professional communicators that their jobs are becoming increasingly dispensable. This creates anxiety about the future of their livelihoods and our wider profession.

Back in 2017, the CEO of Deutsche Bank predicted that half of its workforce could be replaced by robots (Hess, 2017). A study concluded that accountants were highly at risk of losing their jobs to automation in the future (Pistrui, 2018). News stories like this can be frightening and help to explain why people may resist new technologies, as they feel their jobs are at risk. But are these fears really legitimate? There are a lot of things robots can do for us now. They can draft stories for your newsletter or come up with ideas for content for your townhall meeting or create a channels matrix for your organization. But technology is more capable of doing *tactical* work than it is *strategic* work that requires human skills such as creativity, strategic thinking and imagination (Pistrui, 2018).

Perhaps one way we can actively help to allay our fears about new technologies is to regularly learn and develop new skills. We need to adapt, retrain and acquire more digital literacy to keep pace with technology and use it effectively. So, if you've never played around with an AI tool, why not give it a go?

The risks of technological resistance

All of this matters. Really matters. Because there are risks to you, as a professional internal communicator, if you react emotionally to new technology and actively resist it. The world of work has changed and the ability to learn and use new technology is no longer a nice-to-have – it's a need-to-have. You may find yourself quickly becoming irrelevant in the internal communication profession if you are unwilling to keep pace with technological change and the opportunities it brings.

We know that technology has brought us on in leaps and bounds in internal communication, in terms of how we can reach our audiences, how we can segment them, how we can measure our efforts, how we can use a range of media for engaging content. Resisting the utility of this kind of transformative technology may make it challenging for you to stay relevant and effective in your role. Beware the professional stagnation that can creep in if you resist learning new ways of working or trying out new tools.

And for the time-poor internal communicator (which I suspect is *all* of you), resisting new technologies may keep you stuck in an endless to-do list with no space for innovation. New technologies bring the possibility of automation, of increased efficiency, of streamlining workflows and processes so that you have more free time to think, to create and to innovate. Resisting new tech may be harmful to your career in the long run, as other communicators lean into the new technologies available and demonstrate high-value results from their efforts. I spoke with Shaun Randol, founder of Mister Editorial, about this. He shakes his head at the idea of professional communicators resisting technology that could actively help them to communicate better or be more effective in their role. He tells me: 'It's like a baker who refuses to use a stand mixer. It's not just ironic; it's a career-limiting move.'

I talked to an internal communication specialist in the USA about her experimental approach to new technologies and what lessons she is learning. For this book she wishes to remain anonymous, so let's call her Sarah. Interestingly, she asked me not to include her name as she was a bit worried about potential backlash from other internal communicators. 'It seems like AI is such a hot topic in internal comms right now and some people have already decided they hate it before they've even tried it,' she tells me. 'I don't want to be on the receiving end of any negative messages as a result of this interview, plus I'm in quite a junior role so I don't want to harm my job prospects in the future.' Can we pause here and reflect on that? How curious. So I am not the only one who sees the technological resistance in some parts of the internal communication industry.

Sarah tells me that she loves playing around with new tools and tech, partly because she loves gadgets and partly because she really hates admin or tedious work. 'I remember when Zapier came on the market and I began using it to get my software tools to talk to each other for the first time,' she recalls excitedly. 'It acted like duct tape, sticking all my tools together and making a lot less work for me. Anything I can automate, I absolutely will and I'm always looking for opportunities to do less busywork and free up my time for other stuff.'

I ask Sarah her opinion on why some communicators may resist technology, even if it could potentially help them to free up their time or get the job done more efficiently. She tells me that, in her view, some people see creativity and technology as opposing forces. For people who pride themselves on being creative and producing incredible things by hand, they may feel that the introduction of technology reduces the value of their contribution or makes them feel less creative. 'It's a bit of a culture clash maybe,' she muses. 'Like maybe they feel their job will be threatened by tech, but I think it's more than that. I think it's a clash of culture and traditions. They've always done things a certain way, they've had a successful career doing that, so why should they change now?'

Embracing technology in internal communication: A lesson from Microsoft

The pace of digital transformation has created an ever-increasing flow of emails, meetings, notifications and distractions and we're simply not able to keep pace with it. This is what Microsoft have termed 'digital debt' and it's costing us our ability to innovate. According to Microsoft, 64 per cent of people struggle with having enough time and energy to do their job and these people are 3.5 times more likely to also struggle with innovative thinking (Microsoft, 2023).

But, with generative AI, there is the opportunity to reduce this debt and free up more of our time to think, create and innovate, according to Microsoft. Microsoft has positioned AI as a 'copilot', a tool which can automate tedious tasks, reduce administrative work, summarize information concisely and find us the information we need when we need it so we can focus on being more creative and productive.

I speak with Jon Bates, who works with Microsoft as an Employee Communications Lead in Europe. Jon is smart and thoughtful and experimental in his approach to technology. He is what we could class as an 'early adopter' of AI; he ran full throttle towards the new tools as they emerged and began playing with them to see what they could do. He tells me a story of how he used AI to deliver a high-quality documentary production for internal audiences in Microsoft, and this is a masterclass in the innovator's mindset.

Jon wanted to produce something great for his audience of thousands across many countries in Europe. He wanted to do something engaging, something that would capture employees' attention, something *innovative*. He was watching a Netflix documentary one night and it occurred to him that storytelling was the route he wanted to go down. He wanted to create a Netflix-style documentary for Microsoft employees. Not a small undertaking but he was determined to do it.

But Jon had a challenge. He isn't a scriptwriter. He doesn't know how to write a script for a documentary, he's never done it before. He wondered if he could use a technology to help him get over this obstacle and he began experimenting with AI language learning models. He spent some time learning about AI prompting and told the AI model about his audience, about the documentary he wanted to create and about the strategic outcomes he was striving for, and he asked it to draft a script. The first draft was surprisingly good but far too long, so Jon instructed the AI model to make it shorter. He prompted the tool for ideas on visuals he could include in the documentary. He got it to write a voiceover for the introduction narration. He was amazed at how quickly he could pull together a decent script using these tools and began to experiment further. He prompted the tool to create personalized scripts for different countries that would take part in the documentary (for example the documentary for the team in Ireland could show the stunning landscape).

Despite no experience in script writing or documentary creation, Jon was able to leverage technology to create a working script in just a couple of days – he reckons it would have taken him at least a week without the help of AI. His output after one day was a 35-page script split into personalized segments with a clear story and a solid structure. Jon emphasizes that tools like AI language learning models are helpful assistants but won't do all the work for you. 'AI can get you mostly there,' he tells me. 'Then you need the human touch to get you the rest of the way.'

I ask Jon what advice he would have for internal communicators reading this who are nervous or anxious about technologies like AI. 'Just start to experiment,' he suggests. 'Just do it. Don't overthink it. New technologies like AI tools are the way that we will, as communicators, be able to free up time to do more experiments and create space for innovation.'

Communicators who resist technology, Jon asserts, risk getting left behind. If you aren't willing to learn, experiment and play with technology then you face stagnation over time. 'You need to be forward-looking and curious,' he says. 'Experimenting with technology in my role has helped me get stakeholder buy-in, demonstrate value and build my career.'

Applying the innovator's mindset

If you think back to Chapter 6, I suggested that we need an innovator's mindset to succeed in driving innovation in internal communication. This same mindset can be applied when we think about technology. Here's a quick reminder of the key traits of the innovator's mindset:

- curiosity
- open-mindedness

- resilience
- problem-solving
- observation

Apply this mindset when you're thinking about technology as a driver of innovation. Be curious about new technologies that are available and be open-minded about how they can add value for you. Be willing to experiment with them and fail – consider it a learning experience. Use technology to solve problems and identify those problems through observation. Don't use tech just for the sake of it – use it to deliver value.

Adopting the innovator's mindset can help you move from the resistant, angry position of 'This is different and I hate it' to a growth mindset of 'What can I learn about this if I lean in and get curious about it?' Perhaps if you feel overwhelmed by the apparent complexity of a new piece of technology you can borrow from Carol Dweck (2008), who has suggested that the addition of 'yet' helps us move from a fixed mindset into a growth mindset. So your inner dialogue might change like this:

'I can't use this new tool.'

'I can't use this new tool *yet*.'

Or

'AI isn't useful to me.'

'AI isn't useful to me *yet*.'

That's a powerful difference, isn't it? Just by adding that simple three-letter word you can reframe it in your head as a learning experience and something that you need to practise.

Conclusion

I want to leave you with a powerful quote from my interview with Shaun Randol. We discussed the idea that if new technology is making you feel uncomfortable then perhaps you should lean into it rather than shy away from it. This is the key message I want you to take from this chapter. Be curious. Explore the technology. Here's what Shaun says: 'Discomfort is a sign of growth. It's a sign of vitality, of being alive. If we are not challenging ourselves in an environment that sucks up half of our waking hours, then are we even living?'

KEY TAKEAWAYS

- Technology has fundamentally changed our profession and we need to be adept at using it to communicate effectively in a post-pandemic world.

- Innovation through technology should add value or solve a problem, rather than be tech for tech's sake.

- History is littered with examples of resistance to new technology, from the telephone, the motor car, the television and the home computer.

- Resistance may be driven by fear of the unknown, fear of loss, perceived complexity or job insecurity.

- There are risks for internal communicators who actively resist new technologies, including stagnation, ineffectiveness and a lack of time to innovate.

- Take the time to recognize your own source of resistance and make a plan for how to overcome it.

- Get curious about technology and how it can add value to your role or your organization. Experiment with it, play with it and be open to exploring it.

REFLECTIVE QUESTIONS

1 How do you feel about the adoption of new technologies in your professional life?

2 Have you ever resisted a new technology, and can you identify the underlying reason(s) for that resistance?

3 How do you currently approach learning about new technologies in internal communication?

4 What steps can you take to actively stay up to date with technological changes and ensure your skills remain relevant?

5 Have you observed resistance to new technologies among your peers or your colleagues? Can you begin to identify why that resistance occurred?

6 Can you identify any parallels between historical resistance and current attitudes towards emerging technologies in the modern world?

7 Consider a technology you are currently unfamiliar with. What steps could you take to proactively learn about it and decrease any discomfort associated with the unknown?

References

Dweck, C (2008) *Mindset: The new psychology of success*, Ballantine Books, New York

Hess, A J (2017) Deutsche Bank CEO suggests robots could replace half the company's 97,000 employees, CNBC, 8 November

Juma, C (2016) *Innovation and Its Enemies: Why people resist new technologies*, Oxford University Press, Oxford

Kennedy, B and Funk, C (2016) 28% of Americans are 'strong' early adopters of technology, Pew Research Centre, 12 July

LaFrance, A (2015) When people feared computers, *The Atlantic*, 30 March

Microsoft (2023) 2023 Work Trend Index annual report, Microsoft, www.microsoft.com/en-us/worklab/work-trend-index/will-ai-fix-work (archived at https://perma.cc/5CXK-BXW2)

Pessimists Archive (2023) https://pessimistsarchive.org (archived at https://perma.cc/BJ7Q-5MUU)

Pistrui, J (2018) The future of human work is imagination, creativity, and strategy, *Harvard Business Review*, 18 January

Powell, C (2018) Why astronaut Chris Hadfield isn't afraid of death, NBC News, 4 July

PR Newswire (2023) Workforce resistance to change emerges as top challenge for successful digital transformation, PR Newswire, www.prnewswire.com/apac/news-releases/workforce-resistance-to-change-emerges-as-top-challenge-for-successful-digital-transformation-301838163.html (archived at https://perma.cc/AG8J-HQLL)

Raub, J (2021) Knowledge, fear of the unknown, opinion and the pandemic, *American Journal of Health-System Pharmacy*, 79 (5)

Robson, D (2021) Why we're so terrified of the unknown, BBC, 26 October

Syvertsen, T (2017) Resistance to early mass media, *Media Resistance*, Palgrave Macmillan, London

Tversky, A and Kahneman, D (1979) Prospect theory: An analysis of decision under risk, *Econometrica*, 47 (2), 263–92

11

Create a lasting impact

You made it. This is the final chapter of the book. We've covered a lot, right? I hope you feel less intimidated by the idea of innovation and more emboldened to try new things. But maybe you're also feeling a bit overwhelmed and wondering how to digest it all and start putting things into action.

So let's digest together. We've been on quite the journey over the last 10 chapters. Each chapter has been carefully designed to lead into the next, taking you by the hand and introducing more ideas, concepts and practical steps to get you more comfortable with innovation and feeling more confident to begin innovating yourself.

In the previous chapter, we reminded ourselves that you don't *need* technology to innovate, despite common misconceptions that technology and innovation are synonymous. In saying that, we absolutely *can* use technology to innovate in our field. The most important thing is that we are open to exploring new technologies, we get curious about them and experiment with them to see how they can help us in our role. History is littered with stories of resistance to technology and we mustn't let our fears get in the way of trying new things and making improvements. We know that technology has already fundamentally changed how we communicate with employees, and internal communicators have had to innovate by necessity just to keep pace with the changing world. From the plethora of digital comms tools available on the market to new AI technologies appearing online, there's a wealth of opportunities to experiment and explore technology to improve your internal communication. Keep an open mind, be aware that any resistance you feel may be rooted in fear and get curious about your own feelings on the intersection between technology and creativity.

Stepping backwards, we explored the idea of acting like a scientist by using the scientific method. We looked at how measurable experiments can be used to help us iterate and innovate in internal communication. We heard from world-renowned biomedical science expert Professor Patricia Maguire, who emphasized the importance of empirical evidence in decision-making processes and how the scientific method serves as a useful framework for anyone who wants to improve their problem-solving abilities, not just scientists in a lab. We discussed how we, as internal communicators, can create thoughtful measurable experiments to prove or disprove hypotheses about our communication practices, based on observations we note during the course of our work. This chapter emphasized the need to experiment, try new things, measure the results and use the data to generate insights. And we looked at a few stories from non-scientists who are using measurable experiments to innovate and improve in their own work. The iterative scientific process can help you feel confident to try new things in a structured framework, learn to be okay with failure and come up with regular improvements for how you deliver value in your organization.

We saw that innovation can be fuelled by cross-disciplinary learning by getting curious about other industries and other fields and using their insights to generate ideas for how we can improve our work. We looked at practical examples of how other fields can give us inspiration for our work, specifically psychology, science and marketing. Psychology can help us better understand our audiences and influence our stakeholders, scientific studies can help us understand how our brain reacts to messaging and marketing can remind us of the importance of mapping our work to business outcomes and deeply understanding our employee groups. In this chapter we concluded that diversity of knowledge is good – more than good – and that exploring ideas from beyond the internal communication bubble is a great way to brew up ideas for innovation. All we need to do is to indulge our curiosity about other fields and open our minds to learning from others to push beyond the boundaries of conventional thinking in our profession.

The book took a surprising turn when I encouraged you all to get bored. Bet you didn't see that coming. I made the controversial proposition that we should actively make room for moments of boredom in order to allow our minds to wander and be creative. Innovation needs a creative idea, and creative ideas often come when we are doing boring mundane things like ironing a shirt, walking the dog or simply staring out the window. We live in a busy world full of distractions and we have productivity gurus making us feel guilty for moments of idleness. My advice flies in the face of that. I advise you to embrace boredom as a way to connect the dots in your subconscious and come up with your next great innovative idea. Don't feel guilty about it either. Consider boredom an investment in creativity and a worthwhile use of your time.

But it's not enough just to come up with an innovative idea; you also need the mindset to go with it. I proposed five key components for the internal communicators innovator's mindset: curiosity, open-mindedness, resilience, observation and problem-solving. These are areas that all require practice and cultivation and active work to improve. It's worth taking the time to see which of these you are good at, which might be weaker areas for you, and what action you might take to build up the muscle in each area. For example, if you want to actively improve your curiosity then simply start asking more questions. Why is this done that way? Have we ever tried Y? What is Z audience most interested in right now? *Curiosity is the fundamental element of the innovator's mindset*, and it's particularly powerful when combined with the other components.

But it's hard to find time to practice your innovative muscles when you're overworked, overwhelmed and exhausted in the course of your day job. I documented 10 obstacles that are stopping internal communication professionals today from innovating in their roles. These obstacles include a lack of resources, a fear of failure, a lack of autonomy and an adherence to best practices. I suggested practical ways to begin overcoming the obstacles you face to create space for trying new things and innovating.

Key to this is a willingness on our part to fall out of love with best practices and replace it with a deep-seated curiosity. Clinging to methods that worked for other people in the past limits our ability to innovate and truly add value to our organizations. Everything is contextual, everything is situational. This is what makes our jobs so difficult (and ultimately so rewarding). Using a set of best practices as a rigid roadmap for how to do your job won't necessarily result in the outcomes that other people had, and it may not lead you to success. You're better off referring to them as 'good practices', using them as insights and ideas rather than roadmaps, and investing more of your time in getting deeply curious about your own organization and what it truly needs from internal communication. This bravery will help you innovate to create a lasting impact at work.

We explored whether innovation even matters in internal communication. Can't we just keep coasting along as we are? Sadly not. The world is changing fast and the pace of change doesn't seem to be slowing down. If we don't keep up, we'll be left behind. How organizations communicate with employees has changed dramatically over the years and internal communicators have had to innovate and adapt by necessity. Innovation is not new for our profession, nor is it a luxury – it's a requirement.

More broadly I examined the concept of innovation itself, unpacking various definitions and consulting with experts in the field. I settled on three key ingredients for innovation: novelty (there must be an element of newness), action (you must do more than generate a good idea – you must execute on that idea) and value (you must deliver value to the business, it must be genuinely useful). I opted to use this definition of innovation throughout the book:

> 'Innovation is a creative idea brought to application that results in value.'

Innovation is more than a buzzword and it's more than simply having a bright idea. You need a creative idea that you execute on and deliver something useful. That applies to any innovation and not just to our field. This definition again reminds us that innovation does not *require* technology. Innovation and technology are not synonymous.

Anyone can innovate, not just Tech Bros or scientists with scraggly white hair. And innovation doesn't have to be a groundbreaking 'eureka' moment; it can be small, incremental innovations that compound over time to lead to significant results.

And, casting our mind way back to the very start of the book, we got curious about our own profession and what internal communication is all about. We know that internal communication is fundamental to the success of organizations, and that our role is more than just distributing information; it is about alignment, influencing employee behaviour, driving employee engagement and delivering on business goals. We are the oil in the engine, helping things to run smoothly and reducing friction so the car can run efficiently.

This book is an invitation to embrace change. It is a clarion call to organizations and internal communicators alike to embrace curiosity and creativity to create lasting change. We can cultivate an innovation culture where experimentation, exploration and failing is just part of the way we do things. This is not an individual action. This is a collective movement toward a future where internal communication truly makes an impact on how businesses operate and how they succeed in the market. The power to be transformative in our approach lies within your grasp – you simply need to be bold enough to start innovating, experimenting and trying new things.

Key themes of the book

Some key themes have emerged in this book as we've worked our way through all the chapters. These themes include the power of integration, how much our mindset matters and the importance of defying accepted norms.

Theme 1: The power of integration

One of the themes we've explored in the book is the power of integration, with reference to technology and to cross-disciplinary learning.

Getting curious about technology and how it can integrate into our work can be transformational. For some internal communicators who may value our traditional ways of working or find comfort in the manual processes of the creative arts, technology may feel threatening. It may lead to fear or anger or any range of negative emotions. But it doesn't need to feel this way. We don't need to resist technology; we can integrate it into our world and use it to help us improve our work and innovate in our communication practices. We can view technology not just as a tool, but as an enabler that drives efficiency, speed and innovation. Technology can help us to optimize our communication workflows and processes, streamline our communication channels, collaborate asynchronously with colleagues anywhere in the world, target our audiences with increased precision and get important empirical data about communication consumption and impact.

Don't be frightened of new technologies – be excited about them. New technologies are coming to market all the time and the communicator who resists them will get left behind. Getting curious about technology and harnessing it to create a lasting impact will be of critical importance to internal communicators who want to stay ahead of the game and position themselves as valuable assets to employers. Being deft on your feet with technology will help you to feel better equipped to adapt to emerging trends in the digital world. It will help future-proof not just your communication approach in work, but also your career as a comms professional.

My ask is this: don't fear technology. Don't resist it based on an emotional reaction or a desire to cling to the past. Employ your innovator's mindset and be open-minded about how technology can help you.

The theme of integration also emerged when we looked at integrating insights from other fields into our work to enable innovation. Cross-disciplinary learning fuels innovation, and there are endless nuggets of information and practical actions we can take from fields such as psychology, science and marketing. By integrating principles from social or behavioural psychology, we can gain deep insights into the intricacies of human behaviour and motivation. This can help us to innovate in internal communication by going beyond a superficial understanding of our audience or our stakeholders to a deeper, more meaningful understanding to help us make evidence-based decisions and create impactful solutions. We can integrate principles like scarcity and social proof into our work to create communications that not only inform employees but also resonate with them and inspire them to action.

Integrating knowledge from scientific research using trials, brain scans and controlled experiments arms us with data and evidence to sharpen our comms skills and focus on what matters. These studies have rigour and objectivity and are enormously helpful in our ongoing process of learning about what works and what doesn't. Scientific studies can spark ideas for how we can do things differently or how we can improve our existing offerings. Not only that, but we can integrate the scientific method itself into our approach. Let's borrow some of the rigour and objectivity from scientists in the lab and use it ourselves to run some experiments. This encourages us to become more observant as we practise collecting observations and turning them into testable hypotheses. We become scientists ourselves, operating in an iterative cycle of observations, hypotheses, experiments, testing, refinement and evaluation.

And not forgetting how we can integrate the wealth of information we can borrow from the field of marketing. Marketing insights remind us of the importance of getting a deep understanding of our audiences and being able to segment employees effectively for tailored messages and campaigns. You can integrate insights from marketing to improve how to map your work to business outcomes or how to map your employee journey. All of the practices regularly used by marketing are ripe for us to explore and learn from and get curious about.

Imagine the power of integrating the learning from across multiple disciplines as you innovate in internal communication. Your communication practices could leverage technology whilst also incorporating psychological principles which will inspire your audience to action. Or you could use the scientific method to collect data for decision-making to ensure that your communication approach is grounded in empirical evidence, and then also integrate learning from marketing to ensure that you've included a consideration of your target audience in your approach.

The magic happens when all of these elements begin to integrate together. You'll simply be bursting with new ideas and be chomping at the bit to start trying new things. This is because innovation thrives at the intersection of knowledge. Diversity causes the collision of different perspectives and ideas and experiences, and this can brew up new ideas and help you see things differently.

Being open to integrating technology and learning from other fields will help you enormously as you begin innovating in your work.

Theme 2: Your mindset matters

Another theme that emerged in this book is that of mindset. Your mindset matters, it really, *really* matters. We discussed the concept of an internal communication innovator's mindset, one in which you embrace curiosity, open-mindedness, resilience, observation and problem-solving. This isn't just a random collection of traits – it's a collision of powerful practices that will help you level up your game and pave the way for innovation. It will help you go from good to great.

At the heart of the innovator's mindset lies insatiable curiosity. We must have a relentless drive to question, explore and understand our audiences and our organizations. This is what will spark great ideas that you can put into action and deliver value in your roles. By embracing curiosity and not best practice, you open the door to a world of new possibilities in terms of how you work and what you can do. Curiosity is your superpower as a communicator. It will push you to challenge existing norms and interrogate assumptions and try new things and be daring.

Hand-in-hand with curiosity comes open-mindedness. We must be open to other ways of doing things and to accepting that maybe our ideas aren't great. We all have absurd ideas sometimes and that's okay. If you open your mind to diverse perspectives and entertain unconventional ideas, your capacity for innovation will multiply.

Being open-minded can lead to trying new things, and that in turn can lead to failure. As innovative internal communicators, we must be resilient. We must be able to fail, learn from it, get back up and try again. Every time you fail at something or an experiment goes wrong, think of it as a learning experience rather than an embarrassment. Innovators fail all the time. Innovation is inherently risky and there's really no way around that. Building your resilience over time can help you bounce back from failures or setbacks and keep iterating and trying until you succeed.

Observation is also a key part of the innovator's mindset. We need to train ourselves to keenly observe our audiences, our leaders, our environment in order to discern patterns, understand nuances, spot anomalies and identify opportunities that most other people simply do not see. We must be finely attuned to the changing needs of our internal audiences and the shifts in organizational dynamics that will influence our work and how we communicate. Noting and collecting observations can open the way for innovation, as it may spark a creative idea or be the beginning of a testable hypothesis.

We also need our mindset to be in problem-solving mode. Innovation is about delivering value by solving problems – and we need to be able to actively spot and identify problems to do this. We must be both problem solvers and problem finders. We can choose to view challenges as roadblocks or obstacles or we can view them as problems waiting to be solved or opportunities for innovation. They're a reminder that we can constantly improve, we can try new things and solve problems through great communication.

We can see that all of these aspects of the innovator's mindset combine to give us a powerful approach to innovating in internal communication. This mindset will gradually help innovation just became part of how you operate. It will become normal to you.

The other part of our mindset we explored was around our approach to boredom. You may remember Asif ironing his running shorts in Chapter 7. We often forget how powerful boredom can be for generating ideas or sparking an innovative idea – and it's easy in our busy world of internal communications to simply never feel bored as you are firefighting all day long.

It's an unconventional take to say that boredom is great. I'm happy to be the champion of boredom, even if I am a movement-of-one right now. In a world of near-constant digital distraction where we are expected to sacrifice our time to the altar of productivity, there's something dangerously seductive about embracing boredom. Staring blankly out of a window can be good for you! It might just brew up your next great idea. Daydreaming may help you to connect the dots between unconnected ideas you read about earlier this month or may help you to realize that two of your key stakeholders could work together to achieve a powerful win–win outcome.

The brain does amazing things when we allow it to rest. We know from brain scans that the default mode network gets fired up when we allow our mind to wander and to get bored, and this can be a powerful catalyst for creative thinking and generating ideas. Ideas often evolve slowly over time and you need time for them to marinate and percolate. Periods of boredom and rest give your brain the opportunity to do this. So don't think of boredom as the enemy, and don't feel guilty when you're being 'unproductive'. When you're bored, you're actually investing time in coming up with fresh ideas that may be your next valuable innovation.

Think of it as an act of deliberate rebellion in a fast-paced world where rest is demonized. Who wants to join me in the boredom revolution? We could hold an in-person retreat where we get together and do absolutely nothing. It would be glorious!

So that's theme 2 of the book: your mindset. It really, truly does matter.

Theme 3: Defying accepted norms

The third and final theme of the book is about breaking barriers and defying accepted norms. I urge you not to unquestioningly accept advice from others on how to do your job. If someone tells you that you must do X because it is 'best practice', then you should see red flags waving around and know that it's time to get curious and ask questions.

This book is no different, by the way. You might disagree with me or have opposing view to parts of this book. If you do, then great! Keep going. Read every book with a critical eye and through the lens of your own experience. Question all the experts and the advice and the guidance you get and distil from it what is useful and practical for *you*. Because what works for one internal comms team may not work for you at all.

Now, I've always been defying accepted norms, ever since I was a child. My poor parents, bless them, were always so patient and gracious. I was definitely not always a compliant child and I wanted to know *why* things were done a certain way and *why* we couldn't try something new. So it probably wasn't entirely surprising when I began to observe our profession's obsession with best practice and began critically reflecting on why we are so deeply in this love affair and why it is problematic.

In my view, adhering to best practices in internal communication is limiting. It encourages us to take a backward-looking approach to our work by applying what has worked for other people in the past, rather than by thinking about what is going to work for us today or in the future. To me, a best practice approach seems deeply unstrategic as your starting point is outside the organization (what have other people done?) rather than inside the organization (what does our organization need?). And, ultimately, I feel that clinging tightly to best practice stops us from innovating. Why would you try to come up with a new or better way of doing something when there is already a 'best' way? There is no way to improve on 'best', is there?

I urge you to let go of the best practice comfort blanket and get comfortable exploring your own path a bit more. You may want to try something in work that completely defies best practice, because your own data and evidence indicates that it will work. I say go for it! Try something new, test it out, measure it and evaluate it. Then learn from the results and keep iterating. It's a gorgeous cycle of learning and testing and evaluating and learning some more… it never ends. And if you're anything like me, you'll love that.

Sadly for us, there's just no such thing as a silver bullet in internal communication. Best practices are standardized, one-size-fits-all approaches that simply can't account for the multiple cultural and situational nuances in our workplaces. Best practices suggest that a single, ideal solution exists – but this is an illusion. It's not true. What worked for someone else may not work for you. And what worked last year may not work this year. This is where our curiosity, our willingness to experiment, our commitment to ongoing learning will serve us well. We can defy accepted norms and forge our own path. We can confidently try new things and acknowledge that we might fail – and that's okay. We can move from compliance to creativity and celebrate the disruption that it may bring. Questioning norms and disrupting the way things are usually done can be a positive force for driving innovation and creative problem-solving.

Throwing off the shackles of best practice is scary but wildly liberating. You don't need to copy what other people have one before – you can build your own communication practices. You don't need to start from scratch. You can absolutely learn from other people's stories and successes, but calling them 'good practices' instead of 'best practices' can help you to use them as insights and inspiration rather than as rigid roadmaps to follow. So go forth and defy the accepted norms. Be brave and creative and imaginative and bold.

Conclusion: A manifesto for a lasting impact

Ultimately this book is about making a difference and creating lasting impact as an internal communicator. This is my manifesto, the result of many months of getting deeply curious about our profession and how we work. As we conclude the book, I want you to feel ready to drive change in your organization. You can be the catalyst for innovating internal communication, no matter what industry you work in or what size your team is or how many resources you have at your disposal.

You can begin to do things differently after reading this book.

You can commit to innovation by challenging the status quo and inspiring people around you to do the same. You can actively cultivate your innovator's mindset by practising the key skills you need and building them regularly like muscles. You can make curiosity central to how you work by reigniting the inquisitive nature you had as a child and allowing yourself to ask more questions and interrogate assumptions. You can recognize that innovation isn't optional in our field, it's a prerequisite. The world is moving and changing fast and we need to be able to keep up. You can learn to find joy in boredom, in the quiet moments of stillness where your brain can relax and wander and come up with ridiculously brilliant ideas seemingly out of nowhere. And you can become comfortable with failure. Innovation is a risky business. It's not for the complacent communicator. If you can fail, learn from it and try again then you are doing great. If you're not quite there yet, then keep practising. I'm cheering for you.

Here are my parting words of encouragement to inspire you to act as change agents for innovation in your organization:

- **Recognize your influence.** Whether you're a senior leader, a manager or an individual contributor in your organization, as an internal communicator you wield considerable influence. You're shaping communication for every single employee in the company and you have the power to make a significant difference both to the business and to the employee experience. You can act as a force for change by embracing innovation and actively championing it.

- **Be the innovator.** Maybe you work in an organization that isn't exactly known for its innovative approach. Perhaps the leadership team are very conservative or risk averse or old fashioned. This may shape your approach, but it doesn't mean you can't innovate at all. Embrace the innovator's mindset and be fuelled by curiosity to identify ways to innovate and experiment. Remember, innovation can be small incremental changes – it doesn't need to be a huge 'eureka' moment.

- **Seek out diverse perspectives.** We know that innovative ideas can come from the collision of different experiences or perspectives or ways of thinking. So you can actively seek out people who have a different role than you or a different background than you. Or you can even be brave and seek out people who you know are likely to disagree with you. Get curious about their perspectives, learn from them and be open-minded enough to admit you may be wrong about something.

· **Lead with curiosity.** As a change agent, lead with curiosity and encourage others to ask questions. Cultivate a leadership style that celebrates innovation and creativity and imagination to solve business problems. In this way, you'll immediately reduce your reliance on best practices and feel more comfortable identifying the right solution for your problem in your context.

This book is a rallying cry for internal communicators to join a movement of curiosity, creativity and experimentation. I believe we all have the power to shape the experience in our organizations and drive progress towards business goals. You're not a passive participant in this, you are the driving force.

You can define the future of communication in your organization, and you can do this through innovation. This is how you can create a deep and lasting impact.

INDEX

The index is filed in alphabetical, word-by-word order. Acronyms and 'Mc' are filed as presented; numbers are filed as spelt out. Locators in italics denote information within a figure or table.

Looking for another book?

Explore our award-winning
books from global business
experts in Marketing and Sales

Scan the code to browse

www.koganpage.com/marketing

From 4 December 2025 the EU Responsible Person (GPSR) is:
eucomply oÜ, Pärnu mnt. 139b – 14, 11317 Tallinn, Estonia
www.eucompliancepartner.com

www.ingramcontent.com/pod-product-compliance
Lightning Source LLC
Chambersburg PA
CBHW071551210326
41597CB00019B/3189